Claiming the City and Contesting the State

The present book analyzes the relationship between internal migration, urbanization and democratization in Spain during the period of General Francisco Franco's dictatorship (1939–1975) and Spain's transition to democracy (1975–1982). Specifically, the book explores the production and management of urban space as one form of political and social repression under the dictatorship, and the threat posed to the official urban planning regimes by the phenomenon of mass squatting (*chabolismo*).

The growing body of recent literature that analyzes the role of neighborhood associations within Spain's transition to democracy points to the importance and radicalism of associations that formed within squatters' settlements such as Orcasitas in Madrid, Otxarkoaga in Bilbao or Somorrostro and el Camp de la Bota in Barcelona. However, relatively little is known about the formation of community life in these neighborhoods during the 1950s, and about the ways in which the struggle to control and fashion urban space prior to Spain's transition to democracy generated specific notions of democratic citizenship amongst populations lacking in prior coherent ideological commitment.

Inbal Ofer is a senior lecturer in modern European history at The Open University of Israel.

Routledge /Cañada Blanch Studies on Contemporary Spain

Edited by Paul Preston and Sebastian Balfour, Cañada Blanch Centre for Contemporary Spanish Studies, London School of Economics, UK

1 British Volunteers in the Spanish Civil War
The British Battalion in the International Brigades, 1936–1939
Richard Baxell

2 Gunpowder and Incense
The Catholic Church and the Spanish Civil War
Hilari Raguer, translated by Gerald Howson

3 Nazi Germany and Francoist Spain
Christian Leitz

4 Churchill and Spain
The Survival of the Franco Regime, 1940–45
Richard Wigg

5 The Foundations of Civil War
Revolution, Social Conflict and Reaction in Liberal Spain, 1916–1923
Francisco J. Romero Salvadó

6 Ethnicity and Violence
The Case of Radical Basque Nationalism
Diego Muro

7 Medicine and Warfare
Spain 1936–1939
Nicholas Coni

8 The Francoist Military Trials
Peter Anderson

9 The Politics and Memory of Democratic Transition
The Spanish Model
Edited by Diego Muro and Gregorio Alonso

10 Mass Killings and Violence in Spain, 1936–1952
Grappling with the Past
Edited by Peter Anderson and Miguel Ángel del Arco Blanco

11 Claiming the City and Contesting the State
Squatting, Community Formation and Democratization in Spain (1955–1986)
Inbal Ofer

Also published in association with the Cañada Blanch Centre:

Spain and the Great Powers in the Twentieth Century
Edited by Sebastian Balfour and Paul Preston

The Politics of Contemporary Spain
dited by Sebastian Balfour

Claiming the City and Contesting the State

Squatting, Community Formation and Democratization in Spain (1955–1986)

Inbal Ofer

LONDON AND NEW YORK

First published 2017
by Routledge
2 Park Square, Milton Park, Abingdon, Oxon OX14 4RN

and by Routledge
711 Third Avenue, New York, NY 10017

Routledge is an imprint of the Taylor & Francis Group, an informa business

© 2017 Inbal Ofer

The right of Inbal Ofer to be identified as author of this work has been
asserted by him in accordance with sections 77 and 78 of the Copyright,
Designs and Patents Act 1988.

All rights reserved. No part of this book may be reprinted or reproduced or
utilised in any form or by any electronic, mechanical, or other means, now
known or hereafter invented, including photocopying and recording, or in any
information storage or retrieval system, without permission in writing from
the publishers.

Trademark notice: Product or corporate names may be trademarks or
registered trademarks, and are used only for identification and explanation
without intent to infringe.

British Library Cataloguing in Publication Data
A catalogue record for this book is available from the British Library

Library of Congress Cataloging-in-Publication Data
A catalog record for this book has been requested

ISBN: 978-1-138-23771-1 (hbk)
ISBN: 978-1-315-29919-8 (ebk)

Typeset in Sabon
by Taylor & Francis Books

To Miguel, who made the story of Orcasitas come alive for me

Contents

List of figures	viii
Acknowledgments	x

	Introduction	1
1	Social control through spatial segregation: Urban planning under the Franco regime	19
2	Internal migration in a post-Civil War society: From the countryside to the city in search of a better life	39
3	Appropriating urban space: Constructing a *Chabola* and forming a community	58
4	Becoming visible: Neighborhood associations under the Franco regime	80
5	Alternative visions of democracy: Urban space and the Spanish transition	107
	Conclusion: Some thoughts on civic participation, the production of urban space and the meaning of the right to the city	140

Bibliography	148
Index	158

Figures

1.1	A receipt destined to the printer Jaime Barba detailing the cost of printing new street signs in Barcelona (1939)	22
3.1	The entrance to a *chabola* with view to the inside	62
3.2	Cooking outdoors in Orcasitas	64
3.3	A bedroom in one of the *chabolas*	66
3.4	Children playing outside of an open *chabola*	66
3.5	Mothers carrying their children with their school bags on the road leading out of Orcasitas	67
3.6	A toddler being bathed outside his home in Orcasitas	69
3.7, 3.8 and 3.9	Tavern and self-constructed dancing-hall in Orcasitas. The photos are not dated, but they were taken prior to the first wave of mass demolitions in the 1970s. While the taverns and bars catered during the week almost exclusively for men the dance hall was a meeting place for young men and women from both Orcasitas and the neighboring *barrios*	71
3.10	A monument in present-day Orcasitas: A woman carrying her pitcher of water down to the fountain	74
3.11	This photo was taken by an inhabitant of Orcasitas prior to the first mass demolition of *chabolas* in the 1970s. The photo is not dated, and while the women clearly came together in order to be photographed, it reflects the fact that during the mornings the *barrio* was almost an exclusively feminine space. The only exceptions were boys under school age and the occasionally unemployed man	75
4.1 and 4.2	The construction and the opening of the association headquarters, Orcasitas, 1971	90
5.1 and 5.2	The selling of self-manufactured bread in Ocasitas	119
5.3	A list presenting before the neighbors the advantages and disadvantages of living in high-rise towers	127
5.4	The election process of the windows in the apartments.	128

5.5	The structure of a housing nucleus (including towers, four-story apartment buildings and commercial and recreational spaces)	128
5.6 and 5.7	The green march. Neighbors walking to the Ministry of Housing	130
5.8, 5.9 and 5.10	Plaza de la Memoria Vinculante, calle de la Remodelación and Plaza de la Asociación in present-day Orcasitas	132
5.11 and 5.12	The 1986 exposition on the history of the struggle in Orcasitas	134

Acknowledgments

This book has been seven years in the making and there are more people who accompanied me along this long road than I can possibly acknowledge. The book emerged out of a research project that could not have been carried through without the generous funding of the Israel Science Foundation (grant 54/10) and the research authority of the Open University of Israel. I would like to extend special thanks to Dr. Daphna Idelson and to Galit Shulman of the Open University for their tremendous help.

Over a period of seven years the Neighborhood Association of the Meseta de Orcasitas (Madrid) was instrumental in opening before me its archives and putting me in contact with its members (past and present), as well as with other inhabitants of the *barrio*. Special thanks go to Félix López Rey, Eloy Cuéllar Martín and Pura López. I am deeply indebted to all the people who shared with me their life stories and personal memories: to Jesús, Antonio, María Luisa and many others. A special acknowledgement goes to Dr. Cristian Barrionuevo for sharing with me his insights born out of many years of work in Orcasitas.

I would also like to thank the personnel of the Archivo Regional de la Comunidad de Madrid (at the Biblioteca Regional Joaquín Leguina), especially María Nieves Sobrino García and María Inmaculada Campo González, who took time from their regular work in order to guide me through the complex process of using the wealth of available sources without infringing on privacy laws. I would also like to thank all those who aided me in locating necessary documents and in producing workable copies of maps, reconstruction and infrastructure plans.

This book would not have been completed in its current form without the help of Miguel Hernández Soto. Side by side we conducted and transcribed interviews and sifted through an incredible number of primary sources. I cannot imagine completing the database on which the book is based without his immense knowledge not only of Orcasitas but also of many other communities all over Spain from which the people who settled in the *barrio* originally came from. His astute understanding and personal knowledge of the events that took place in Madrid during the years of the transition to democracy provided me with insights that greatly enhanced my work. Alongside Miguel I would like to thank Ángela and Adday, who opened their home to me and turned Orcasitas into my home away from home through long periods of research.

Acknowledgments xi

Special thanks go to many colleagues, who accompanied along the way, providing support, suggestions and feedback. To Tamar Groves, who collaborated with me in numerous conferences and publications and never tired of reading and discussing parts of my work. To Professor Paul Preston, who inspired me through years of research and study of Spanish history and was relentless in encouraging me to bring this manuscript to publication. To Raanan Rein, who was always there to read, correct and discuss both history and theory. To my colleagues at the University of Valencia (and especially to Ismael Saz), who were part of the project titled "De la Dictadura Nacionalista a la Democracia de las Autinimias: Política, Cultura, Identidades Colectivas (HAR2011–27392)." To my colleagues at the Open University of Israel and abroad: special thanks to Iris Shagrir (who read and shared with me her comments on several chapters in this book). To Guy Miron, Varda Wasserman, Ishay Landa, Pamela Radcliff, Ángela Cenarro, José Babiano Mora, José Álvarez Junco, Adrian Shubert, Nigel Townson and many others.

Finally, I would like to thank Ilan, Adam and Arielle for all their patience and love and for the willingness to accompany me on more research trips than they can remember. I hope they have come to appreciate and understand this particular piece of history as I have.

Introduction

The present book analyzes the relationship between internal migration, urbanization and democratization in Spain during the period of General Francisco Franco's dictatorship (1939–1975) and Spain's transition to democracy (1975–1982). Specifically, the book explores the production and management of urban space as one form of political and social repression, and examines the relationship between the dictatorship's urban planning regimes and the phenomenon of mass squatting (*chabolismo*). The growing body of recent literature that focuses on the role of neighborhood associations within Spain's transition to democracy, points to the importance and radicalism of associations that formed within shantytowns (such as Orcasitas in Madrid, Otxarkoaga in Bilbao or Somorrostro and el Camp de la Bota in Barcelona).[1] However, relatively little is known about the formation of community life in these neighborhoods during the 1950s or about the ways in which the struggle to control and fashion urban space prior to Spain's transition to democracy generated specific notions of democratic citizenship amongst populations lacking in coherent ideological commitment.

In order to shed light on the links between political repression and spatial control and between squatting and political resistance the present book focuses on the history of Orcasitas: the largest of the shantytowns that formed around the Spanish capital during the years of the Franco regime. What is known today as the *barrio* of Orcasitas was originally made up of three different neighborhoods: *Meseta de Orcasitas*, *OrcaSur* and *Poblado Dirigido de Orcasitas*. The first two formed between 1955 and 1962 as a result of illegal self-construction. The third was built as a temporary dormitory suburb in 1958 and was never dismantled. This section of Madrid was for many years the embodiment of urban alienation. By the early 1970s the *barrio* expanded so as to include over 10,000 inhabitants (mostly newly arrived migrants from *Castilla la Mancha* and *Andalucía*) all of them living under dire material conditions and in an extreme state of social marginalization.

The patterns of squatting and of community life in Orcasitas were representative of hundreds of other shantytowns all over Spain. The uniqueness of Orcasitas lies in the way in which its dwellers struggled against eviction and challenged legal notions of entitlement already under the dictatorship. By

2 Introduction

forcing the local authorities to acknowledge their claim to the land they had occupied, and their status as a community of neighbors, the inhabitants set a legal precedent. They also established their right to take an active part in any process of urban renovation pertaining to their *barrio*. As the struggle for urban renovation merged into a process of political transition in the mid 1970s, what started off as local experiments of self-management and of grass-roots activism matured into a struggle for a more participative and democratic political system.

The story of Orcasitas highlights the centrality of space to the study of the Franco regime and the formation of an entire spectrum of oppositional practices under the dictatorship (from individual and communal acts of subversion to more comprehensive, ideologically grounded resistance). The current book aims to situate the specific (and at times ground breaking) events that took place in Orcasitas within the narratives of migration, squatting and resistance that emerged within other areas of Spain, mainly in Barcelona and Bilbao. In doing so it attempts to point to the specific conditions under which the appropriation of space can turn into a comprehensive act of political resistance.

In order to better comprehend the relationship between spatial practices and historical processes the book builds on the theoretical framework offered by Henri Lefebvre regarding the three-dimensional production of space: space as perceived (materially produced); conceived (ideologically/institutionally produced); and experienced (symbolized through everyday use).[2] Especially significant for my purpose are his claims that space is the product of state spatial strategies and that its transformation entails transformations in political practices, institutional arrangements and political imageries.

The book is structured around three main arguments. The first chapter explores the relationship between the spatial practices of the Franco regime and its mechanisms of repression. My claim is that the dictatorship embraced urban space as a focal point of accelerated economic growth and instituted a policy that drew industry, services and capital into the city. With the same intensity, however, it also labored to distance the Spanish working class from the center of most Spanish cities. The regime's policies in terms of political repression and of urban planning can only be understood by paying careful attention to this simultaneous drive for industrialization and spatial segregation.[3]

The second and the third chapters examine the process of internal migration and of community-formation within shantytowns (*barrios chabolistas*) in the 1950s and early 1960s. My argument is that the act of squatting both complemented and challenged the regime's spatial practices. It complemented such practices in the sense that it offered the most basic housing solutions to large working-class populations on lands that were situated close to the industrial complexes constructed following the Spanish Civil War (1936–1939). Until the late 1950s much of that land was not claimed for formal residential use. The illegal status of the *chabolas* and the precarious living conditions within shantytowns such as Orcasitas led the authorities to think that they could be easily evacuated in case the need arose. At the same time the continued existence of squatter settlements led their inhabitants, urban planning professionals and even the

Francoist courts to critically reconsider the existing notions of entitlement during the final years of the dictatorship.

The last two chapters in the book focus on the formation of neighborhood associations within shantytowns and on their civic and political role during the years of Spain's transition to democracy. As Pamela Radcliff demonstrated, neighborhood associations functioned as an interim model between the regime-sponsored associations and other, more ideologically conscious entities that were linked to the democratic opposition.[4] Neighborhood associations functioned as primary entities of socialization and mobilization and as platforms for processes of democratization, which took place within urban society in the final years of the dictatorship. From the late 1960s some neighborhood associations started to establish mechanisms of cooperation and of information sharing, while expressing similar goals in relation to specific projects of urban renovation within their respective cities. During the first year of Spain's transition to democracy individual neighborhood associations merged into a Citizens' Movement (*movimiento ciudadano*) which became one of the most important channels of popular expression and mobilization at the time. My claim is that at this point dispersed projects of consensual self-management were gradually reframed in relation to a larger political project—that of direct / radical democracy.

The concluding section of the book reflects on the conditions that enable local struggles for improved living conditions to mature into a full-scale battle for a different urban regime. The history of neighborhood associations (and of the Citizens' Movement in general) sheds light on the nature of Spanish democracy. During the transition neighborhood associations operated within a relatively short window of opportunity. Administrative transparency and consensual decision-making were prerequisites for the creation of a different kind of city. During a brief period of time they were also useful tools in the fight to dismantle the remaining structures of the dictatorship. But the new political regime, which evolved out of the Spanish transition, was a far cry from the project of radical participatory democracy that many of these associations strove to implement. Within the framework of liberal democracy the Spanish state took upon itself to guarantee an extended list of essential rights (such as the right for housing, employment, education and health). Continued civic participation at all levels of governance, however, was never perceived as one of those rights. The concluding section of the book analyzes the reasons for this.

The current study is based on several types of primary sources, including architectural and urban planes, written texts and visual materials collected from the archives of the National Institute of Housing (located at the *Archivo Regional de Madrid*) and from private collections and publications of architects and planners such as Pedro Bidagor, Luis Laorga, Francisco Javier Sáenz de Oiza and Fernando de Terán. Another important source includes a database which I constructed and which contains information about 1,680 families that settled in the *barrios* of Orcasitas between the years 1940 and 1965. The database draws on two sets of files that were produced by the Francoist Ministry of Housing: the first set was compiled between the years 1957 and 1961 and

4 *Introduction*

documents the legal and socio-economic status of the families who lived in Orcasitas during that period. This information was used by the authorities in later years in order to determine the priorities for the expropriation of land and the compensation offered to the inhabitants. A second set of files was produced between the years 1962 and 1966 during the process of land-expropriation and demolition of the existing *chabolas*. All files contain details concerning the families' origin; household composition; employment conditions; plans of the self-constructed homes and the legal standing of the property. The processed database was compiled in such a way so as to allow me to examine possible links between people's socio-economic status and community of origin and the profile of their post-migration lives. The database is supplemented by a series of 20 in-depth interviews with members of the Orcasitas Neighborhood Association and with individuals (7 women and 13 men) who migrated to the *barrios* during the 1960s and 1970s either as children or as young adults.

Producing space: Henri Lefebvre and the politics of spatial change

In view of the tremendous depth of Henri Lefebvre's work (and of the rapidly expending literature on his contribution to the fields of sociology, political geography, the study of urban social movements and of urban planning) it would seem almost presumptuous to try and "condense" an appraisal of his theory of spatial production and of social change into a few pages. This indeed is not my intention here. By concentrating on four of Lefebvre's essays (*The Critique of Everyday Life, The Production of Space, Right to the City* and *The Urban Revolution*) I briefly explore the ways in which the concept of produced space and his notion of "right to the city" provide important tools for the analysis of social and political change in Spain.[5]

> Curiously, space is a stranger to customary political reflection. Political thought and the representations which it elaborates remain "up in the air," with only an abstract relation with the soil and even the national territory ... Space belongs to the geographers in the academic division of labor. But then it reintroduces itself subversively through the effects of peripheries, the margins, the regions, the villages and local communities long abandoned, neglected, even abased through centralizing state-power[6]

The above quotation, taken from Lefebvre's work on the state (*De l'État*), reflects the importance of spatial analysis to any discussion on the formation and consolidation of power relations within modern states. In the time in which Lefebvre wrote these words they also reflected a difficulty in engaging with space, as a meaningful analytical category, within most disciplines. This tendency was reversed in the past decade mostly through the work of scholars such as Neil Brenner, Stuart Elden and Mark Purcell, who employed Lefebvre's spatial analysis from the perspective of both geography and political theory. In the field of history space, while often referred to, is still looked upon more as a container of social relations than as an element that constitutes and is being constituted by them. This is despite the fact that Lefebvre's work offers a productive platform for integrating spatial and historical analysis.

Spatiality is central to our understanding of each of the three processes with which this book is concerned: migration, urbanization and democratization. Spatial analysis contributes to our ability to historicize each of these phenomena independently. It allows us to examine the ways in which urban and what Lefebvre calls "state spaces" (*l'espace étatique*) are produced and reproduced through processes of migration and of urbanization in Franco's Spain. Most importantly it makes explicit the ties that existed between the production of different spatial regimes and the production of the political and the economic order under the dictatorship.

In order to understand the relationship between the production of space, the constitution of power relations and the emergence of different practices of resistance it is essential first to examine the concepts of everyday life, alienation and domination / appropriation in Henri Lefebvre's work. In his 1947 essay *The Critique of Everyday Life* Lefebvre wrote:

> Everyday life, in a sense residual, defined by "what is left over" after all distinct, superior, specialized, structured activities have been singled out for analysis, must be defined as a totality. Considered in their specialization and their technicality, superior activities leave a "technical vacuum" between one another which is filled by everyday life. Everyday life is profoundly related to all activities, and encompasses them with all their differences and their conflicts; it is their meeting place, their bond, it is their common ground.[7]

Everyday life is characterized as unspecialized and spontaneous by nature. It is the basis for the formation of social bonds and therefore has the potential to function as an arena of resistance. It concerns:

> a level in contemporary society defined by: 1) the gap between this level and levels above it (those of the State, technology, high culture); 2) The intersection between the non-dominated sector of reality and the dominated sector; 3) transformation of objects into appropriated goods.[8]

In direct relation to everyday life Lefebvre also discussed the concept of "alienation," which he viewed as central to the understanding of the development of human society. Alienation to him was not exclusively economic in nature. Rather it was the general inability to grasp and to think of the "other," an inability that resulted from the fragmented nature of modern life.[9] While viewing traditional everyday life as mostly based on the principle of on non-separation (of functions, spaces, generations, genders, etc.) he pointed to the tendency of modern everyday life to become more and more fragmented and therefore also highly alienated. Lefebvre viewed "alienation" as a historically grounded process that resulted from the tendency towards separation (which culminated in social

6 *Introduction*

phenomena such as the division of labor and specialization of the spheres of human activity) and abstraction (which resulted in the stripping off of human action from substance in favor of signs and symbols).

The uniqueness of Lefebvre's analysis, however, does not emerge simply from his definition of the everyday. Rather it is located in the claim that the private and social functions that are associated with everyday life, and the structures that are constructed for their performance, are all embedded in space and should be analyzed spatially. In the *Production of Space* (1974) Lefebvre developed his theory of space as produced on three levels: the level of spatial practices, which assign the functions of production and of reproduction to particular locations with specific spatial characteristics; the level of representations of space that "order" and legitimize the allocation of space and the construction of spatial practices through academic and/or professional discourses; and the level of representational space, which is lived space that embodies the complex symbolism of its users.[10]

This spatial shift in Lefebvre's work moved the focus of his analysis from the working class to the more general category of the users of space. As Teresa Hoskyns noted, the assertion that the power relations concern also built space opened the way for an extension of the concept of "alienation." If the production of space may be carried out away from the sphere of influence of the users and independently of them, then alienation may also occur between individuals and their environment.[11] In order to explain how exactly this process takes place Lefebvre called into use the concepts of "domination" and "appropriation."

According to him both domination and appropriation transform space. Dominated space is transformed by technology, which introduces onto it new forms of use, often closing, sterilizing and emptying it in the process.[12] Appropriated space, on the other hand, is transformed by use in order to serve the needs of its inhabitants.[13] Modern everyday life, then, despite its tendency to succumb to processes of separation and abstraction, is in many ways also the final frontier in the struggle against them. The space of everyday life (especially that of urban everyday life) while not free of domination also holds great potential for resistance. The city must be thought of as a work of continued production. In that sense it is not simply organized and instituted, but can also be remodeled and appropriated by its inhabitants in ways that challenge the dominant political and economic arrangements.

From the perspective of my own research, Lefebvre's analysis raises several important questions. The first and perhaps the most important one has to do with the way in which one can begin to historicize processes of spatial domination and / or appropriation. As I show in the first and third chapters of the book, thinking in terms of practices and representations, and the ways in which the two affect representational space, allows us to break down these processes into analyzable units. In a tightly monitored and regulated society such as the one that existed in Spain during the years of the Franco regime, urban space was no doubt a resource to be controlled and fashioned by the authorities according to their ideological and economic needs. What were these needs? How were they

Introduction   7

translated into a spatial reality, which affected decisions regarding housing priorities, infrastructure planning and so forth? How were such decisions explained professionally and politically? What populations benefited from the spatial practices of the regime and under what conditions?

Lefebvre not only proposes three levels of spatial analysis, he also points to three spatial scales which such an analysis must take into consideration: A "private" realm that includes a family's living space as well as entrances, thresholds and reception areas; an interim level, which is made up of avenues and squares, medium-size thoroughfares and the passageways leading to the houses; and finally, a global level divided into spaces open to the public and closed institutional spaces. As he notes in *the Production of Space*, in the best of circumstances the outside space of a community is dominated, while the indoor space of family life is appropriated. In the context of the current study this, again, raises several questions: how did the regime define its right to act and through what type of interventions did it attempt to dominate global, intermediate and private spaces? Was it more successful in dominating certain spaces and if so why? Was its failure to implement certain spatial practices the result of intended oppositional practices? To what extent did the partial appropriation of private and intermediate spaces that took place within shantytowns (such as Orcasitas) contribute to the creation of such opposition?

In the introduction to *the Urban Revolution* Neil Smith wrote:

> In the present text he [Lefebvre] makes a synchronic distinction between the "global," "mixed" and "private" levels of society, which are roughly equated with the state, the urban and "habiting" respectively. In contemporary parlance this represents a halting effort at what might now be called "politics of scale," but Lefebvre's reluctance, in deference to the openness of space, to allow this production of "levels" to crystallize into anything approaching coherent spatial entities forecloses our understanding of the political processes by which social assumptions are written unto the scaled cartography of everyday places.[14]

While Smith might be right in his criticism regarding the clarity of Lefebvre's scalar categories, I feel that thinking in terms of private, intermediate and global spaces enhances our understanding of the ways in which power relations are constituted spatially. A central question raised in the final chapter of the book, for example, has to do with conditions that enable oppositional spatial practices that emerge within private and intermediate communal spaces to be translated into civic and political resistance within global spaces of the city. This question is of special importance since it is all too easy to assume a direct link between the act of squatting (that is of taking control over land in opposition to the spatial practices of the regime) and claiming one's right to the city. Such a link, however, is not a straightforward one. In the case of Orcasitas squatting indeed led to the creation of "counter-spaces" that catered to the needs of the newly formed community. This process, while empowering in some ways, did

8 Introduction

not immediately lead to a questioning of the economic and political power relations under the dictatorship. Only in the final years of the dictatorship, and following the threat of forced eviction did squatter communities tie their concrete material demands with the need for extensive political change.

It was only at this stage that squatters in Spain started to claim their right to the city in the Lefebvrian sense: the right of all the inhabitants to live in the city and to use the services it offered, and more importantly to shape the city after their own manner and according to their own needs. "Right to the city" is a concept that emerged out of Lefebvre's sociological research and his analysis of the conditions that led to the mobilizations of May 1968 in France and beyond. The concept encompasses two distinct rights: the right of appropriation and the right for participation. As Mark Purcell rightly noted Lefebvre's right to the city was not a suggestion for reform. Rather, it was a call for:

> a radical restructuring of social, political, and economic relations, both in the city and beyond. Key to this radical nature is that the right to the city reframes the arena of decision-making in cities: it reorients decision-making away from the state and toward the production of urban space. Instead of democratic deliberation being limited to just state decisions, Lefebvre imagines it to apply to *all* decisions that contribute to the production of urban space. The right to the city stresses the need to restructure the power relations that underlie the production of urban space[15]

Within this context the empowerment of some urban communities might very well go against the existing rights of others, and different sets of rights may be in direct confrontation with one another (such as the right of ownership and the right of use).

Looked at from Lefebvre's point of view the struggle to define and appropriate urban space under the dictatorship can be broken down into three interrelated processes: the institution of spatial practices by the regime and their legitimization on a discursive level; the resistance to them through the everyday use of space by individuals and different social groups; and the framing of spatial resistance in political terms. The final phase of the struggle in Spain provides as example of the ways in which the appropriation of space can lead to a reconsideration, or a rescaling, of the concept of citizenship itself. In liberal democracies political participation is linked to formal citizenship in the nation-state. Formal citizens have some institutionalized say in the decisions the state will take. Because their participation is linked to *state* decisions and policies, citizens' participation is scaled in a very particular way. In Lefebvre's conception as expressed in the *Right to the City*, however:

> enfranchisement is for those who *inhabit the city*. Because the right to the city revolves around the production of urban space, it is those who live in the city – who contribute to the body of urban lived experience and lived space – who can legitimately claim the right to the city. Whereas

conventional enfranchisement empowers national *citizens*, the right to the city empowers urban *inhabitants*. Under the right to the city, membership in the community of enfranchised people is not an accident of nationality or ethnicity or birth; rather it is earned by living out the routines of everyday life in the space of the city.[16]

The principle of inhabitance, therefore, imagines a scalar arrangement in which the urban is the hegemonic scale at which political community is defined. Under the right to the city other scales of community are subordinate to the urban scale. One might still be part of a national community, but since one can equally inhabit the city regardless of nationality, urban inhabitance must come first in defining the political community.

Under the Franco regime formal enfranchisement (limited in its expression and meaning) was based on the status of national citizenship. Throughout its existence, however, the dictatorship limited most forms of political representation and intervention. When it granted certain rights of representation and of intervention to its citizens those were channeled through specific, sub-national entities. In the years immediately following the Civil War the dictatorship had put into place representational structures that engaged citizens as members of "organic" or corporative entities (the family, syndicate and municipality). The ability of citizens represented within these entities to impact political decision-making processes on a local or national level was limited. At the same time I would like to suggest that the very existence of these platforms highlighted in the minds of many people the need to think of an effective exercise of citizenship as something that could and should be carried out also within sub-national levels.

Social control, political repression and spatial segregation: The Franco regime and space

The diverse historiography on the subject of social and political repression during the Franco period is lacking in substantial studies that examine the regime's spatial policies in urban areas and in the Spanish countryside.[17] While many works allude to the urban expansion of the late 1950s and 1960s, especially in the metropolitan areas of Barcelona and Madrid, there is little systematic analysis of the regime's planning policies on a national level and of their impact of different populations. Furthermore, only one recently published monograph examines the changes that occurred in Spain's urban planning regimes during the years of democratic transition.[18]

As the first chapter in this book reveals, close ties existed between the regime's spatial practices and its mechanisms of repression. In the case of Spain's major urban centers the regime instituted spatial practices which strove to maintain strict separation between the functions of production and reproduction. The regime attempted to segregate urban space according to function and to class lines: from the center (where administrative, leisure, consumption and residential spaces of the higher and middle classes congregated) to the periphery

10   *Introduction*

(where heavy industry and the bare residential necessities of the working classes and newly arrived emigrants were met). This was especially apparent in large cities that underwent extensive processes of reconstruction following the Civil War.

The Franco regime's conception of urban space was greatly influenced by its oppressive social and ideological outlook. At the same time this book also points to the extent to which urban planning policies in Francoist Spain drew on the theoretical debates that took place in other parts of Western Europe in the interwar years and again following 1945. During the 1940s Spanish architects and urban planners adopted for the most part a conservative architectural discourse which praised functionalism for its efficiency. It was proposed that separating work from family space would better serve the needs of production and provide a "healthier," "safer" and more moral environment for women and children. Consequently, the regime instituted an array of planning strategies that strove to remove working-class populations from the urban centers with their wealth of social services and cultural and educational opportunities. Even worse was the fact that the marginal spaces that were assigned for the use of those populations only allowed for one basic function: sleep. Working-class neighborhoods and workers' colonies were designed almost exclusively as dormitory suburbs devoid of spaces for leisure, consumption or social interaction as part of the regime's strive to crush the existing social networks of the Spanish working class.

The planning policies of the 1940s generated extraordinary imbalances in terms of urban development. Such imbalances were noted most of all in relation to the housing market and to the construction of infrastructures. In an attempt to partially remedy the situation the period between the years 1956 and 1964 saw the publication of a new Land Law (*ley de suelo*) and private capital became increasingly important for the formulation of Spain's housing policy. During those years the regime operated in accordance with a National Social Emergency Plan (*Plan de Urgencia Social*—PUS), which strove to eradicate illegal construction and provide mass low-cost housing. The success of this plan was modest at best.

The third period in Spain's planning history spanned the final decade of the dictatorship and the years of the transition to democracy. This period marked a move towards urban planning on a regional scale. It was characterized by social volatility and rapid political change. In terms of urban planning it signified more flexibility and attention to the needs of different populations. However, implementation of the new policies was severely limited by the onset of an economic crisis which constrained the ability of the authorities to establish new and radically different spatial practices. The first chapter in the book analyzes the effects of the regime's changing policies on the urban fabric in Spain and provides a context for understanding the phenomenon of squatting.

Squatting: Between necessity and subversion

Squatting is not a new phenomenon in human history. There is no doubt, however, that the extent and visibility of squatting greatly increased since the

1950s.[19] Throughout the second half of the twentieth century different forms of squatting became the means through which growing numbers of immigrant families and newly formed households acquired their first home in urban regions. Newly arrived migrants solved the problems of homelessness and of unemployment through a variety of self-help (and often illegal) initiatives.[20] The existing literature on the subject tends to differentiates between squatter settlements or slums (that emerge from land invasion) and informal settlements (where dwellers have the consent of the owner of the land but the land itself is not approved for construction and housing purposes). While a key referent in both types of settlements is the quality of the housing and of services, the legal status of home owners and renters and the authorities' tolerance towards them may vary radically in the two cases.

In a recently published volume titled *Public Goods versus Economic Interests: Global Perspectives on the History of Squatting*, Thomas Aguilera and Alan Smart referred to the differences in the ways in which the concept of "squatting" was understood and investigated in the global South and North. According to them:

> In the North, "squats" and "slums" are distinguished, representing two different situations. "Squat" designates the illegal occupation of a building without authorization by the owner. "Slum" is used to designate illegal occupation of land without the owner's authorization, usually accompanied by self-built housing without legal access to basic services and infra-structures ... What Northern researchers refer to as "slums" is very close to the core meaning of "squatter settlement" in the South.[21]

The shantytowns with which this book is concerned belonged for the most part to the category of informal settlements. That is their inhabitants either bought or rented land or self-constructed houses that should not have been sold or leased since they were situated in areas that were designated as "rural" and were not intended for development. With the passing of the years (due to the emergency plans launched for the clearing of the shantytowns and the con-struction of low-cost housing on those same lands) the profile of squatter communities evolved. By the 1970s *barrios* such as Orcasitas included families that continued to occupy their original shanty homes alongside families that inhabited poor quality, high-rise *chabolas* built by the state.

The difference in the legal status of the property clearly affected the lives of the dwellers. Those differences became especially meaningful when the authorities started to launch expropriation campaigns. However, it is important to keep in mind that in the Spanish case, both squatter settlements and slums lacked adequate services and infrastructures. Furthermore, most of the people who lived in mixed neighborhoods such as Orcasitas referred to themselves as *chabolistas* (squatters) regardless of the formal status of their homes. Even more important, in my view, is the fact that self-constructed settlements (whether built on land invaded or legally bought) played a similar role in the expansion of Francoist

12 Introduction

cities and of the Francoist economy. Regardless of individual differences it was the element of self-construction which affected most the nature (and the future) of the communities that formed within shantytowns such as Orcasitas.

In the preface to another recently published volume titled *Squatting in Europe: Radical Spaces, Urban Struggles* Margit Mayer introduced another distinction into the debate regarding the typology of squatting:

> Squatting – simply defined as living in or using a dwelling without the consent of the owner – occurs in many different circumstances, and as such, even if it occurs with the intention of long-term use, is not necessarily transformative of social relations ... Thus, squatting as a tactic can be used by individuals to improve their housing situation outside of any social movement, or it can be used, as a technique or action repertoire, by a variety of different social movements (including right-wing movements).[22]

Mayer differentiates squatting, as an act of radical resistance (often tied to social movements' activism) from other types of land seizure by stressing the ways in which the former facilitates collective living arrangements, new forms of self-management and organization and a variety of counter-cultural activities. In another chapter in the same volume Miguel Martínez López discusses the Spanish Squatter Movement. He identifies three phases in the Movement's activism starting in 1980 and ending in 2006. Martínez López states:

> The emergence of the squatters' movement in Spanish cities in the 1980s coincided with the first important crisis of the Neighborhood Movement. The latter, a protagonist movement for a great part of the transition period between 1975 and 1982, has been studied by several scholars ... who have emphasized its combination of demands for collective facilities and democratic reform.

However, according to Martínez López the squatters' movement of the 1980s must be differentiated from earlier forms of squatting since it adopted a radicalized set of goals and repertoires of action:

> The practice of squatting in abandoned buildings was initially a way of finding spaces to strengthen the most radical aspects of the New Social Movements ... but also of other more fringe and alternative movements ... It immediately spread as a movement with the characteristic features of an urban movement, an alternative political scene and counter-cultural practices that distinguished it from other social movements.[23]

Like Mayer and Martínez López, other contributors to the volume *Squatting in Europe* implicitly assume low levels of radicalization and political consciousness amongst those engaged in individual squatting as a means of improving their housing situation. They therefore view the act of squatting under these conditions as having a limited transformative capacity. This perspective, however, is problematic since it assumes that the initial goals and conditions that propel people to opt for the illegal occupation of space determine the nature of squatting as a process. This assumption ignores the transformative capacity of squatting as an ongoing, day-to-day form of existence that may modify both the occupied space and the perceptions and political agendas of the people involved in its occupation.

Recent research into the historical antecedents of contemporary squatter movements (such as *Occupy* and *M-15*) explored their links to earlier social movements that proliferated in the 1970s.[24] Works on squatter movements in Germany, Italy, France and the UK analyze their engagement with a variety of civic entities (such as feminists, students, workers and ecological movements). However, the existing literature largely ignores the legacies and repertoires of actions inherited from earlier squatter communities that formed in the late 1950s and 1960s in response to accelerated processes of internal migration and industrialization. The third chapter in the book examines the ways through which individual, deprivation based squatting can turn into a communal endeavor by pointing to the transformative capacity of squatting and its effects on the formation of social networks and community structures.

Producing political change: Neighborhood associations and the Citizens' Movement within Spain's transition to Democracy

Since the death of General Francisco Franco, historians have been engaged in a lively debate concerning the nature of the Spanish transition to democracy and of the concept of democratic citizenship that emerged out of it.[25] The framework that dominated most spheres of research throughout the 1990s presented the transition to democracy in Spain as a process propelled primarily by a consensual pact "from above." This framework, however, was challenged by both ordinary citizens and by professionals in the past decade.[26]

There is a wide-ranging agreement amongst historians today that the economic reforms fostered by the dictatorship during the 1960s and the progressive opening of Spanish society to outside influences (in the form of growing international cooperation as well as through the influence of tourism) generated new spaces for cultural and civic activism. In this respect it could be said that from the mid 1960s the ground was progressively prepared for a significant political change in Spain. However, the decade preceding the dictator's death also included periods of intense political repression (from the Burgos trials in 1969 to the backlash following the assassination of Franco's designated successor Admiral Luis Carrero Blanco in 1973). Against this background much research is still needed in order to understand how people's ideological identifications and their patterns of civic and political mobilization were affected by economic liberalization and socio-cultural changes.

The present book belongs to a growing body of literature that views the dictatorship as a regime that evolved significantly over time. It identifies the

14 *Introduction*

roots of political democratization in socio-economic processes and cultural change that took place within Spanish society well before the death of the dictator. Chapter 4 in the book explores the forms of public activism that were available to the various civic entities that operated under the dictatorship. It focuses on the ways in which activism within neighborhood associations enabled ordinary citizens to expand their interactions with the authorities and gain a clearer understanding of their needs as inhabitants of the city and the users of its space.

Chapter 5 examines how during the final months of the dictatorship neighborhood associations merged into what contemporaries labeled as the "Citizens' Movement." The term "Citizens Movement" first appeared in the Spanish press in the summer of 1975. It was used to describe the joint action of neighborhood and housewives' associations in their struggle against the rising cost of living and the deficiencies in urban infrastructures.[27] Throughout the years of the transition the Citizens' Movement grew in size and diversified so as to include professional and civic associations, students, feminists and various pressure groups. While all these entities strove to bring about a political change many of them were not directly affiliated with the parties of the clandestine opposition such as the Spanish Socialist Party (PSOE) and the Spanish Communist Party (PCE).

The Spanish Citizens' Movement, as the final chapter of the book demonstrates, can be situated at the crossroads between the definition of old and new social movements. An important theoretical foundation for the "new social movements" paradigm sharply distinguished between the classic protest movements of capitalist societies and those that emerged since the late 1960s. Classic protest movements were strongly attached to identities formed in relation to the economic arena; expressed material concerns and interests and put forward distributive demands; were led or supported by the organized working class; and deployed highly institutionalized practices, usually linked to hierarchically organized labor unions or left-wing parties.[28]

The new social movements, by contrast, were seen as associated with emerging identities formulated on the basis of cultural distinctions and lifestyle, and raising demands that mainly related to post-materialist values and the recognition of distinct identities.[29] Even when some of the issues dealt with by these movements had a clear distributive dimension, their demands were primarily framed in terms of the recognition of distinct culturally based identities and of excluded and oppressed groups. The main support base of the new social movements was identified as the educated middle classes, especially their younger cohorts. The movements were most often characterized by a rejection of institutionalized politics; a fluid and seemingly non-hierarchical organizational structures; participatory democracy and deliberative procedures of decision-making; and creative and innovative protest practices.

The present study, centered as it is on one of the principal forces behind the Spanish Citizens' Movement, raises questions relating to the tenability of a clear-cut distinction between old and new social movements. Throughout 1976 individual neighborhood associations merged into a movement that was made up of a variety of entities with their specific agendas. It operated as a network

Introduction   15

whose different "command centers" shared similar discourses regarding the desired meaning of citizenship and engaged in common practices of communication and consensual decision-making. More than anything the workings of the Spanish Citizens Movement could be identified with the network properties of social movements referred to by Mario Diani. According to Diani:

> Dense informal networks differentiate social movement processes from the innumerable instances in which collective action takes place and is coordinated, mostly within the boundaries of specific organizations. A social movement process is in place to the extent that both individual and organized actors, while keeping their autonomy and independence, engage in sustained exchanges of resources in pursuit of common goals. The coordination of specific initiatives, the regulation of individual actors' conduct, and the definition of strategies all depend on permanent negotiations between the individuals and the organizations involved in collective action. No single organized actor, no matter how powerful, can claim to represent a movement as a whole.[30]

While many of the Citizens Movement's leading activists belonged to the working class, most were not members of the Spanish Workers' Movement. This did not prevent the Citizens' Movement from presenting demands regarding the need for the distribution of communal and national assents. At the same time these demands were not formulated in classical class terms, partly due to the fact that both neighborhood and housewives associations presented a mixed class profile. Analyzing the workings of an important sector within the Citizens' Movement (and the nature of the relationships between neighborhood associations and other entities within the movement) is essential to our understanding of the ways in which popular mobilizations affected the framework of a political transition.

The current book does not attempt analyze the relationship between the nature of the transition and the quality of democracy in Spain nowadays. It does wish, however, to contribute to a process of reframing the process of transition itself by presenting it as a struggle over different versions of democracy, versions that enjoyed support within Spanish society of the 1970s, but whose voices were suppressed during the following two decades, versions that can no longer be suppressed or ignored, partly due to their re-emergence within contemporary, popular discourses and the socio-political agendas of entities such as the 15-M movement.

Notes

1 M. Castells, *The City and the Grassroots: A Cross-Cultural Theory of Urban Social Movements*, Berkeley, CA: University of California Press, 1983; N. Calvita and A. Ferrer, "Behind Barcelona's Success Story: Citizen Movement and Planners' Power," *Journal of Urban History*, 2000, 26(6), pp. 793–807; M. Toral, J. del Vigo, J.

16 Introduction

Eguiraun, J. M. Paredes, A. Izarzelaia (eds.), "Movimientos ciudadanos en Bilbao: Rekaldeberri, Otxarkoaga, S. Francisco," *Bidebarrieta*, 2011, pp. 229–248; V. Urrutia Abaigar, "La ciudad de los ciudadanos, Actas del VI Symposium: Movimientos Ciudadanos y Sociales en Bilbao," Bidebarrieta, 10, 2001, pp. 11–23.

2 H. Lefebvre, *The Production of Space* (translated by D. Nicholson-Smith) Oxford: Blackwell, 1991.

3 On the topic of repression and class, see for example: M. Richards, *Un Tiempo de Silencio. La Guerra Civil y la Cultura de la Represión en la España de Franco 1936–1945*, Barcelona: Critica, 1999; C. Barciela (ed.), *Autarquía y Mercado Negro. El Fracaso Económico del Primer Franquismo 1939–1959*, Barcelona: Critica, 2003; E. E. Barranquero and L. Prieto, *Así Sobrevivimos el Hambre: Estrategias de Supervivencia de las Mujeres de la Posguerra Española*, Málaga: Diputación Provincial de Málaga, 2003; M. A. del Arco Blanco, *Hambre de Siglos. Mundo Rural y Apoyos Sociales del Franquismo en Andalucía Oriental (1936–1951)*, Granada: Comares, 2007.

4 P. Radcliff, *Making Democratic Citizens in Spain: Civil Society and the Popular Origins of the Transition 1960–1978*, New York: Palgrave Macmillan, 2011.

5 For further analysis of Lefebvre's work see for example: M. Purcell, "Excavating Lefebvre: The Right to the City and Urban Politics of the Inhabitants," *GeoJournal*, 58, 2002, pp. 99–108; N. Brenner and S. Elden, "Henri Lefebvre on State Space and Territory," *International Political Sociology*, 3(4), 2009, pp. 353–377; L. Stanek, *Henri Lefebvre on Space: Architecture, Urban research, and the Production of Theory*, MN: University of Minnesota Press, 2011; N. Brenner, P. Marcuse and M. Mayer (eds.), *Cities for People not for Profit; Critical Urban Theory and the Right to the City*, London: Routledge, 2012.

6 H. Lefebvre, *De l'État*, Paris: UGE, 1976–78, vol. 4, p. 164.

7 H. Lefebvre, *Critique of Everyday Life* (translated by John Moore) London: Verso, 1991, vol. 1, p. 130.

8 H. Lefebvre, "Les mythes dans la vie quotidienne," in *Key Writings*, edited by Stuart Elden, Elizabeth Lebas and Eleonore Kofman, London: Continuum, 2003, p. 100.

9 M. Trebitsch in H. Lefebvre, *Critique of Everyday Life*, p. xvi.

10 Lefebvre, *The Production of Space*, pp. 33–34.

11 T. Hoskyns, *The Empty Place: Democracy and Public Space*, London: Routledge, 2014, pp. 74–75.

12 Lefebvre, *The Production of Space*, p. 165.

13 Ibid.

14 N. Smith, Foreword to H. Lefebvre, *The Urban Revolution* (translated by R. Bonnano), Minneapolis, MN: University of Minnesota Press, 2003, p. XIV.

15 Purcell, "Excavating Lefebvre: The Right to the City and Urban Politics of the Inhabitants," p. 102.

16 Ibid.

17 A few notable exceptions are: A. Terán, *Planeamiento urbano de la España contemporánea. Historia de un proceso imposible*, Barcelona: Alianza, 1982; C. Sambricio, *Madrid, vivienda y urbanismo: 1900–1960*, Madrid: AKAL, 2004; Z. Box Varela, La fundación de un régimen. La construcción simbólica del franquismo doctoral thesis, Universidad Complutense de Madrid, 2008, pp. 353–415; J. M. Beascoechea Gangoiti and F. Martínez Rueda, "La creación del 'Gran Bilbao' en el franquismo y el alcalde Joaquín Zuazagoitia (1942–1959)," *Bidebarrieta: Revista de humanidades y ciencias sociales de Bilbao*, 22, 2011, pp. 79–92; I. Bordetas Jiménez, *Nosotros somos los que hemos hecho esta ciudad. Autoorganización y movilización vecinal durante el tardofranquismo y el proceso de cambio político*, doctoral thesis, Universidad Autónoma de Barcelona, 2012.

18 L. Coudroy de Lille, C. Vaz and C. Vorms (eds.), *L'urbanisme espagnol depuis les années 1970*, Rennes: Presses Universitaires de Rennes, 2013.

Introduction 17

19 For more information and statistics on squatting and squatters' settlements in Asia, Africa and Latin America see the volume published in 2010 by Habitat International Coalition: A. Sugranyes and C. Mathivet, *Cities for All: Proposals and Experiences towards the Right to the City*, Santiago de Chile: HIC, 2010.

20 In this respect see: L. Leontidou, "Urban Social Movements in 'Weak' Civil Societies: The Right to the City and Cosmopolitan Activism in Southern Europe," *Urban Studies*, 47, 2010, pp. 1179–1203; P. R. Pinto, "Housing and Citizenship: Building Social Rights in Twentieth Century Portugal," *Contemporary European History*, 18(2), 2009, pp. 199–215.

21 T. Aguilera and A. Smart, "Squatting, North, South and Turnabout: A Dialogue Comparing Illegal Housing Research," in F. Anders and A. Sedlmaier (eds.), *Public Goods versus Economic Interests: Global Perspectives on the history of squatting*, London, Routledge: 2017, p. 30.

22 M. Mayer, "Preface" in Squatting Europe Kollective (eds.), *Squatting in Europe: Radical Spaces, Urban Struggles*, New York: Minor Compositions, 2013, p. 2.

23 M. A. Martínez López, "The Squatters' Movement in Spain: A Local and Global Cycle of Urban Protests," in ibid., p. 113.

24 In this respect see for example: B. Van der Steen, A. Katzeff, and L. Van Hoogenhuiuze (eds.), *The City is Ours: Squatting and Autonomous Movements in Europe from the 1970s to the Present*, Oakland, CA: PM Press, 2014.

25 For some of the more recent works see for example: R. Quirosa-Cheyrouze (ed.), *Historia de la Transición Española. Los inicios del proceso democratizador*, Madrid: Biblioteca Nueva, 2007; C. Molinero (ed.), *La Transición treinta años después. De la dictadura a la instauración y consolidación de la democracia*, Barcelona: Atalaya, 2006; M. Ortiz Heras (ed.), *Los movimientos sociales en la crisis de la dictadura y la Transición*, Ciudad Real: Almud Ediciones, 2008; D. A. González Madrid (ed.), *El franquismo, y la Transición en España. Desmitificación y reconstrucción de la memoria de una época*, Madrid: Catarata, 2008.

26 See for example: X. Doménech, *Clase Obrera, Antifranquismo y Cambio Político. Pequeños Grandes Cambios, 1956–1969*, Madrid: Catarata, 2008; J. Foweraker, *Making Democracy in Spain: Grass-Roots Struggle in the South 1955–1975*, Cambridge: Cambridge University Press, 2003; N. Townson, *Spain Transformed: The Late Franco Dictatorship, 1959–1975*, New York: Palgrave Macmillan, 2007; P. Radcliff, *Making Democratic Citizens in Spain: Civil Society and the Popular Origins of the Transition, 1960–78*, New York: Palgrave Macmillan, 2011; T. Groves, *Teachers and the Struggle for Democracy in Spain 1970–1985*, London: Palgrave Macmillan, 2015.

27 The earliest reference I was able to find appeared in E. Garrido Treviño, "Mientras el ayuntamiento se irrita los vecinos recobran la legalidad," *Doblon* (7.6.1975). See also S. Molina, "Participación democrática," *Ciudadano* (15.12.1975).

28 See for example: G. Evans (ed.) *The End of Class Politics? Class Voting in Comparative Context*, Oxford: Oxford University Press, 1999; H. Kitschelt, *The Transformation of European Social Democracy*, Cambridge: Cambridge University Press, 1994; F. Piven and R. Cloward *Poor People's Movements: Why They Succeed, How They Fail*, New York: Vintage Books, 1977.

29 On the new social movements, see: M. Castells, *Networks of Outrage and Hope: Social Movements in the Internet Age*, Cambridge: Cambridge University Press, 2012; D. Della Porta and A. Mattoni (eds.), *Spreading Protest: Social Movements in Times of Crisis*, Colchester: ECPR Press, 2014; C. Flesher Fominaya, *Social Movements and Globalization: How Protests, Occupations and Uprisings Are Changing the World*, London: Palgrave Macmillan, 2014; H. Kriesi, R. Koopmans, J. Willem Duyvendak and M. G. Giugni, *New Social Movements in Western Europe: A Comparative Analysis*, Minneapolis, MN: University of Minnesota Press, 1995; E. Laraña, H. Johnston and J. R. Gusfield, *New Social Movements: From Ideology to Identity*, Philadelphia, PA: Temple University Press, 1994; G. Steinmetz, "Regulation Theory,

18 Introduction

Post-Marxism, and the New Social Movements," *Comparative Studies in Society and History*, 36(1), pp. 176–212; B. Tejerina and P. Ignacia Perugorria (eds.), *From Social to Political: New Forms of Mobilization and Democratization, Conference Proceedings*, Bilbao: Universidad del País Vasco, 2012.

30 D. Della Porta and M. Diani, *Social Movements: An Introduction*, Victoria: Blackwell, 2006, p. 20.

1 Social control through spatial segregation

Urban planning under the Franco regime

The *new town* was the typical significant phenomenon in which and on which this organisation could be *read* because it was there that it was *written*. What, apart from such features as the negation of traditional towns, segregation and intense police surveillance, was inscribed in this social text to be deciphered by those who knew the code, what was projected on this screen? The organisation of the everyday neatly subdivided (work, private life, leisure) and programmed to fit a controlled, exact time-table[1]

The "centre-periphery" relation, in spite of its importance, is neither the sole nor the essential connective relation. It is subordinate to a deeper conflictive relation: the relation between, on the one hand, the *fragmentation* of space (first *practical*, since space has become a commodity that is bought and sold, chopped up into lots and parcels; but also *theoretical*, since it is carved up by scientific specialisation), and, on the other hand, the global capacity of the productive forces and of scientific knowledge to produce spaces on a planetary and even interplanetary scale.

This dialectised, conflictive space is where the reproduction of the relations of production is achieved.[2]

Between the years 1936 and 1939 Spain was torn apart by a civil war that took the lives of over 400,000 soldiers and civilians.[3] The war severely damaged national and urban infrastructures all across the country and set the development of the Spanish economy back by nearly two decades. Post-war reconstruction projects in Spain were carried out under dire material conditions and within the context of a highly repressive, nationalist dictatorship.

Throughout the years of the dictatorship a growing gap could be noted between the aims and the scope of urban planning schemes and the demographic changes undergone by Spanish society. If in 1900 only 33.3 percent of the Spanish population lived in cities with over 10,000 inhabitants. By the end of the twentieth century the percentage had risen to 75.67 percent. The city of Madrid, for example, registered 576,538 inhabitants in 1900. By 1940 (and despite the ravages of the Civil War) the number rose to 1,326,647 and had almost doubled itself by 1960. Barcelona exhibited the same demographic trend. During the first decade of the twentieth century it was home to 537,354 people. By 1940 this number increased to 1,081,174. Barcelona reached its demographic

20 *Social control through spatial segregation*

peak in 1974 with 1,816,623 inhabitants, a number that had decreased steadily ever since due to falling birth rates and increased migration within Cataluña. The city of Bilbao (much smaller than the first two) included in 1950 236,565 inhabitants. By 1970 the number reached 1970 410,490.[4] The numbers all point to the fact that despite great variations in size planners throughout Spain were faced with a reality of urban expansion all through the twentieth century. Following the Civil War this process of expansion overwhelmed the authorities, who thought that they could direct and control it and instead found themselves belatedly reacting to it.

The Franco regime's conception of urban space was greatly influenced by its oppressive social and ideological outlook. At the same time it is surprising to discover the extent to which its urban planning policies also drew on the theoretical debates that took place in other parts of Western Europe in the interwar years and again following 1945. This was partly due to the background of some of the architects that headed the central planning agencies during the 1940s and 1950s. Architects like Pedro Bidagor, Carlos de Miguel and Pedro Muguruza trained and worked in Spain and abroad during the years of the Second Republic (1931–1936).[5] Once they became affiliated with the planning agencies of the new regime they brought with them not only technical knowledge, but also a certain level of continuity in terms of theoretical concerns.

Urban planning under the Franco regime can be divided into three periods. The first period spanned the years 1939–1956. This period was characterized by centralized planning initiatives controlled by the state through its various organs. During these years the institutions and laws that governed urban planning were formed through complex negotiations between the regime's leading ideological "families." In the second period, the years 1956–1964, a new Land Law (*ley de suelo*) was put into effect and private capital became increasingly important to the formulation of Spain's housing policy. During those years the regime operated in accordance with a National Social Emergency Plan (*Plan de Urgencia Social*—PUS) which was meant to eradicate illegal construction and provide mass, low-cost housing. The third period in Spain's planning history spanned final decade of the dictatorship and the years of the transition to democracy. This period marked a move towards urban planning on a regional scale. It was characterized by social volatility and rapid political change. In terms of urban planning it signified more flexibility and attention to the needs of different populations. However, implementation of the new policies was severely limited by the onset of an economic crisis that greatly constrained the ability of the authorities to establish radically different spatial practices.

The General Plan: Spatial practices and representations of space in the shadow of a civil war

During the decade following the Civil War Spanish architects and urban planners had to face the enormous task of reconstruction. For this purpose the nationalist authorities created already during the final year of the war the National

Service for Devastated Regions and Reconstruction (*Servicio Nacional de Regiones Devastadas y Reparación*). A census taken by the Service in mid 1939 concluded that in 192 of Spanish cities over 60 percent of the building stock and infrastructures were damaged beyond repair.[6] Reconstruction, however, was not viewed by the new regime solely in material terms. The process of material reconstruction, of re-forming the state, had to also reflect a process of moral regeneration.

In symbolic terms regeneration was almost immediately manifested in the massive change in the names of streets and plazas. In Madrid the most significant changes included la *Castellana* which was changed to *Avenida del Generalísimo*; la *Gran Vía* which became *Avenida de José Antonio Primo de Rivera* (commemorating the founder of the Spanish Falange who was executed by the Republican authorities during the first months of the Civil War); and *Plaza de las Cortes* which was changed to *Plaza José Calvo Sotelo* (commemorating the conservative minister and former Finance Minister under the Primo de Rivera dictatorship who was assassinated in July 1936). Barcelona's *Gran Vía* was also renamed after José Antonio Primo de Rivera, while its *Avenida Diagonal* became *Avenida Generalísimo Franco*. In Bilbao besides renaming existing streets the authorities capitalized on the construction of six new bridges leading into the city in order to immortalize General Franco, José Antonio Primo de Rivera as well as the Generals José Sanjurjo (who headed the failed rebellion against the Spanish Republic in August 1932) and General Emilio Mola (who led the forces of the nationalist uprising in Northern Spain during the Civil War).

In structural terms the National or General Plan of Reconstruction (which was published in 1939) expressed a new and highly organic vision of the Spanish State. According to the Plan the "body of the nation" was made up different organs, each with its own function: from the city to the metropolitan area and all the way up to the scale of the region. Pedro Muguruza (who headed the National Service of Architecture) closed the First National Assembly of Architects in June 1939 by declaring: "Our transcendental mission is to ... urbanize Spain and systematically rebuild the New State from the foundation."[7] Architect Luis Pérez Mínguez during the same assembly expounded a plan for national reconstruction. For Pérez Mínguez unity of planning and of execution was essential. Highly critical of liberal planning, he demanded that the process of reconstruction be carried out throughout the national territory by "adhering to plans defined by the state ... We should put an end to all confrontations resulting from liberty of action and move ahead by forming precise organizations with defined tasks that will work towards a unified national mission."[8]

The wish for unity, however, was frustrated almost from the start by the creation of multiple planning organs. In September 1939 the National Service of Architecture was founded within the Ministry of the Interior. The service was to oversee the work of all the architects and technical auxiliaries working for the state. A month later the National Institute of Housing was created within the Ministry of Labor, which was to implement all housing schemes subsidized by the state. On a regional level the 1945 Law of Local Administration (*Ley de*

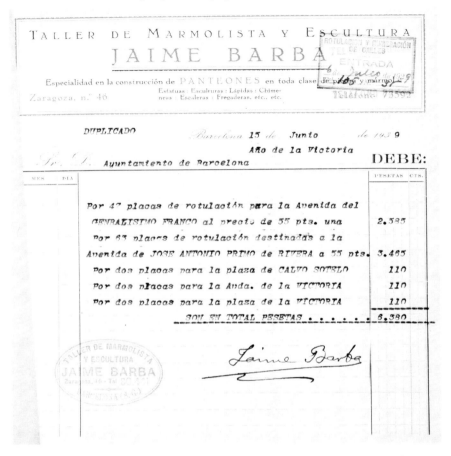

Figure 1.1 A receipt destined to the printer Jaime Barba detailing the cost of printing new street signs in Barcelona (1939)
Source: http://www.bcn.cat/bcnpostguerra/exposiciovirtual/es/1.6-represion-cultural-y-linguistica.html

Bases de Régimen Local) defined the "province" as an entity in charge of executing the state's policies in terms of urban planning. However, in the absence of adequate budgeting and of administrative autonomy many competencies that should have been under the control of city councils and the provincial deputations were soon transferred to the local representatives of government ministries and of different national services.

Against this confused administrative background some of the cities that were identified with the new regime (such as Salamanca, Burgos and even Madrid following the decision not to rob it of its status as Spain's capital) fared better than others. The Junta for the Reconstruction of Madrid, for example, was created as early as 1940. Its technical commission was headed by the well-known architect

Pedro Bidagor (who was also the head the department of Urbanism within the National Service of Architecture). Bidagor's goal was to formulate a series of General Plans as platforms for the reconstruction of Spain's major cities and he started with Madrid's General Plan that was published in 1941. Cataluña and the Basque region, on the other hand, were identified by the new regime as centers of political subversion. As a result they were castigated and intentionally deprived of sufficient resources for reconstruction throughout the 1940s.[9] Consequently the General Plan for the city of Bilbao was only published in 1945 followed by that of Barcelona in 1953.

The General Plan of Madrid divided the capital and its surroundings into two categories of land: urban and rural. To the first category belonged parcels of land that could be developed for housing and infrastructure uses. The second category included lands of limited development potential. The plan split Madrid into three circles and five zones, each with a distinct function. The first circle included the historical center of the capital. This space comprised a mixture of small residential and commercial zones but was dedicated for the most part to national monuments and administrative spaces. The second circle (*extrarradio*), bordering on the historical center of the city, included residential zones built mostly during the last decades of the nineteenth century as well as additional commercial zones. Finally, the outer circle (that in 1941 was mostly made up of undeveloped land and half destroyed villages) was to be dedicated to residential and industrial uses.[10]

The residential nuclei within the outer circle were called Satellite Suburbs, a term that pointed to their ambivalent relationship with the city. The neighborhoods of the *extrarradio* were connected to the historical center of Madrid via a series of roads. The Satellite Suburbs, on the other hand, were isolated both from the center and from each other. According to the Bidagor Plan Satellite Suburbs were supposed to exist as self-sufficient units. Just how this was supposed to happen was never made clear, since none of the neighborhoods was to have commercial spaces or basic health or education services.[11]

The General Plan of the city of Bilbao was initiated by the city's mayor Joaquín Zuazagoitia Azcorra in cooperation with Pedro Bidagor. Since the early 1920s local architects and politicians debated the desirability of planning for the "Great Bilbao" by encompassing within a single Plan both banks of the river Nervión. While liberals, republicans and socialists called for the annexation and integration of new residential areas on both banks of the river directly into the city's parameter, conservatives strove to contain the growth of the metropolitan area of Bilbao by channeling low-income and migrant populations into independent localities outside of the city's boundaries. The 1945 General Plan adopted an intermediate position by classifying the city and its metropolitan area as two separate entities, while at the same time planning for both within the same framework.

According to the General Plan the metropolitan area of Bilbao was to include 22 municipalities along the Nervión River and the Valley of Asúa. In 1945 the area covered by the Plan housed 350,000 inhabitants, 200,000 of them within

24 *Social control through spatial segregation*

the city of Bilbao itself. The Plan divided the city into five sectors or zones similarly to the Madrid Plan. The historical center of city was reserved for symbolic and administrative uses and was to include only limited residential zones (mostly catering for the needs of the affluent middle classes). The second circle covered the extension or *ensanche* of the old town. It included a mixture of middle-class and traditional working-class neighborhoods (such as Deusto, Rekaldeberri, Artxanda and Begoña) as well as some small-scale industries. All future residential expansion of low-income populations, as well as large-scale industry, was to be directed towards the left bank of the river and a belt of Satellite Suburbs.

Beascoechea Gangoiti and Martínez Rueda assessed Bilbao's General Plan in the following words:

> Despite the law's amplitude its defined sphere of action and most of its concrete recommendations constituted no more than an attempt to reorganize planning suggestions that were heard since the early 1920s. The Plan advocated specific changes to the urban fabric. In general terms, however, it rested on the [logic] of socio-functional zoning, the same logic that guided long-term urban development processes in Bilbao since the initial stages of its industrialization. The [General Plan] benefited the existing elites: local merchants, those engaged with the port of Bilbao, and the affluent classes of the city who maintained their residential privileges.[12]

Like other General Plans the Bilbao one was selectively implemented through a series of Partial Plans (*planes parciales*): the Partial Plans of Deusto (1947) and Begoña (1954) developed a specific sector within the *ensanche* for residential uses. While the partial plan of San Adrián – Rekaldeberri (1949–52) expanded the network of access roads to the center of town. None of these attempted to remedy the acute housing shortage in the city.

In the case of Barcelona a commission for the re-ordering of its metropolitan area was convened by the Civil Governor in 1945. In 1953 the commission finally produced a General Plan that was approved, but only partially implemented by 1960. The General Plan for the Metropolitan Area of Barcelona was intended to:

> define and regulate the desired scope of urban expansion. The Plan limited the size of the city and ensured the absorption of surplus [population] within satellite suburbs that were defined as independent residential units. Both within the parameter of the capital itself and within the metropolitan area the Plan strove to separate residential spaces from civic centers and administrative, cultural and commercial spaces with their unique profile.[13]

Similar to the Bilbao case, the General Plan of Barcelona also encompassed an area larger than the city itself. Here too the relationship between the provincial capital and its metropolitan area was defined hierarchically: from the center of

Barcelona where all the symbolic and administrative functions congregated to an outer residential circle that included between 100,000 and 200,000 inhabitants grouped within 26 municipalities, and all the way through to buffer zone which was made up of complexes of heavy industry and segregated residential areas designated for the working classes.[14] Within the context of a planning discourse that emphasized both hierarchy and the organic relationship between a city and its surrounding metropolitan area the plan ensured that certain functions would be catered for solely within the city of Barcelona. While transportation infrastructures, for example, were greatly improved in order to connect the city with the neighboring municipalities, many other services (in the fields of education, health and culture) were only partially provided for outside of the city center.

All of the General Plans that were published throughout the 1940s and early 1950s relied heavily on the concept of functional zoning. Functional zoning first received wide professional diffusion during the Fourth International Congress of Modern Architecture (CIAM IV) that took place in Marseilles and Athens in 1933. Four functions of the modern city were set forth in what would become known as the Athens Charter: living, working, recreation and circulation.[15] Functional zoning assigned specific spaces to each of those and determined accordingly different systems of circulation or transport. Later on, under the extreme circumstances that characterized everyday life in many post-World War II cities in Europe, the concept of functional zoning became the basis for policies of mass construction of infrastructures and of standardized housing. This highly rational planning module was aimed at maximizing the use of space and reducing to a minimum the cost of urbanization.

Abelardo Martínez de Lamadrid, an industrial engineer who worked alongside Pedro Bidagor on the formulation of the Madrid General Plan, reflected on the social function of zoning in the Spanish case:

> The division into zones went hand in hand with the accepted planning criteria of the time: facilitating the access of primary material; enabling the distribution of products; and minimizing the inconveniences of industrial production. But zoning also facilitates the location of a mass population of workers in Satellite Suburbs – spatially independent of the city itself and with easy access to the countryside. In this way the green zones and industrial zones provided a bulwark against the invasion of the masses[16]

In Spain, functional zoning acquired an additional goal – that of social segregation. Throughout the years of the dictatorship the authorities perceived urban space as a hotbed of social subversion.[17] Workers, essential as they were to the process of production, had to be excluded from the heart of the city. This vision was central to the creation of a new Francoist city where the spatial practices of the Second Republic would be eradicated. In the words of Nil Santiáñez:

26 Social control through spatial segregation

> Republicans changed radically the stable and traditional definition of "place" ... Within anti-Republican ideology, on the other hand, the meaning of "place" resulted from a ... unitary, classist and hierarchical system of meanings that defined spaces, places ad movements: stations went back to being stations, convents to being convents, colleges to being colleges and asylums to being asylums.[18]

Pedro Bidagor himself when referring to the reconstruction of Madrid declared that it could not consist of simply rebuilding that which had been destroyed. In 1941 he stated:

> Alongside material destruction we are witnessing the moral destruction of the entire urban fabric. This is the result of century long planning policies that lacked in tradition and were devoid of an organic understanding [of life]. If we limit ourselves to material reconstruction without taking into consideration the need for total urban reorganization it will be as if we are rebuilding the chaos of the past. We need to reform the city of Madrid and convert each of its existing sectors ... into a specifically defined part of a whole with exact dimensions and an exact function.[19]

Despite the attempts to present Francoist urban space as neat, orderly and radically different from the so called chaotic Republican city, in reality the process of "reforming" the Francoist city took place through an integration of several elements that were referred to and debated by the Spanish planning community since the 1920s. The General Plans strove to enlarge the residential areas bordering on the classical center of the city. They paid much attention to the relationship between the size of the population and the required volume of infrastructures. Their greatest contribution, however, was in the transition to a planning regime on a metropolitan scale, which situated "the city" within its spatial sphere of influence.

At the same time it is important to keep in mind the fact that the General Plans of the 1940s were not primarily concerned with the users of urban space and their needs. In this respect it would be reasonable to assume that the development of metropolitan infrastructures had more to do with a need to rationalize production and transportation and to facilitate the needs of national industry than with an attempt to cater to the needs of the urban population. All General Plans considerably restricted the number and the size of communal spaces, especially in the periphery of large urban centers. Green zones and recreational spaces where exalted for their healthy and tranquilizing effects on the population. However, as the General Plans were translated into Partial Plans most of these spaces, as well as other communal spaces dedicated for commercial and cultural uses, disappeared. According to the regime this was the unfortunate result of restricted financial resources. In reality this was mostly due to the authorities' fear that such spaces would provide an opportunity for subversive congregation.

Social control through spatial segregation 27

In this respect one can say that Francoist cities of the 1940s and early 1950s embodied what Henri Lefebvre defined as the central paradox of the spatial practices under late capitalism: an association that "includes the most extreme separation between the places it links together."[20] The mutual relationship between a much desired process of industrialization and the much feared presence of the working classes was never fully discussed during the post-war years. Nor were the consequences of adopting a planning regime, which oscillated between organic visions of the city, ideological paranoia and a harsh material reality. Against this background the General Plans often became a site of an intense struggle between the professional interests of the architects, the planning visions of urban planners and the economic and ideological interests of the political elites. The Falangist architect Víctor D'Ors warned in 1947 that this situation instead of leading to the creation of a rich architectural culture would bring about the institution of quasi-traditionalist style, disconnected from the here and now.[21]

During the first decade of the dictatorship ideological conflicts, budgetary limitations and administrative chaos prevented the full implementation of the General Plans. When the plans were implemented they generated extraordinary imbalances in terms of urban development. Such imbalances, as I mentioned before, were noted most of all in relation to the housing market and to the construction of infrastructures. This situation, in its turn, brought about an increase in illegal, self-construction all over Spain. In the case of major urban centers (such as Madrid, Barcelona and Bilbao) self-construction took place mostly within the outer industrial belt that was supposed to limit the expansion of the city. This area was especially attractive for squatters who came to seek work in the city due to its proximity to the industrial complexes and to the fact that in the early 1940s it was still sparsely inhabited.

As we shall see, squatting was one of two forms of settlement open to migrant families who moved into the major urban centers of Spain during the second half of the 1950s. A survey conducted in the southern periphery of Madrid in 1956 qualified 65 percent of the dwellings in the districts as *infraviviendas*, i.e. homes that did not meet the basic residential needs of the inhabitants. By 1976 12 percent of them did not yet have a toilet or a bath and only 35 percent had access to electricity.[22] A similar inquest conducted in Bilbao in 1959 concluded that 40,000 people in the city lived in *chabolas* and a further 100,000 were sub-renters. Students at the University of Duesto conducted interviews amongst the dwellers of 4,987 *chabolas*, which indicated that 69 percent lacked electricity and running water. The average number of inhabitants was 5 (for a 1–2 room *chabola*). 17 percent of the constructions included only one bed or had no bed at all and 27 percent did not have cupboards or storage units of any type.[23] In Barcelona the situation appeared to be much worse. As early as 1949 the Service for the Repression of Squatting (*Servicio de la Represión del Barraquismo del Barcelona*) indicated the existence of 15,000 shanty-homes all over the city, which housed over 60,000 persons. By 1957 (three years following the publication of the General Plan for

28 Social control through spatial segregation

the Metropolitan Area of Barcelona) the number of persons living in shanty-homes rose to over 120,000.[24]

Despite the rhetoric which qualified *chabolismo* as a manifestation of social and moral disintegration, the authorities were unwilling to eradicate the phenomenon before the 1960s. Squatting provided housing for a much needed urban work force at a minimal cost and soon became a profitable business. In the words of historian Luis Bilbao Larrondo:

> Faced with the scarcity of housing-solutions and the elevated prices of the existing housing stock, exploitation and speculation soon followed. The land that housed the squatters was bought off, illegally parceled and sold to third parties ... The squatters themselves ended up in a pitiable situation whereby they had bought with good money land or a house over which they were not able to provide a proof of legal ownership.[25]

As we shall see in Chapter 3, despite the harsh living conditions squatter settlements all over Spain developed extensive networks of communal life and mutual aid. By "misusing" space their inhabitants created residential enclaves that connected the outer zones of metropolitan areas with the heart of the city. Throughout the 1940s and 1950s squatter settlements progressively undermined the logic and implementation of the General Plans. Their very existence constituted a compromise: not only between the authorities and the squatters themselves but also between the regime's representations of urban space and its spatial practices.

The 1956 Land Law and the 1957 Social Emergency Plan: The construction of a periphery

> Having become political, social space is on the one hand centralized and fixed in a political centrality, and on the other hand specialized and parceled out. At the same time space is distributed into peripheries which are hierarchised in relation to the centers; it is atomized ... Around the center there are nothing but subjected, exploited and dependent spaces: neo-colonial space.[26]

In a rather delayed response the dictatorship attempted to adjust its urban planning regime by publishing in 1956 a new Land Law (*Ley de suelo*) followed in 1957 by the Social Emergency Plan (*Plan de Urgencia Social* – PUS). The publication of the new legislation coincided with a major ideological shift within the regime that had profound effects on the direction of urban planning policies. In 1957 Franco restructured his cabinet with a view to reorienting the Spanish economy and guiding the nation toward a modern fiscal system. He appointed a number of talented young bankers and economists. The "technocrats" as they were called, who were members of the lay Catholic organization Opus Dei. They were largely responsible for introducing and administering the Economic Stabilization Plan that formed the basis of Spain's future economic development. The new Stabilization Plan was intended to reduce inflation through the introduction of monetary discipline. Public spending was curbed and so was public debt. Domestic markets were partially liberalized and the prices of goods and services supplied by state monopolies were adjusted (mostly upward).[27]

The 1956 Land Law was born out of an understanding that all future urban expansion in Spain had to be supervised through a centralized planning process that took into consideration the reality on the ground, and especially budgetary issues. A central aim of the new legislation was to define once and for all the status and uses of different types of land, a step that had implications for all future housing policies. It was clear to all of the professionals involved in the drafting of the law that the strict distinction between urban and rural land was becoming less and less tenable. In the case of urban areas such as Madrid and Barcelona it was apparent that the city was "coming together" in a process that reflected both industrial expansion and accelerated urbanization. Illegal self-construction as we shall see in the following chapters became an urbanizing force in its own right, which changed the de facto status of large segments of land. Land, whether urbanized or rural was fast becoming a desired commodity.

The distinction between urban and rural land in the General Plans defined the first category as including parcels of land within the internal parameter of a city or a village that were reserved for future development or settlement. Rural land was defined as land not intended for residential development. Such land was reserved for agricultural and industrial uses, as well as for the construction of "communal infrastructures" (such as hospitals, roads, military compounds, etc.). The 1956 Law created a further category, that of Urban Reserve Land. Under this category were grouped all parcels of land that were not defined as "urban" but were already included within existing General and Partial Plans. The Law attempted to rationalize the process of urban planning by creating a system of hierarchical planes: National; Regional / Provincial; Metropolitan / General; and Partial. However, one of the law's main problems stemmed from the fact that the metropolitan level (unlike the provincial one) was never recognized as a unit of governance within the exiting political system. Of the 1,116 metropolitan plans that were approved between the years 1956 and 1975 many, therefore, lacked planning precision and execution capacity.

Following the publication of the new Land Law (and in view of the massive increase in illegal construction throughout Spain) the regime launched in 1957 its Social Emergency Plan. The Plan's aim was to accelerate the construction of housing units in general—and of low-cost housing units specifically—through cooperation with private developers. In doing so the regime hoped to both clear up the space taken by illegal settlements and offer support to the growing construction industry. The plan called for the construction of 60,000 new housing units in Madrid, 50,000 units in Bilbao and 51,000 units in Barcelona all within five years. Three different organs were responsible for the Plan's execution: the local Commissions for Urban Development were in charge of determining the

30 *Social control through spatial segregation*

location of future housing complexes; of freeing land through expropriation; and of constructing all communal infrastructures. The National Institute of Housing was charged with ensuring the provision of long-term mortgages and financial incentives for private developers. Finally the Syndicate of Home and architecture (*Obra Sindical del Hogar y la Arquitectura*—OSH) was charged with formulating and executing all "social housing" schemes.

At the heart of social housing schemes during the years of dictatorship was the Law of Protected Housing (*Viviendas Protegidas*, 1939). The houses constructed under the auspices of this law were defined as units of "reduced cost." This meant that rent could not amount to more than six days' pay or to a fifth of the renters' monthly salary. In 1954 a further law (*Ley de renta limitada*) specified three types of apartments to be constructed under the supervision of the authorities: reduced (74–100 m^2); minimal (35–58 m^2); and social (42 m^2).

While the regime did not commit itself to the construction of mass, low-cost housing prior to the late 1950s, the desired structure of minimal housing units generated heated debates as early as 1939. Immediately following the Civil War Pedro Muguruza outlined the three essential criteria to which minimal housing units had to adhere: the parents' sleeping area had to be separated from that of the children and the children had to be separated according to their gender; each apartment had to include a family room, where social interaction and moral instruction could take place; the apartments would be designed so as to provide appropriate ventilation and light, and the provision of running water.[28]

The designs of minimal housing units that Spanish architects produced during the post-war years drew on a model that was put forth during the second meeting of the International Congress for Modern Architecture (CIAM II) that took place in Frankfurt in 1929. However, while the model adopted at CIAM II set the bare limit of the "minimal house" at 50 m^2, the units constructed in Francoist Spain comprised 35–42 m^2. The houses were intended for the use of families with an average of four children and under these circumstances could hardly comply with the requirements indicated by Muguruza himself. In reality not only were most of social housing units constructed with only a single children's bedroom but most of the living-rooms acquired a double function: during the day they functioned as a space for socialization and eating while at night they were converted into an additional sleeping space.[29] The corridor (which was viewed as an essential component of all minimal apartments and was supposed to provide a "healthy" separation between the spaces designated for socialization and those designated for sleep) was dispensed with by most architects.[30]

The new housing units were incorporated into the Social Emergency Plan within two distinct modules: that of Absorption Suburbs (*Poblados de Absorción*) and that of Controlled Suburbs (*Poblados Dirigidos*). Despite the fact that historians sometimes confuse the two the planning modalities of these suburbs were distinct from each other. Absorption Suburbs were meant (as their name indicated) to absorb much of the population that lived in illegal, self-constructed neighborhoods. Most Absorption Suburbs were designed prior to 1957 and their

Social control through spatial segregation   31

construction was an essential step in clearing the area surrounding the pathways leading into major cities such as Madrid. These suburbs were envisioned from the start as transitory solutions and were therefore built using the cheapest materials and included the smallest housing units possible (between 24 m^2 and 35 m^2).[31] Both the internal structure of the houses and the external structure of the suburbs themselves were meant to meet what Lefebvre defined as the lowest possible threshold of sociability, "beyond which survival would be impossible because all social life would disappear."[32]

Controlled Suburbs, on the other hand, were envisioned as a more permanent solution.[33] Within the framework of Controlled Suburbs the state took upon itself to provide urbanized land, construction materials and mortgages for suitable buyers. The buyers, on the other hand, had to cover the price of the land and a percentage of the general costs of construction. Unlike the Absorption Suburbs, which lacked all public spaces, Controlled Suburbs were designed from the start around a principle road that was to connect the different housing nuclei and functioned as a commercial space of sorts.[34] Another characteristic that distinguished the Controlled Suburbs from all other forms of social housing during that period was the idea of a participatory construction process. The houses were destined to pass into the ownership of the inhabitants within 50 years, during which they paid reduced monthly rent. Upon occupation the inhabitants had to provide an initial down payment of about 20 percent of the total price. Families that could not afford the required amount could participate instead in the construction process, thus saving a significant portion of the cost. Luis Cubillo, one of the architects involved in the construction of the Controlled Suburbs in Madrid, recorded:

> The aspect I loved most in the Controlled Suburbs' project had to do with our own personal involvement. It required tremendous efforts because we had to spend our Saturdays and Sundays sitting down with a bunch of people who had no idea what they were doing. One gentleman was a butcher another was a hairdresser, and so forth and so on ... But it was a very special experience for all of the architects that took part ... It was a miracle that things actually worked out ... but they did.[35]

In *barrios* such as Entrevías, Fuencarral, Canillas, Caño Roto and Orcasitas in Madrid and in the Controlled Suburb of Otxarkoaga in Bilbao, future inhabitants, social workers, architects and representatives of the construction companies came together to form working groups. The structure of the houses and the suburbs' general design could not be altered by the neighbors. But the process nonetheless highlighted in the minds of both the inhabitants and the professionals involved the importance of popular participation. It also aided in the creation of a strong sense of community prior to the occupation of the suburb.

It is difficult to assess the long-term impact of the varied projects that were executed under the title of "Controlled Suburbs" on Spanish urbanism in general. Architect Ana María Esteban Maluenda claimed that the experience of the

32 Social control through spatial segregation

Controlled Suburbs constituted the first step in a renewed dialogue between Spanish architects and their colleagues abroad.[36] In the minds of the architects involved in the planning of Controlled Suburbs (such as Francisco Javier Sáenz de Oíza y Alejandro de la Sota and Julián Laguna) they designed residential units that offered better housing solutions under dire material constraints. Throughout the 1950s those architects were engaged in debates regarding the desired nature of the "neighborhood" as a planning unit: should it be an interclass unit that would cater for the needs of different populations and encourage their hierarchical cohabitation (as suggested by some of the Falangist architects such as Muguruza)? Or should the regime direct its energies and economic resources to the construction of mass working-class neighborhoods at a minimal cost (as suggested by some conservative architects such as César Cort)?[37]

A second debate revolved around the relationship between the structure of a minimal apartment and the nature of family life that took place within its walls. In some respects minimal housing units sponsored by the regime constituted an improvement over the self-constructed *chabolas* that will be analyzed in the third chapter. For both the authorities and the squatters a move from a self-constructed *chabola* to a "proper" house signified a move from chaos to an orderly built environment. It soon became apparent, however, that in certain cases the newly built apartments undermined some of the inhabitants' most basic definitions of well-being. The scarcity of space dictated the use multi-functional furniture (kitchen benches and sofas that could be transformed into beds; cooking spaces that could be transformed into dining tables and spaces dedicated for home-work) which was perceived as unaesthetic and mechanical in nature. Originally, spaces dedicated private activities (such as sleep and bathing) were assigned to the back of the house. The requirements of water provision, however, forced many architects to locate the bathroom next to the kitchen in a way that was perceived as both unhygienic and undermined the inhabitants' sense of privacy. The lack of space also forced many of the architects to eliminating the corridor (which constitutes central attribute in many modern Spanish houses to this day). By doing so they also eliminated the possibility for a gradual transition from spaces designated for social activities to those designated for private ones. This had implications not only for the inhabitants' sense of privacy but also for the ability to protect the most intimate spaces of the house from odors, noises and other types of intrusion.

In order to ensure high profit for the private developers most of the new polygons included buildings of up to ten stories high (instead of two and four as was originally intended). Green spaces and civic centers were eliminated and most of the new suburbs looked more like a collection of buildings constructed in proximity to each other than a neighborhood. The low quality of construction materials was soon evident. Worst of all was the fact that the suburbs lacked access roads that would connect them with the cities of which they were part. The new dwellers of these neighborhoods often did not understand the internal structure of their apartments and were intimidated by the scale of the buildings. What started off as a well-intentioned enterprise by socially minded architects ended up in the construction of what would become known to the inhabitants as *high rise chabolas*.

Urban planning in transition: Regional planning and private investment

The final decade in the history of the dictatorship was marked by two trends in terms of urban planning: the formulation of long-term, regional development plans and an increased reliance on private developers and private capital in the field of housing. In 1961 the regime approved a National Housing Plan whose goal was to build a million and a half new housing units throughout the country spread over 16 years. Reviewing the rate of urban growth it is clear that the Plan, even if carried through to perfection, could not keep up with the increasing demand for housing in the urban sector. Indeed, by 1968 over 60,000 people in Madrid alone still lived in illegally constructed homes.[38] Along the capital's south-eastern periphery a mixture of housing solutions and land-uses existed side by side:

> Between Usera and Villaverde one can find the Absorption and Controlled Suburbs of Orcasitas, Zofio and Villaverde. In between you can spot different nuclei of self-constructed houses or *chabolas*. And on the other side of the highway is the largest industrial zone of Madrid, where private developers constructed the Euskalduna and Boetticher Workers' Colonies.[39]

The responsibility for this uncoordinated urban disaster lay squarely on the shoulders of the Francoist administration. An examination of the regional plans of Madrid (1963) and Bilbao (1964) provides some clues as to the reasons behind the regime's inability to bring about sustainable change in its planning regime. Both plans pointed out to the need to clear spaces for residential uses and "decongest" the city center. In the case of Madrid this was supposed to be done by expanding the traffic infrastructures that connected the capital with the Alcala de Henares–Jarama–Tajo triangle and constructing more dispersed residential areas around the sierra of Guadarrama. A further concern of the regional plan was to enlarge and protect the agricultural zones that surrounded the capital and played an important role in its provisioning. These aims were only partially fulfilled due to the lack of financial means, but mostly because the different municipalities encompassed within the plan refused to cooperate with Madrid's planning agency, which they felt did not represent their own interests.

In the case of Bilbao the 1964 regional plan did not significantly diverge from the 1946 General Plan. Both were characterized by continued friction, which emanated from an all too rigorous application of the concept of functional zoning. The regional plan adhered to the division of Bilbao into different sectors: the classical town center, areas of intensive construction and those of controlled development, new suburbs, areas dedicated to large-scale industries and those dedicated to small-scale industries, and parks and cultural spaces. However, following a rigid functional approach often meant that planners ignored the specific profile of established neighborhoods both within the center of Bilbao

34 *Social control through spatial segregation*

and within the *ensanche*. The lack of coordination generated a chaotic urban panorama and the lack of funds undermined the construction of adequate collective infrastructures that were required for civic use.[40]

By 1970, overwhelmed by the pressure from low-income populations (through illegal construction) and from the construction sector and the urban middle classes (who were no longer looking for the regime to solve their housing problems but solely to provide land for private development) the government launched the ACTUR (Urgent Urban Intervention Plan).[41] Two ACTUR plans were implemented in Barcelona and one in Madrid. Along with other plans in Valencia, Sevilla, Zaragoza and Cádiz they provided housing solutions for nearly a million people within five years. However, the ACTUR also exposed the fact that the discursive reference to a new regional scale did not translate into a new planning regime. All of ACTUR projects were assigned to areas far beyond the metropolitan sphere of previous plans. The land on which the projects were constructed was rural land, situated between 15 and 25 kilometers from the center of the cities of which they were part. While the roads and transportation services of these new agglomerations were far better than the ones designed for the use of the older Satellite Suburbs, they too functioned mostly as dormitory suburbs.

Both the plans of the 1960s and the ACTUR reflected the fact that the regime was unable to make the transition towards a truly regional planning regime. This happened for several reasons. First, Spain's planning regime during the 1960s was guided by the dictates of the first Development Plans (*Planes de Desarrollo*) launched between the years 1964 and 1972. The plans followed the recommendations of the World Bank by attempting to generate economic growth on a global level and implementing a strategy of development poles (*polos de desarrollo*). Development poles were relatively limited geographical zones in which intensive industrial activity was promoted in the hope of activating the economy of the region surrounding them.[42] Implemented correctly, the notion of development poles could have helped in decongesting Spain's major cities and providing employment on a regional level. However for this to happen it was not sufficient to connect areas of intense industrial activity with the residential nuclei surrounding them. It was also necessary to construct new residential areas that would be self-sufficient in terms of other services such as health, education, culture, etc. As long as this was not done it was not reasonable to expect a voluntary spread of the population within the regional unit. Pablo Gigosos and Manuel Saravia, in their study of Spanish urbanism indicated a further reason for the failure of the regional plans.[43] For planning to be effective the plans had to be flexible and to anticipate rather than control urban growth. However, even the most advanced plans published throughout the 1960s attempted to mold both urban space and the population into a rigid grid rather than fashion urban space in ways that would respond to the needs of the population.

The new Land Law and the Law of Local Administration (*Ley de Régimen Local*) that were published in 1975 reflected the understanding of architects, planners and the authorities that a radical change of perspective was needed. The Law of Local Administration finally closed the gap between governance and planning theory by creating regional and metropolitan entities with their corresponding administrative organs. The implementation of the new Land Law was greatly enhanced by the new administrative framework. The 1975 Land Law was the first piece of legislation in four decades to step beyond functional grid. Concerned with the need to increase the supply of developed land, it encouraged the local authorities to come up with "open plans, without a fixed time of validity, evolutionary and non-homogeneous ..."[44]

In organizational terms, the new Land Law situated the supervising bodies at the regional level. At the same time it allowed for more flexibility at the level of municipal planning. This, as we shall see in the final chapter of the book, made the authorities more susceptible to popular pressure and to the notion of citizens' incorporation into urban decision-making processes. At the same time the Law acknowledged the inability of the state to shoulder the financial burden of planning and construction. It, therefore, called for the accelerated incorporation of private capital and enterprises into urban planning processes.[45] Fernando Terán, who was involved in the implementation of the new Land Law, wrote:

> It is interesting to note that most of the criticism directed against the Law was derived from the fact that its authors recognized the impotency of the authorities when it came to the implementing previous [legislation]. Only a few were willing to acknowledge the fact that the willingness to renounce past fantasies was the first step on the way towards constructing an urban regime capable of facing the tasks ahead of it.[46]

According to Terán, despite the fact that the law was published only months before the death of the dictator, it did not take into account the possibility of a radical political change. The more flexible and socially oriented Land Law borrowed some concepts from the new currents of urban planning in other Western European countries and in the USA. This piece of legislation timidly echoed within the Spanish context voices that had been heard in the French and Italian architectural worlds since the early 1960s. It borrowed indirectly from the work of French architects and planners in Bogota and Chandigarh, and especially the work of Michael Ecochard in Morocco. Those architects produced new paradigms for urban planning by planning under dire conditions and for "great numbers." Most of all they accentuated the need to take the existing urban structures into account and to conduct sociological and building surveys in order to get to know the city's history and ethnic fabric, and to "humanize" its future structure. In the Spanish context, however, the adoption of such ideas still took place within a strict technical framework that did not adopt a more democratic and socially critical perspective.

***

Following the death of General Franco, Spain entered a long and complex process of transition to democracy. The democratic constitution, which was approved

36 Social control through spatial segregation

in October 1978, acknowledged a large array of fundamental rights that were not formally acknowledged under the dictatorship. Article 45 of the constitution decreed that all citizens have the right to make rational use of society's natural resources and therefore should be allowed to benefit from their environment. Article 47 declared the right of all citizens to dignified housing. Against this background it is tempting to identify 1975 as a year of transition from a rigidly oppressive and conceptually limiting form of urban planning to a more flexible and democratic one. The dictatorship's spatial practices indeed had several distinct features: classist segregation of both the spaces of production and of reproduction and the creation of a massive urban periphery; the negation of public space as an open space where cultural production and social interaction could take place; and the acceptance of mass, illegal construction, which could be forcefully cleared out at the authorities' will.

However, one should be careful not to assume that a clear-cut dichotomy existed between the planning regimes before and after 1975. The subjection of urban planning regimes to economic goals, for example, was to continue throughout Spain's transition to democracy and beyond. This tendency was severally aggravated as Spain sank into economic depression following the second petroleum crisis in 1979. At the same time, some of the more flexible and participatory processes of urban planning that were envisioned by neighborhood associations and the architects that worked with them, resulted from cooperation that took place already during the final years of the dictatorship. Furthermore, as ineffective as the Franco era planning was in managing urban growth, its achievements did not differ significantly from those of other, democratic, regimes during the 1950s and 1960s. The singularity of the dictatorship's planning policy was derived from a simultaneous drive for modernization and spatial segregation. While this dual pattern was especially apparent in the case of Madrid and Barcelona, it could be detected throughout the country. The spatial practices of the regime, however, constituted only one aspect in the production of urban space. The dictatorship's spatial practices were shaped against constant popular attempts to define, manage and divide urban space. Popular pressure, as we shall see, progressively invaded and reshaped the Francoist city despite the regime's best intents. In doing so it created intermediate spaces that escaped the disciplinary strategies of the dictatorship, spaces where new communities were founded and new political practices emerged.

Notes

1 Lefebvre, *Everyday Life in the Modern World*, p. 59.
2 H. Lefebvre, *The Survival of Capitalism: Reproduction of the Relations of Production* (translated by F. Byrant), New York: Editions Anthropos, 1976, p. 241.
3 For a detailed account of war casualties and extermination of civilians during the war, see: P. Preston, *The Spanish Holocaust: Inquisition and Extermination in Twentieth-Century Spain*, London: Harper Press, 2012.
4 V. Simancas and J. M. Elizalde, "Madrid, Siglo XX," in *Madrid: cuarenta años de desarrollo urbano (1940–1980)*, Madrid: Ayuntamiento de Madrid, 1980, p. 11. For

more information on Barcelona, see A. Walker and B. Porraz, "The Case of Barcelona," available at http://www.ucl.ac.uk/dpu-projects/Global_Report/pdfs/Barcelona.pdf. On Bilbao, see: J. A. Pérez Pérez, "La configuración de nuevos espacios de sociabilidad en el ámbito del gran Bilbao de los años 60," *Studia historica. Historia contemporánea*, 18, 2000, pp. 117–147.

5 On the professional background of these architects, see: V. Pérez-Escolano, "Arquitectura y política en España a través del Boletín de la Dirección General de Arquitectura (1946–1957)." *Revista de Arquitectura*, 15 (2013), pp. 35–46.

6 F. Terán, *Planeamiento urbano de la España contemporánea. Historia de un proceso imposible*, Barcelona: Alianza, 1982, p. 118.

7 Terán, *Planeamiento urbano de la España contemporánea*, p. 121.

8 Ibid., p. 138.

9 Beascoechea Gangoiti and Martínez Rueda, "La creación del 'Gran Bilbao' en el franquismo y el alcalde Joaquín Zuazagoitia (1942–1959)," p. 83.

10 On the construction of monuments and administrative spaces in Madrid, see: Z. Box Varela, "La fundación de un régimen. La construcción simbólica del franquismo," doctoral thesis, Universidad Complutense de Madrid, 2008, pp. 353–437.

11 For more on Madrid's General Plan see: "Madrid, 1941: Tercer año de la victoria," in C. Sambricio, *Madrid, Vivienda y Urbanismo: 1900–1960*, pp. 314–328.

12 Beascoechea Gangoiti and Martínez Rueda, "La creación del "Gran Bilbao" en el franquismo y el alcalde Joaquín Zuazagoitia (1942–1959)," p. 88.

13 I. Bordetas Jiménez, "Nosotros somos los que hemos hecho esta ciudad. Autoorganización y movilización vecinal durante el tardofranquismo y el proceso de cambio político," doctoral thesis, Universidad Autónoma de Barcelona, 2012, p. 74.

14 M. Valenzuela Rubio, "Notas sobre el desarrollo histórico del planeamiento en España," *Cuadernos de investigación: Geografía e historia*, 4(2), 1978, pp. 51–52.

15 For more information on the formulation of the Charter of Athens see Le Corbusier, *The Athens Charter* (translated by A. Eardely) New York: Grossman Publishers, 1973. On reconstruction projects in Western Europe, see: A. S. Milward, *The Reconstruction of Western Europe 1945–1951*, Berkeley, CA: University of California Press, 1984.

16 Terán, *Planeamiento Urbano en la España Contemporánea*, p. 173.

17 I. Ofer, "The Concept of Mobility in Migration Processes: The Subjectivity of Moving towards a "Better Life," in Fernández Montes, M. and La Barbera, M. C. (eds.), *Negotiating Identity in Migration Processes*, Dordrecht: Springer, 2014.

18 N. Santiáñez, "Cartografía crítica del fascismo español: *Checas de Madrid* de Tomás Borrás," *Res publica*, 13–14, 2004, pp. 189–190.

19 P. Bidagor, "Primeras problemas de la Reconstrucción de Madrid," in Sambricio, *Madrid, Vivienda y Urbanismo*, p. 312.

20 Lefebvre, *The Production of Space*, p. 38.

21 V. D'Ors, "Estudios de Teoría de la Arquitectura, I. Sobre el Ábaco y el equino," in *Revista Nacional de Arquitectura*, 70–71, 1947, p. 338. Cited by Varela, *La fundación de un régimen. La construcción simbólica del franquismo*, p. 405.

22 J. Montes Mieza, M. Paredes Grosso and A. Villanueva Paredes, "Los asentamientos chabolistas en Madrid," *Ciudad y Territorio. Revista de ciencia urbana*, vol. 2–3, Madrid, 1976, p. 172. For further information concerning the district of Villaverde (including family size, housing and infrastructures) see also: COPLACO, *Villaverde*, Madrid: Colección Documentos de Difusión y Debate, 1980.

23 L. Bilbao Larrondo, *El poblado dirigido de Otxarkoaga: Del plan de urgencia social al primer plan de desarrollo (La vivienda en Bilbao 1959–1964*, Bilbao: UDALA Ayuntamiento, 2008, p. 34.

24 Ibid., pp. 95–96.

25 Ibid., p. 35.

26 H. Lefebvre, *The Survival of Capitalism* (Reproduction of the Relations of Production, translated by F. Bryant), New York: St. Martin's Press, 1976, pp. 84–85.

38 Social control through spatial segregation

27 For more on the 1959 Stabilization Plan and its effects see: L. Prados de la Escosura, J. R. Rosés and I. Sanz-Villarroya, "Economic Reforms and Growth in Franco's Spain," *Working Papers in Economic History, Universidad Carlos III de Madrid*, 2011.

28 P. Muguruza and L. Gutiérrez Soto in A. Santas Torres, "Un reto para la vivienda social en España: el hogar sin pasillo," *Actas del congreso internacional Los años 50: La arquitectura española y su compromiso con la historia*, Pamplona: T6 Ediciones, 2000, p. 174.

29 A. M. Esteban Maluenda, "La vivienda social española en la década de los 50: Un paseo por los poblados dirigidos de Madrid," *Cuaderno de Notas*, 7, 1999, pp. 55–80.

30 Santas Torres, "Un reto para la vivienda social en España: el hogar sin pasillo," pp. 171–180.

31 Montes Mieza, Paredes Grosso and Villanueva Paredes, "Los asentamientos chabolistas en Madrid," p. 172.

32 Lefebvre, *The Production of Space*, p. 316.

33 Interview with J. Laguna in L. Fernández Galiano, *La quimera moderna. Los Poblados Dirigidos de Madrid*, Madrid: Hermann Blume, 1989, p. 171.

34 Bilbao Larrondo, *El Poblado Dirigido de Otxarkoaga*, pp. 106–110.

35 Ibid., p. 58.

36 Esteban Maluenda, "*La vivienda social española en la década de los 50*," p. 57.

37 For more on this debate see: J. López Díaz, "Vivienda Social y Falange: Ideario y Construcciones en la Década de los 40," *Scripta Nova*, 8(146), 2003, available at http://www.ub.es/geocrit/sn/sn-146(024).htm .

38 M. Valenzuela Rubio, "Iniciativa oficial y crecimiento urbano en Madrid 1939–1973," *Estudios Geográficos*, 137, 1974, p. 625.

39 R. Moneo, "*El Desarrollo Urbano de Madrid en los años Sesenta*" in *Ayuntamiento de Madrid, Madrid: cuarenta años de desarrollo urbano (1940–1980)*, Madrid: Temas Urbanos, 1981, p. 103.

40 E. Mas Serra, "El urbanismo del período desarrollista en las capitales vascas," *Rev. int. estud. vascos.* 50(2), 2005, p. 477.

41 For more information on the ACTUR, see: L. Parejo Alfonso, "L'évolition du cadre juridique de la production de la ville depuis 1956," in L. Coudroy de Lille, C. Vaz and C. Vorms (eds.), *L'urbanisme español depuis les années*, 1970, pp. 28–31.

42 The first Development Plan signaled out Valladolid and Vigo as development poles of the automobile industry; Huelva as a development pole of the chemical industry; and Burgos, La Coruña, Zaragoza and Sevilla as poles of general industrial development. The second Development Plan shifted its focus to Granada, Córdoba and Oviedo. For more on Spain's Development Plans see: R. Alsina Oliva, "La estrategia de desarrollo plantificada en España 1964–1975," doctoral thesis, Facultad de Ciencias Económicas y Empresariales, Universidad de Barcelona, 1987, chapters 2–3.

43 P. Gigosos and M. Saravia, "Relectura del Planeamiento Español de los Años 80: Generación de Planes, Generación de Urbanistas," *Ciudades*, 1, 1993, p. 41.

44 Ministerio de Vivienda, *Reforma de la ley del Suelo y Ordenación Urbana*, Madrid, 1975, p. 9. See also: C. Blain, "Team 10, the French Context," presented at the International Conference *Team 10—between Modernity and the Everyday*, organized by the Faculty of Architecture TU Delft, Chair of Architecture and Housing. June 5–6, 2003. See also: B. Highmor, "Between Modernity and the Everyday: Team 10," in ibid.

45 Ibid.

46 Terán, *El Planeamiento Urbano en la España Contemporánea*, p. 544.

2 Internal migration in a post-Civil War society

From the countryside to the city in search of a better life

> Today, the town and country relation is changing, an important aspect of a general transformation. In industrial countries, the old exploitation by the city, centre of capital accumulation, of the surrounding countryside, gives way to more subtle forms of domination and exploitation, the city becoming centre of decision-making and apparently also of association. However that may be, the expanding city attacks the countryside, corrodes and dissolves it ... Urban life penetrates peasant life, dispossessing it of its traditional features: crafts, small centres which decline to the benefit of urban centres (commercial, industrial, distribution networks, centres of decision-making etc.).[1]

In order to understand the distinct socio-economic profile and the nature of community life that formed within shantytowns in Francoist Spain it is essential to examine first the processes of internal migration that led to their formation. In this chapter I examine the profile of internal migration from small towns and rural communities to the periphery of Madrid. I focus specifically on the concept of mobility and look at the ways in which movement was represented (by the Francoist authorities and the migrants themselves). I then examine the social networks that enabled individuals and families to carry through the act migration and the conditions that enabled them to translate the movement across space into social mobility.

Throughout the decades of the 1950s and 1960s over 20 percent of the general Spanish population changed its place of residence within the country. While rural Spain bled demographically the major urban centers gained more than 7 million new inhabitants. Sociologist Miguel Siguán wrote in 1966:

> Migration is probably the most important social phenomenon we are witnessing nowadays in the Spanish countryside. This is made clear by the wealth of statistics that are published in relation to demographic changes ... Its importance can also be noted on a subjective level. Migration has turned into an issue of major public concern and is referred to in every conversation.[2]

And yet, despite its great volume and the long-term effects it had on the structure of Spanish society this exodus received relatively little attention from

40 Internal migration post-Civil War

historians.[3] Until recently it was seen as a mere footnote in another history—that of external migration. If analyzed at all, it was mostly in economic terms. And it was not sufficiently integrated into the narratives that explain the massive changes undergone by Spanish society throughout the second half of the twentieth century.[4]

A common narrative situates the phenomenon of internal migration under the Franco dictatorship at the crossroads between two processes: the abandonment of the autarchic regime throughout the second half of the 1950s, and the "miraculous" economic recovery of the 1960s. The first process, according to many, served to "push" large segments of the unemployed rural population out of the countryside, while the second "pulled" precisely that same population into the growing industrial and service sectors in the cities. As attractive as this line of explanation might sound much work is still needed in order to validate it. Not enough is known, for example, about the motivations for internal migration during the years of the Franco dictatorship. Nor about the social networks that enabled migrants to transform movement across space into social mobility. A simplistic push and pull theory also ignores the fact that during the height of economic growth in Spain about a third of all internal migration was directed towards towns or villages that were classified as rural or intermediate in size (that is including a population of less than 10,000 persons).[5] Finally, it does not account for the fact that internal migration in Spain never ceased following the Civil War and peaked well before the effects of economic growth could be felt.

Massive population movements between countryside and urbanized areas in Spain were recorded throughout the first three decades of the twentieth century. Following the Civil War, however, the nature and motivations for migration changed. Under the dictatorship the four regions of Andalusia, Extremadura and the two Castillas generated 86 percent of all migratory flows, while Cataluña, Madrid, Valencia and the urbanized Basque region absorbed almost the entire migrating population. The scale of migration generated social and structural tensions within all of these regions. These were most noticeable in the case of Barcelona and Bilbao, where linguistic disparities raised questions regarding the effects of migration on Catalan and Basque identity.[6]

The most thorough analysis of this period was conducted by Alfonso García Barbancho, who indicated that about 1.05 million people changed their place of residence between the years 1941 and 1950.[7] According to Horacio Capel Sáez and García Barbancho about 2.29 million people changed their place of residence within Spain during the 1950s and additional 2 million did so between the years 1960 and 1965.[8] In the case of Madrid a study carried out by sociologist Miguel Siguán shows that some of the city's largest self-constructed *barrios* (such as *el Pozo del Tío Raimundo* or *el Cerro del Tío Felipe Pío*) attracted migrants as early as 1942.[9] In these *barrios* the flow of newcomers peaked in 1954 and slowed down in 1957, following the publication of new decree that called for the deportation and incarceration of migrants who did not possess "adequate" housing and imposed fines on the companies that contracted them.

By the mid 1960s Madrid lost its status as a favored destination due to a considerable decrease in its economic growth rates. From that point onwards the brunt of migration from Andalusia and Extremadura was absorbed by the Basque region, while Barcelona absorbed most of the Catalan migrants. While internal migration during the 1960s constituted mostly a movement from rural to urban regions and greatly enhanced regional economic differentiation, the migratory wave of the 1970s included patterns of returned migration and professional relocation and therefore generated increased movement between developed areas.[10]

During the 1940s and 1950s internal migrate was often linked to shifts in patterns of inheritance, land allocation and work in the countryside. The decision to migrate was backed up by concrete knowledge of the social and medical benefits that some of the urban centers were able to offer newcomers already in the immediate post-Civil War years and was clearly influenced by images of modernity and material progress that were associated with urban space. However, internal migration in Spain was also affected by more specific conditions that related to the installation of the dictatorship. Power relations between the victors (*vencedores*) and the vanquished (*vencidos*) of the Civil War were played out differently in small, agricultural communities and in dense, urbanized regions. Many migrants, therefore, perceived spatial mobility as a way of escaping a limiting socio-economic environment. This view helped them proceed with a project that during its initial phases often worsened their living conditions rather than improved them.

Mobility, movement and space

Increased mobility has been viewed by many as a central attribute of modern life. Some of the first sociologists who discussed the relationship between modernity and mobility viewed mobility, like modernity itself, as highly directional. If the idea of "first modernity" was connected with the notion of the nation state and with an anticipated linear progress in economic and institutional terms, then modern mobility was viewed as movement with origin, direction and destination, a strive forward in a spatial and social terms. However, with the emergence of what some call second modernity mobility, as a social concept, transformed itself.[11]

The "new mobilities paradigm" emerged in the past decade out of the work of sociologists like Mimi Sheller, John Urry, Vincent Kaufmann and Sven Kesselring. These writers highlighted the non-directional nature of modern mobility while focusing on rapid changes in all aspects of contemporary social life. The "new mobilities paradigm" in general emphasizes the fluidity of places as inseparable from the people who move through them. It views space, therefore, not as a fixed container of social lives but as constantly changing and as made up of zones of connectivity which empower some and exclude others. Vincent Kaufmann specifically highlights the relationship between three concepts instrumental to our understanding of modern mobility: the concept of movement

42 *Internal migration post-Civil War*

(which refers strictly to a geographic dimension and occurs between an origin and one or several destinations); the concept of a network (that can be defined as the framework of movement and can be social or technical in nature); and the concept of motility (which relates to the capacity of an actor to move socially and spatially). This capacity is clearly reinforced by the existence of networks and the availability of skills.[12]

The "new mobilities paradigm" is a useful framework for the analysis of internal migration for several reasons: the conceptual division between movement, network and motility highlights the fact that one can move without being mobile (in cases where the movement in space does not change the state of the actor) and at the same time that one can be mobile without moving (in cases where social practices and new forms of communication can lead to an association with new social universes). The paradigm also emphasizes the need to explore the discourses, practices and infrastructures of mobility and the ways in which they affect both movement and stasis. As Mimi Sheller indicates, critical mobilities research interrogates who and what is demobilized and remobilized across many different scales.[13] It also raises the issue of 'mobility capital,' or the uneven distribution of capacities and competencies, in relation to the physical, social and political affordances for movement.

Barak Kalir has argued that one of the limitations of the "new mobilities paradigm" has to do with the fact that much of the emerging work in the field has been fixated on the lives of people who become mobile across national borders. Kalir claims that the "… recurring reference to national borders and an emphasis on states as points of departure and arrival for both migrants and our analysis of them keeps the mobilities paradigm captured within the perceived omnipresence of the state with its interests and categories."[14] However, the new paradigm goes well beyond the state in analyzing the power relations behind mobility. As this chapter demonstrates mobility regimes that are instituted within the boundaries of national territory can be just as coercive as those applying to the movement between national territories. A framework through which one can deconstruct the relationship between movement and mobility, and which focuses on the differentiated nature of mobility itself, is therefore useful to our understanding of migration as a complex social phenomenon. Such a framework facilitates the study of both mobility regimes and of ways in which these regimes are viewed and negotiated by the migrants themselves.

The fear of unsupervised movement: Internal migration in Francoist rhetoric and legislation

As Tim Cresswell noted, a multitude of representations have been attached to the concept of mobility throughout history:

> Mobility has been figured as adventure, as tedium, as education, as freedom, as modern, as threatening. Think of the contemporary links made between

immigrant mobilities and notions of threat ... Or alternatively, the idea of the right to mobility as fundamental to modern Western citizenship[15]

How was mobility discursively constituted by the Spanish authorities following the Civil War? Before answering this question it is important to note that in the decade preceding the installation of the Franco dictatorship Spanish society experienced extensive changes in its relation to the concept of mobility. Under the Second Republic spatial mobility was acknowledged as a universal right of both men and women regardless of their marital or socio-economic status. This right, however, was contested by some sectors. A proof of this can be found in conservative and nationalist rhetoric that singled out the "chaotic" mixing of genders and classes as a danger to the potency and moral integrity of the nation. During the Civil War spatial mobility was greatly constrained (by the construction of new borders, the emergence of frontlines, the damage transport infrastructures, etc.). At the same time, movement across space was often the only possible response in face of life threatening situations.

Following the war the regime attempted to "restore" order by designating individuals and social groups to their "appropriate" place within the national territory and the newly founded social order. Unsupervised spatial movement, therefore, constituted a threat to the highly regimented society, which the dictatorship attempted to mold. However, an examination of Francoist rhetoric reveals that in the case of external migration references to mobility were often positive ones and linked to debates about labor and foreign affairs policies. Internal migration, on the other hand, was mostly referred to in relation to the growing problem of illegal construction on the outskirts of urban centers. Internal migration did not exhibit the advantages attributed to external migration. It did not minimize the threat of political unrest, nor did it significantly increase the buying power of the Spanish population, although it did decrease the overall levels of national unemployment.

The authorities viewed the migrants who moved across the national territory simultaneously as a much-needed work force and as disorderly and potentially subversive masses. Nowhere was this better expressed than in the words of José Luis Arrese, the Minister of Housing, who in 1956 stated:

If we do not stop even in an artificial and provisional way this tremendous rural exodus we will end up ruining the countryside. And what is worse, such a disaster will not solve the problems underlying [migration]. It will only serve to create around our cities a suffocating belt [of shanty-towns].

We must do our best in order to change the panorama of small-town life and recreate a sense of harmony between Man and the landscape around him. We must keep men away from the turbulent, proletarian city of the masses.[16]

The regime's fears were further expressed in a document of the Spanish Ministry of the Interior, which stated:

> The intense demographic and industrial development of Madrid, and of other urban centers, is enhanced first and foremost by those who arrive from rural areas into the big cities. This process is causing grave imbalances in the division of the population, which must be [amended].[17]

Keeping certain segments of the population in "designated" spaces (from small rural communities to urban dormitory suburbs) enabled the regime to maintain better control over them. In small, intimate communities in the countryside the authorities could make use of more indirect forms of social control: priests, teachers and neighbors were used to monitor individuals and their families. In these communities, where the economic wealth and employment opportunities were controlled by a handful of families that were loyal to the regime, many informal sanctions could be used in order to keep people "in line" both morally and politically. Spatial mobility, therefore, quite literally undermined the mechanisms of political repression and of social control instituted by the dictatorship.

While martial law stayed in vigor in Spain (1946) the population's movement was severely limited, especially in the frontier provinces. But even in the early years following the Civil War the authorities did not manage to stop internal migration altogether. During the 1950s the regime continuously struggled to distinguish between legal and illegal migrants. To belong to the first group, individuals had to possess an income sufficient to maintain themselves and anyone else that had joined them in the city, and prove that they had adequate housing and stable employment. Some migrants tried to adhere to such requisites by sending first one member of the family (usually the husband) while all the others had joined him only after he found housing and employment in his new place of residence. But in reality only a minority of the migrants could fulfill these legal requirements. As far as the regime was concerned, therefore, internal migrants were almost a priori assigned the position of criminals. In the case of those who settled in illegally, self-constructed neighborhoods, the lack of infrastructures and services created real deprivation, dirt and antagonism, which only reinforced their status as dangerous "others."

Under these conditions one may ask what were the motivations of the people, who nonetheless chose to internally migrate? The distinction between a city and a village or a small town in post-Civil War Spain was a very clear one. Francoist censuses defined a city as an area that encompassed a population of more than 10,000 inhabitants. In a highly scrutinized and repressed society large cities, therefore, offered anonymity. They also offered distinct types of employment and access to different (though not necessarily improved) life styles. While rural space was identified with work in the primary sector, "city work" was identified with employment opportunities in the secondary and tertiary sectors.[18]

In the countryside the basic family and work unit was often one and the same. The "casa" (or *baserría* as it was called in the Basque regions) was the basic unit of agrarian family life. In many areas the *casa* included three generations: a retired or semi-retired couple (the grandparents), a married couple and their children. While the *casa* remained a central family unit in the Spanish countryside throughout the 1950s, the world around changed rapidly. As Susan F. Harding noted in her research on rural communities in Aragon:

> The central transformative process ... was an expansion of capitalist agriculture that was orchestrated by agrarian reform measures enacted under the regime of Francisco Franco. Villagers dismantled pre-industrialized forms of agriculture and constructed a form of mechanized capitalist agriculture through a series of separate, seemingly unconnected, individual decisions to alter their productive strategies ... The collective effect of these decisions was to dissolve the village and its homesteads as ecological, social and moral universes ... At the same time villagers constructed a world in which agriculture was more a livelihood than a way of life, in which interdependencies within and between village families, and between families and the land, were eclipsed by more urban and market oriented ties, and in which local domains of authority and solidarity gave way to more secular, regional and national commitments.[19]

Under these conditions marriage became less a means of reproducing the *casa* than a way of establishing one's own nuclear family. At the same time impartible inheritance laws (that were meant to protect the essential land unit on which the *casa* could subsist) drove the non-inheriting siblings into a state of landlessness. Consequently many had joined an already existing population of day laborers, who by 1975 made up 50 percent of the countryside's inhabitants.

Political repression during and following the Civil War was also responsible for an increase in the countryside's landless population. Francoist repression was based on two fundamental procedures: physical punishment and economic penalties, of which the seizure of assets was the most common. Economic repression was regulated by the Law of Political Responsibilities of February 1939.[20] The scope of investigation according to the Law of Political Responsibilities was wide, and the confiscation of assets forced entire populations back to an economic "point zero." In such cases any chance of economic recovery often depended on the ability of the accused and their families to escape the repressive environment in their community of origin.

Political repression and economic deprivation provided powerful motivations for internal migration despite the existence of highly coercive mobility regimes in Franco's Spain. As the following pages show, however, the option of spatial movement was not open to everyone. Following the Civil War Spanish society was loosely divided into two camps: that of the victors and that of the vanquished. Internal migration was an option open only to certain types of *vencidos*. Individuals and families had to develop specific strategies in order to facilitate the process of migration under highly unfavorable conditions. They did so by relying both on social networks that emerged in their community of origin and within their new place of residence. And even then spatial movement was not necessarily equated with significant social mobility. Under such conditions the

46 *Internal migration post-Civil War*

framing of the migratory process as a process of self-improvement raises several questions: how did the most deprived populations under the dictatorship define mobility? What capacities did these populations possess for moving spatially within Spain? And finally, what was the correlation between spatial movement and social mobility?

The politics of location: Subjective stories of self-improvement

Statistics relating to internal migration from rural to urban areas in Spain during the decade of the 1950s reflect the fact that it was mostly professionally unqualified populations that tended to migrate. A census conducted in 1954–1955 indicated that migrants who arrived into the Madrid area were divided along the following lines: 49 percent women and 51 percent men; 49 percent defined themselves as actively employed in their former place of residence; of this population 71 percent were day laborers and 11 percent were employed in the field of domestic service; 7 per cent-8 percent were illiterate and about 20 percent lacked any former professional training.[21]

Migrants into the Barcelona areas represented a slightly different profile. There the bulk of migrants that arrived from Valencia and Aragon were qualified laborers. Many of whom were integrated into the transport industry. Migrants arriving from smaller urban centers in Cataluña usually occupied qualified positions within the secondary sectors, as well as within the banking and sanitation sectors. On the other hand many of the migrants from Murcia and Almeria (much like those from Andalusia and Extremadura in the case of Madrid) were classified as unqualified laborers and were integrated into the construction sector and into the lower spheres of mechanized industry (mostly the textile and the chemical industries).[22] In the case of Bilbao the more qualified migrants from La Rioja, Cantabria and Navarra (who made up over 80 percent of all migrants to the city in the decade of the 1940s) were replaced between 1955 and 1965 by growing number of migrants from Andalusia, Extremadura and Castilla La-Mancha. In Bilbao too unqualified laborers found work in the lowest levels of industry, in the construction sector and as dock workers.[23]

Michaela Benson, in her ethnographic work of lifestyle migration, referred to the importance of understanding people's decision to migrate:

> The decision to migrate remains important, revealing the basic characteristics of the lifestyle sought … However, while accounts of the decision to migrate can give early insights into the characteristics of the lives sought, it is pertinent to move beyond this descriptive material to explore and explain the culturally framed meanings that particular destinations have for individuals and experiences of life following migration.[24]

The majority of the people who settled in the district of Villaverde (of which the neighborhood of Orcasitas is part) were day laborers who lacked economic security in their place of origin. However, the interviews I conducted expose certain motivations behind the migratory projects that go beyond the purely economic push and pull factors. Ángela was born in Madrid. Her parents arrived in Villaverde from the town of *La Roda* near Albacete. She recounted:

> My father's family owned meat shops. Following the war the regime confiscated our business for having provisioned the Republican Army. Since he was unable to find work in *La Roda* my [father] got into business with someone from his hometown. They founded a paint factory close to the *Poblado Dirigido de Orcasitas*.[25]

Ángela tells a typical story of Francoist economic repression. Her grandfather was a supporter of the Spanish Republic, but he was not accused of specific crimes by the nationalist authorities. He and his son, therefore, did not lose their freedom only their business. Founding a new business was a difficult task, but it was within the family's realm of possibilities. However, migrating away from the town where they were well known was the only way to go about it.

Gregorio arrived in Orcasitas at the age of 9 from the village *San Roque* in the province of Cadiz. He and his family were "tagged" as deviants, albeit from a different perspective. For them too migration was the only option:

> I tell you, we suffered so many disasters over there, between those two rivers. So much hunger and suffering. That was the Franco era and we gypsies, we weren't treated then the way we deserved to be treated. Everyone over there looked at us funny, superior sort of.[26]

Jesús, originally from the Toledo countryside, settled in the district of Villaverde in 1955. In his interview with historian Julio Fernández Gómez he recounted another typical story of migration in search of anonymity:

> This guy who was in charge of everything back there [in Toledo] started a sausage factory ... Many of us worked there, but the guy did not pay us social security, making but the most basic payments. I denounced him in 1954. And what a surprise! Since everyone in the village worked with him I was left with no employment, no one would hire me.[27]

Jesús did not come from a background of political activism, and it is important to note that his actions were not framed within an oppositional discourse. He did, however, come from an area where agrarian reform plans were implemented during the years of the Second Republic. This period, which he experienced as a very young child, was described by him as "a time of social security" that clearly shaped his conceptions of right and wrong and his expectations of communal help. Acting on such expectations he soon found himself unemployed. Migration was his only choice.

48 *Internal migration post-Civil War*

José López de Pablo arrived in Orcasitas in 1952 from the town of Manzanres in the Province of Ciudad Real. He recorded:

> I came here because there was no regular work in the village, and since we dared to complain they labeled us as "troublesome" ... One day we sat, some laborers, around the village square. It was the time for Mass and the priest came out and called us to come in. We did not say anything, nor did we move. And he said "Not one of you is going to stay here."[28]

When analyzing the causes for mass internal migration in the 1950s it is important to note that the image of the countryside as a place characterized by harsher living conditions and lacking in secure employment was not a new one. Under the government Second Republic, however, there was a general sense that the state was working in order to minimize the disparities in living conditions and economic output. Under the dictatorship such disparities were perceived as part of a planned strategy, against which movement across space was the only remedy.

Those who made the decision to migrate to Madrid soon found out that life in the city was not intrinsically better or easier to manage. Primary products were often cheaper in the countryside and so were some free-time activities. While other more modern diversions (such going to the cinema or to a musical event) were accessible only in the city, they were often beyond the economic reach of most of the migrant families. As far as education was concerned, primary school placements were harder to secure in the city, where some peripheral neighborhoods had no classes at all. Secondary education, on the other hand, was more diversified and more easily financed through scholarships.

In terms of work, too, migration to Madrid cannot be viewed as a process of absolute improvement. Upward mobility work-wise could mean several things: it could mean better pay, more possibilities for professional training and advancement or different working conditions. Sociologist Isidro Alonso Hinojal, who interviewed migrant families in Orcasitas in 1965, pointed out that half of the men he talked to found work in Madrid only as non-qualified laborers. Of those 40 per cent, indicated that they would be interested in finding better jobs—that is jobs that necessitated further professional training. The rest stressed that they were happy with their current employment.[29] From the interviews I conducted it is clear that employment stability and the predictability of working hours were valued above all else by first-generation migrants. Possibilities for professional training and advancement were perceived as less important. A man who had migrated to Madrid in 1954 explained in an interview he gave years later:

> In the countryside we worked endlessly. Between the middle of June and the middle of September, for example, I could not take a single day off ... Then we got to the factories [in the city] and clearly we had to work hard. But at 19:30 you would go home, and [your work the next day] would be

secure. This was unheard of [in the countryside] where we worked like slaves and with no prospect [of security].[30]

Of course not all men worked an 8-hour day in the city. By the mid 1960s, 31 percent of the men in Orcasitas reported they worked between 8.5 and 10.5 hours a day and 22 percent reported working over 10 hours. A major difference for those who did so was the fact that they now earned extra pay for their overtime work.[31]

A carpenter who had migrated to Madrid in 1952 at the age of 28 from a village of the Toledo countryside recounted:

> In the countryside we worked more and lived under worse conditions. I was made aware of that when I arrived in Madrid [1946] in order to complete my military service. And I was one of those with a permanent job. I worked all year around ... But I did my math and it came out I was earning 7 pesetas a day in the countryside in 1951. It was then that I decided I couldn't go on. And the worst thing is that I worked day and night, no holidays. This is why I came to Madrid.[32]

Connections of hope: The role of social networks in internal migration

One factor that clearly affected the willingness of individuals to consider migration was the amount of the information they possessed regarding the place in which they wished to settle. Studies concerned with different forms of internal migration provide ample evidence of the existence of varied social networks that tie urban and rural communities, providing migrants with extensive information and practical assistance. Social networks might be based on different affiliations: blood-relations, professional ties, personal friendships or common geographical origins.

Paradoxically it would seem that some of the most useful networks in the case of internal migration in Francoist Spain were put in place by the regime itself. Of all the families interviewed in 1959 by sociologist Miguel Siguán 5 percent of the men stated that they first contemplated the idea of moving to the capital during their military service. It was in Madrid that they received their first professional training. As young, unmarried men who were fed and housed by the state they were able to make use of their small salaries to enjoy the city's cinemas and bars. In both cultural and economic terms life in the city seemed to offer advancement. However, it is significant that none stayed on after their service. It was only after they were married that the final move to the city was made. Study periods and sporting events sponsored by the regime's Youth Movement also provided an excellent opportunity to get to know the capital.

All migrants, and especially women, soon became adept at using new channels of information and of mutual aid offered to them by the city in their search for shelter, education and livelihood. When analyzing the relationship of working-class communities with the dictatorship, especially to its education and welfare

50 *Internal migration post-Civil War*

agencies, it is important to keep in mind that the engagement with aid and charity agencies was often a double-edged sword. Following the Civil War the Franco regime entrusted a wide range of its social welfare activities to the Female Section of the Spanish Fascist Party (Sección Femenina de la FET).[33] As the regime moved away from its first phase, characterized by the use of brute force, and into a phase of more subtle forms of control and supervision it increasingly used welfare agencies as tools of "soft" indoctrination. Such agencies were expected to initiate contact with "problematic" populations by providing them with material assistance (food coupons, medical aid, housing solutions). In doing so they were able to gain firsthand information about the personal lives of their clients and facilitate their participation in social and cultural activities of an ideological nature fostered by the regime. Migrant women often spent large portions of their day standing in line in soup kitchens and government ministries; or petitioning, begging and cajoling social workers and priests; or filling in documents and balancing the various demands that qualified them for aid from a variety of private and public organizations.[34] Their skill in manipulating this system no doubt earned their families additional income. Such skills were passed on to other, newly arrived women, in countless encounters within the neighborhood.

My research in the case of Orcasitas has demonstrated that geographical affiliations played a central role in the decision to migrate to Madrid and in determining the form of settlement once there. There is no doubt that for some people the decision to settle in Orcasitas was arbitrary. The neighborhood was simply the last cheap, unsupervised frontier before the actual capital. But the fact that some streets, and later on entire buildings, were populated by different households belonging to one extended family or arriving from the same village indicates that many migrants purposely made their way into an area where they already had acquaintances.

Of the 1,680 households that comprise my database, 14 percent moved into the *barrio* from the center of Madrid itself. This information highlights the fact that shantytowns provided housing solutions not only for newly arrived migrants, but also to the younger cohorts of the capital's working-class. Other municipalities provided smaller numbers of migrant families. However, relative to the size of these municipalities there is no doubt that the percentage of people who chose to settle in Orcasitas was significant. Especially striking is the case of the municipality of *Belvís de la Jara* in the province of Toledo. In the early 1950s the municipality numbered about 4,000 inhabitants, of which 52 households migrated to Orcasitas.[35] The villages *Bohonal del Ibor* and *El Gordo*, in the province of Caceres, and *Campo de Criptana*, in the province of Ciudad Real, were even smaller than Belvís. Between the years 1950 and 1970 both were destined to lose about a third of their population through migration. A significant number of these migrants found their way to Orcasitas.[36]

When focusing on specific streets in Orcasitas, the importance of geographical affiliation becomes even more pronounced. *Calle Anguita*, for example, consisted in 1958 of 28 households: 33 percent of the families on that street came from the small town of *Ubeda* in the province of Jaen, and a further 10 percent from the city of Jaen itself.[37] *Calle Antonio Cordobes* in 1957 consisted of 91 households; of those 10 percent came from the small town of *Andujar*, also in the province of Jaen, and a further 12 percent from the towns of *Belvís de la Jara* and *Herencia* in the province of Ciudad Real.[38] The road leading into Orcasitas, *Carretera de Villaverde*, registered 60 households in 1958, 20 percent of those families came from the small town of *Bohonal del Ibor* in the province of Caceres.[39]

Historians José Babiano and Julio Fernández Gómez noted that geographical affiliation played a similar role in determining the migrants' decisions regarding their initial work place.[40] In Madrid and elsewhere across Spain, employers and job seekers used existing social networks as a recruitment tool as can be seen in the following extract:

> I learnt of the job from Manolo … He told me that in *Boetticher* there were several openings and that they paid well. We talked quite a bit and told each other things. I actually earned more where I was working at the time, but they did not let us do [other things] and I was very young and I wanted to move up in life. Also I could trust Manolo to tell me exactly what things were like *Boetticher* so I knew what to expect.[41]

The above extract points to the mutual advantages of recruiting through existing social networks. Workers benefited from fast-circulating information about vacancies, they could filter those that they knew would be relevant to them and had detailed information about the expected pay and working conditions. Since these applicants came recommended by people who already worked in the company, they also stood a better chance of securing the post they applied for. Employers, on the other hand, obtained employees who were aware of the working conditions in the company and therefore were more likely to stay on permanently. This form of recruitment also helped to exclude undesired elements and to discipline newcomers. In the words of one interviewee:

> Employers and business owners benefitted from the situation. There was always a chance that one of the guys [that you helped bring in] would be more rebellious than the others. In which case they could count on you to [help them] control the situation. You had more seniority and the guys would come to you with their problems. And you could tell them: 'It's not important, let it go, it's not worth losing your job over something like this.' They would ask for your opinion because they held you in high esteem, since you were the one who arranged the job for them.[42]

In October 1940 the company Boetticher y Navarro S.A. acquired a large parcel of land in the district of Villaverde for its future installations. It was followed the same year by the electronics company Marconi Española and the glass manufacturer Giralt Laporta S.A. These industries were joined in 1948–1949 by Barreiros Diesel S.A. and Ferrovial-Agromán (that already had an assembly line

52 Internal migration post-Civil War

in Madrid) and by Laboratorios Llophar (or Llofar), S.A. From the second half of the 1950s the last three companies provided part-time or full-time employment for almost one-third of all the heads of households in Orcasitas. However, having crossed the information in my database regarding the migrants' place of origin and their place of work in Madrid I was unable to find a correlation between the two. It would therefore seem most likely that the networks through which job opportunities were secured in these larger companies emerged out of their geographical proximity to the *barrio* itself, and drew upon the newly formed social relations within the community rather than on older geographically based ties.

At the same time it is important to note that the fragmented professional profile of the community in Orcasitas limited the role that could be played by social networks (of any kind) in enhancing people's professional socialization. Only 2.3 percent of the heads of households that comprise my database defined themselves as qualified laborers. The largest group of employed persons (35 per cent) defined themselves as day laborers and 5 percent as working from home with no specified profession (mostly households headed by women). Bricklayers made up the second largest professional group in the *barrio* (5.9 per cent), followed by independent business owners (5.4 per cent), mechanics (3.4 per cent), carpenters (3 per cent), waiters (2.9 per cent) and general assistants (2.8 per cent). A third of all those who provided information regarding their professional background indicated that they did not have stable employment. Under these conditions one can deduce that at least during the 1950s most of the working population in Orcasitas did not undergo meaningful processes of professional socialization in a way similar to other working-class populations in Madrid (in the neighboring *barrios* of Usera or Carabanchel for example). As we shall see in the following chapters, this situation reduced the ability of the inhabitants to capitalize on professional networks (especially direct access to the clandestine labor movement and its organizational resources) in order to extend and consolidate their political and civic activism in later years.

Geographically based social networks forged within the migrants' community of origin had an effect not only on their choice of residence once in the city, but also on the structure of cultural and community life in Orcasitas. Felicitas (aged 91) arrived at Orcasitas from Albacete. In her interview she explained how the presence of her husband's friends from *La Roda* dominated the couple's social life in Madrid:

> Look, my husband came from Albacete and he kept in touch with some friends that also got away and lived here. Some intimate friends. We celebrated birthdays together, we all got together and each year we celebrated Christmas in a different home. It was wonderful.[43]

Daniel (aged 61) arrived in Orcasitas at the age of 17 from *Belmez*, near Cordoba. He stated proudly:

> One of the most important things for me is the fact that I was never uprooted from the old land. After forty something years here [in Madrid] I

still keep my accent and I have no intention of losing it. I come from a miners' village in the province of Cordoba and when my final moment comes they will say – here lies a man from the village of Belmez.[44]

The view that the life and culture of the city and that of the countryside were positioned along a continuum rather than as two dichotomous experiences was further enhanced by material and affective ties. About a third of all those who owned some sort of property prior to migration chose to retain it even though they were often hard pressed to pay for their new home in the city. Some people were afraid of leaving behind the small patch of land and few animals that had supported them economically so far. Others simply left their property in the hands of family members while making use of the possessions of other family members already in the city. The countryside (both as a memory and as a concrete location) was visited and revisited during holidays and summer vacations. For children who were born in Madrid or arrived there at a very young age, it often emerged as a space in which they could experience a different life and reconnect with the memories that shaped the lives of their parents. The remnants of a so-called "rural culture" were maintained because of their usefulness, mainly their capacity to provide migrants with practical assistance and a sense of psychological security. And this modified sense of community and of kinship, as well as other elements of village culture (especially cooking practices and regional fiestas) were retained and incorporated into a new, hybrid urban culture.

**

As this chapter demonstrates internal migration under the Franco regime was a complex experience. It constituted a movement across space, mostly (although not always) from smaller geographical units (such as villages and small towns) to larger ones. Spatial movement was undertaken with an explicit wish to improve one's life, but hardly ever resulted in unequivocal upward mobility. Nowhere was this better exemplified than in the words of Antonio Egea Gil, who arrived in 1957 to Orcasitas from the town of La Coronada in the province of Badajoz. In 1986 he reflected back:

> Orcasitas [started off] as a transit station, the last one on our journey to Madrid. This is what we wanted most of all – to enter the city, the 'promised city.' It did not matter how we did it, even under the poorest conditions. But we never attained our goal. We were left there – in that final transit station ... From afar we saw tall buildings and city-lights. They were there for those who managed to get their foot in the door, those who made it into the city. For years that was our only dream.[45]

The above quotation encompasses, in my view, an entire spectrum of reflections regarding the nature of migration and its relation to the concept of "mobility." It points to mobility as imagined and as something to be achieved. It highlights the fact that unlike movement, mobility is assessed less in terms of a distance traveled, or the distance left for traveling—and more in relation to a specific material and a psychological reality, which one strives to attain or produce.

In the Spanish case the complexity of everyday life, the socio-political status of most of the migrants and the spatial practices of the regime frustrated the hope for improvement across all walks of life almost from the start. Under the dictatorship different forms of political, social and economic repression affected the lives of Spaniards both in the cities and the countryside. The most extreme examples of repression included execution, imprisonment and forced migration. However, during the 1940s and 1950s the ample category of *vencidos* included many more than just those executed or imprisoned by the regime. It included a multitude of men and women who suffered from different forms of surveillance and acute exclusion within their communities of origin during the first decade following the Civil War. Imposed immobility, therefore, served the dictatorship both politically and the economically. This situation changed drastically in the early 1960s, but even before then the regime was unable to completely stem the free movement and resettlement of its citizens.

The reasons behind internal migration in Spain varied. However, a simplistic city / countryside dichotomy that associates each of the two locations with specific cultures and lifestyles did not exist in reality in Spain of the 1950s. Small and intermediate rural communities and large urban communities often shared patterns of employment and socialization. When differences did exist, therefore, it is important to note the ways in which they were interpreted by the migrants themselves. The city did not necessarily offer more or better paid work but rather stable work with a clearer professional identity. It did not necessarily offer better housing arrangement, but rather more independence for the nuclear family unit and the ability to make better use of educational and social services offered by the state. It was not a space free of repression, but rather a space that due to its size and diversity offered anonymity.

As Antonio Egea Gil's words well reflect, even when the material gains of migration proved to be modest, migrants often did not opt for further movement across space if they sensed that some of their psychological needs were met and that they achieved a sense of belonging in their post-migration lives. In this sense, the existence of material and affective ties between migrants and their communities of origin proved highly important. Such ties not only enabled migrants to move spatially, they also enhanced the presence of the "village" within "city life" and generated a modified sense of community and of kinship, which was an essential part of a new, hybrid urban culture.

Notes

1 H. Lefebvre, "Town and Countryside," in *Writings on Cities* (translated and introduced by E. Kofman and E. Lebas), Oxford: Blackwell, 1996, p. 119.
2 M. Siguán, "Las raíces de la emigración campesina," *Estudios Geográficos*, 27, 1966, p. 533.

3 For a recent example, see: J. de la Torre and G. Sanz Lafuente, *Migración y Coyuntura Económica del Franquismo a la Democracia*, Zaragoza: PUZ, 2008.
4 In the case of the literature on Madrid it is possible to distinguish one line of research that critically examines the phenomenon of internal migration within the context of the more general socio-cultural changes undergone by the Spanish society. This line was developed in several anthropological and sociological manuscripts that were published in the 1960s and 1970s. These works provide critical information concerning the changing needs and everyday lives of the newly arrived migrants. See for example: J. García Fernández, "La atracción demográfica de Madrid," *Estudios Geográficos*, 1957, pp. 87–91; M. Siguán, *Del campo al suburbio. Un estudio sobre la inmigración interior en España*, Madrid: C.S.I.C., 1959; A. Cabo Alonso, "Valor de la inmigración Madrileña," *Estudios Geográficos*, 22(5), 1961, pp. 353–374; I. Alonso Hinojal, *Algunos aspectos sociológicos de un barrio Madrileño de incorporación*, Madrid: Conferencias, Discursos y Estudios Monográficos, 1969. One neighborhood that received much attention from investigators is Vallecas. See for example: E. Lorenzi, "Aportaciones de los nuevos pobladores a la cultura local," in P. Cirujano and A. Lucena Gíl (eds.), *Vallecas. Cultura de Vallecas 1950–2005. La Creación Compartida*, Madrid: Distrito de Villa de Vallecas, 2007, pp. 257–284. In the case of migration to other Spanish cities see: C. Borderías, "Emigración y trayectorias sociales femeninas," *Historia Social*, 17, 1993, pp. 75–94; V. E. Bustillo Merino, "Bilbao 1940–1975: del auge al inicio del declive. Un estudio histórico demográfico," Doctoral thesis, Universidad del País Vasco, 2005; X. M. Cid Fernández, X. C. Domínguez Alberte, and R. Soutelo Vazquez (eds.), *Migracions na Galicia contemporanea: desafíos para a sociedades actual*, Santiago de Compostela: Sotelo Blanco, 2008.
5 V. M. Pérez Díaz, "Nota sobre migraciones rurales internas y disparidades regionales en el medio rural," *Revista de Estudios Agrosociales*, 58, 1967, p. 74.
6 A. Puig i Valls, "De Granada a Sabadell: la emigración una experiencia vivida," *Historia y Fuentes Orales: Memoria y sociedad en la España Contemporánea: actas III Jornadas*, 1996, pp. 275–284.
7 A. García Barbancho, "Los Movimientos Migratorios en España," *Revista de Estudios Agrosociales*, 33, 1960, p. 9. For a more general analysis of the censuses conducted during the dictatorship years, see: J. Azagra Ros, P. Chorén Rodríguez, F.J. Goerlich Gisbert and M. Mas (eds.), *La localización de la población Española sobre el territorio. Un siglo de cambios*, Bilbao: BBVA, 2006.
8 H. Capel Sáez, "Las Migraciones Interiores Definitivas en España," *Estudios Geográficos*, 24, 1962, pp. 600–602; A. García Barbancho, *Las migraciones interiores españolas en 1961–1970*, Madrid: Instituto de Estudios Económicos, 1974.
9 Siguán, *Del Campo al suburbio: un estudio sobre la inmigración interior en España*, pp. 211–216.
10 C. Ródenas "Migraciones Interiores 1960–1985: Balance de la investigación y análisis de las fuentes estadísticas," in de la Torre and Sanz Lafuente (eds.), *Migraciones y coyuntura económica del franquismo a la democracia*, pp. 69–70.
11 U. Beck, W. Bonss and C. Lau, "The Theory of Reflexive Modernization Problematic, Hypotheses and Research Programme," *Theory, Culture & Society*, 20(2), 2003, pp. 1–33.
12 V. Kaufmann, M. Bergman and D. Joye, "Motility: Mobility as Capital," *International Journal of Urban and Regional Research*, 28(4), 2004, pp. 745–756.
13 M. Sheller, "Mobility," Sociopedia.isa, 2011, available at http://www.sagepub.net/isa/resources/pdf/mobility.pdf/.
14 B. Kalir, "Moving Subjects, Stagnant Paradigms: Can the 'Mobilities Paradigm' Transcend Methodological Nationalism?" *Journal of Ethnic and Migration Studies*, 39(2), 2013, p. 312.
15 T. Cresswell, "Towards a Politics of Mobility,"*Environment and Planning D: Society and Space*, 28, (1), 2007, p. 19.

56 Internal migration post-Civil War

16 J. Luis Arrese in Terán, *El Planeamiento Urbano en la España Contemporánea*, p. 323.
17 BOE Presidencia del Gobierno, "Decreto de 12 de diciembre de 1958 por el que se crea una Comisión Interministerial para estudiar y proponer los núcleos urbanos de descongestión de Madrid y demás comarcas de inmigración interna."
18 A. Higueras Arnal,*La Emigración Interior en España*, Madrid: Ediciones Mundo del Trabajo, 1967, p. 15.
19 S. F. Harding, *Remaking Ibieca: Rural Life in Aragon under Franco*, Chapel Hill, NC: University of North California Press, 1984, p. v.
20 F. Martínez López and M. Gómez Oliver, "Political Responsibilities in Franco's Spain: Recovering the Memory of Economic Repression and Social Control in Andalusia 1936–1945," in A. G. Morcillo (ed.),*Memory and Cultural History of the Spanish Civil War: Realms of Oblivion*, Leiden: Brill, 2014, p. 116.
21 FOESSA—Cáritas Diocesa de Madrid, *Informe sociológico sobre la situación social en Madrid*, Madrid: Euramèrica, 1967.
22 S. Balfour, *La dictadura, los trabajadores y la ciudad. El movimiento obrero en el área metropolitana de Barcelona (1939–1988)*, Valencia: Generalitat Valencia, 1994, p. 68.
23 J. A. Pérez Pérez, "La configuración de nuevos espacios de sociabilidad en el ámbito del Gran Bilbao de los 60," *Studio Historia*, 18, 2000, p. 123.
24 M. Benson, "The Movement beyond (Lifestyle) Migration: Mobile Practices and the Constitution of a Better Way of Life," *Mobilities*, 6(2), 2011, p. 224
25 Ángela, interview (Orcasitas, Madrid).
26 Gregorio, interview (Orcasitas, Madrid).
27 J. A. Fernández Gómez, *Buscando el pan del trabajo. Sobre la industrialización Franquista y sus costes sociales en Villaverde (Madrid 1940–1965)*, Madrid: Miños y Davila Editores, 2007, p. 261.
28 J. López de Pablo, *Del barro al barrio. La Meseta de Orcasitas*, Asociación de vecinos de la Meseta de Orcasitas, Madrid, 1986, p. 38.
29 A. Isidro Hinojal, *Alguno Aspectos Sociológicos de un Barrio Madrileño de Incorporación*, Madrid: Servicio Central de Publicaciones, Ministerio de la Vivienda, 1969, pp. 33–34.
30 Fernández Gómez, *Buscando el pan del trabajo*, p. 265.
31 Isidro Hinojal, *Alguno Aspectos Sociológicos de un Barrio Madrileño de Incorporación*, p. 62.
32 Fernández Gómez, *Buscando el pan del trabajo*, p. 255.
33 On the SF of the Falange see: M. T. Gallego Méndez, *Mujer, Falange y Franquismo*, Madrid: Taurus Ediciones, 1983; I. Blasco Herranz, *Armas femeninas para la contrarrevolución. La Sección Femenina en Aragón (1936–1950)*, Málaga: Universidad de Málaga, 1999; I. Ofer, *Señoritas in Blue: The Making of a Female Political Elite in Franco's Spain. The National Leadership of the Sección Femenina de la Falange (1936–1977)*, Brighton: Sussex University Press, 2009.
34 Borderías, "Emigración y trayectorias sociales femeninas," pp. 75–94.
35 Archivo Regional de Madrid, Fondo: Instituto Nacional de la Vivienda, *Signatura* 216927/2, fichas 2024–2032; Signatura 219475(1), fichas 905; Signatura 219402 (1), ficha 285; Signatura 19408 (2), ficha 486–489 and 1123.
36 Archivo Regional de Madrid, Fondo: Instituto Nacional de la Vivienda, signatura 217301 (1), ficha 1248–1250.
37 Archivo Regional de Madrid, Fondo: Instituto Nacional de la Vivienda, signatura 217301 (1), ficha 1215–1249.
38 Archivo Regional de Madrid, Fondo: Instituto Nacional de la Vivienda, signatura 219451(1), ficha 1252–1267.
39 Archivo Regional de Madrid, Fondo: Instituto Nacional de la Vivienda, signatura 216942(2), ficha 1679–1700.

40 J. M. Babiano, *Emigrantes, Crónometros y huelgas. Un estudio sobre el trabajo y los trabajadores durante el Franquismo (Madrid 1951–1977)*, Madrid: Siglo XXI, 1998, p. 153. See also Fernández Gómez, *Buscando el pan del trabajo*, p. 289.
41 Ibid., p. 287.
42 Ibid., p. 288.
43 Felicitas, interview (Orcasitas, Madrid).
44 Daniel, interview (Orcasitas, Madrid).
45 *Del Barro al Barrio*, pp. 46.

3 Appropriating urban space
Constructing a *Chabola* and forming a community

> The city can be read because it writes, because it was writing. However, it is not enough to examine this without recourse to context. To write on this writing or language, to elaborate the *metalanguage of the city* is not to know the city and the urban. The context, what is *below* the text to decipher (everyday life, immediate relations, the *unconscious* of the urban, what is little said and of which even less is written), hides itself in the inhabited spaces – sexual and family life – and rarely confronts itself and what is *above* this urban text (institutions, ideologies), cannot be neglected in the deciphering[1]

The first chapter in this book was mostly concerned with what Henri Lefebvre defined as the "upper urban text": the ideologies that shaped the policies of urban development, the institutions that were charged with executing them, and the ways in which those policies were translated over time into the spatial practices. The current chapter, on the other hand, examines the "unconscious of the urban": everyday life and the ways in which it shaped and was embedded in the most marginalized and least supervised spaces—those of self-constructed shantytowns.

Recent research on the emergence and internal dynamics of squatter movements in Western Europe highlights the mixed profile of their members and their engagement with a wide range of civic entities (such as ecological and feminist movements, student associations, professional pressure groups, etc.). However, the existing literature largely ignores the legacies and repertoires of actions inherited from earlier squatter communities that formed in the late 1950s and 1960s in response to accelerated processes of internal migration and indus-trialization. One of the aims of this book is to try to understand the conditions that led squatter communities to join the waves of social protest that swept Spain starting in the mid 1960s. In order to assess the distinct contribution of those communities to the new social movements that emerged in Spain it is important to examine first the ways in which individuals engaged in "deprivation-based squatting" came to think of themselves as a community.[2]

In this context the concept of "appropriation," as defined by Lefebvre, proves extremely useful. Lefebvre did not view spatial proximity in itself as a guarantee for the creation of social bonds. Rather he tried to theorize the ways in which dwelling (as a continued practice) reinforces collective identification. In his 1967 publication *L'Urbanisme aujourd'hui*, he wrote:

> For an individual, for a group, to inhabit is to appropriate something. Not in the sense of possessing it, but as making it an oeuvre, making it one's own, marking it, modeling it, shaping it ... To inhabit is to appropriate space, in the midst of constraints, that is to say, to be in a conflict – often acute – between the constraining powers and the forces of appropriation.[3]

In *The Production of Space* Lefebvre noted the appropriative potential of squatter communities, but did not discuss the strategies through which squatting could in fact lead to the creation of spaces truly appropriated by their users. My contention is that under specific conditions the very nature of squatting (the context of illegality, the lack of pre-existing infrastructures, the practices of self-construction) may facilitate a more critical and purposeful engagement of people with their lived space. In order to understand under what conditions such a process may take place it is useful to consider the relationship between appropriation and spatial scales. As mentioned before, Lefebvre proposed three scales for the analysis of space: a "private" realm, an interim level and a global level. He rightly noted that even in the best of circumstances—when the indoor space of family life is truly appropriated by its users—the outer spaces of a community life are still mostly dominated. In the current chapter I show how squatting (as an ongoing daily process) can extend the scope of appropriated space from the private to the intermediate level, thereby creating new communitarian "counter-spaces" where new subjectivities are formed.

Self-construction and the investment of values: The case of Orcasitas

Until the late 1920s many of the low-income families that migrated to Spanish cities such as Barcelona, Madrid or Bilbao settled into existing working-class neighborhoods. In these neighborhoods they rented single rooms with the right to use common kitchen and bathroom space. During the final years of the Primo de Rivera dictatorship (1923–1930) a new phenomenon, called *chabolismo* or *barraquismo*, started to manifest itself around the periphery of some cities. A working paper composed in 1977 by the Commission for Planning and Coordination of the Madrid Metropolitan Area (COPLACO) stated:

> With the passing of time the word *chabolisimo* came to signify any type of housing that was built bypassing the official procedures of urban planning ... Initially, however, *chabolismo* was simply an *ad hoc* way in which migrants and newly formed households responded to the unsolvable housing problem.[4]

Chabolismo was relatively restricted in size prior to the years of the Second Republic (1939–1936). In 1927 there were approximately 6,500 *barracas* in

60 Appropriating urban space

Barcelona and less than 2,000 in Madrid.[5] Most of the *chabolas* that were built prior to 1936 did not survive the Civil War. By the mid 1940s, however, squatting changed its face in Spain. It was no longer made up of individual constructions that were scattered throughout the peripheries of large cities, but rather of dense areas covered by mass self-constructions. By 1957 the city of Barcelona registered 15,352 *barracas*, mostly in the neighborhoods of Montjuïc, Carmel and el Levante. In Bilbao over 40,000 people lived in *chabolas* by 1959 and in Madrid the numbers were even higher.

The term *chabolismo* referred to two interrelated aspects: the status of the land and the state of services and infrastructures. As indicated in the first chapter, most of the land occupied by squatters in Francoist Spain was defined under the 1956 Land Law as rural or as urban reserve land. Despite the fact that many squatters bought their *chabolas* and the land on which they were erected, the transactions often had no legal standing. The illegality of these transactions, however, worried neither the authorities nor the buyers throughout the early 1950s. The authorities (represented by the Civil Guard) turned a blind eye to construction as long as it was carried out during the night and accompanied by the payment of substantial bribes. The migrants (arriving as they did from areas where mixed land uses constituted a norm) completely disregarded the formal distinctions between different types of land.

Spanish urban planner and historian, José Montes Mieza, described the selling of land throughout the southern periphery of Madrid. His words reflect the fact that the parceling and selling of rural land constituted a first step in the formation of an informal system of land and home ownership:

> The selling of agricultural plots of dry land, about 80 square meters in size, was the first step in the colonization of marginal urban areas. This was done with the full knowledge of everyone. In the middle of the plot the seller would situate a table. He was usually accompanied by a witness and a self-appointed surveyor ... Both parties signed contracts that specified payment installments. This meant that the failure to provide a single installment, be it the last one, rendered the entire contract void.
>
> The buyers also purchased construction materials in one of the makeshift stores that mushroomed all around. The buyer then had to construct the actual *chabola*. This was usually done at night, which was termed "a time of tolerance."[6]

Chabolismo did not refer to the adequacy of the house itself, although many of the houses originally constructed in *barrios* such as *Orcasitas* clearly fell under the definition of *infraviviendas* (homes that did not meet the basic residential needs of their inhabitants). A survey conducted in the southern periphery of Madrid in 1956 qualified 65 percent of the dwellings as *infraviviendas*. By 1976 12 percent of them did not yet have a toilet or a bath and only 35 percent had access to electricity.[7] Many *chabolas* were made of wood and cardboard. The crude materials and hasty construction made the opening of doors and especially windows difficult. All the houses were badly ventilated. In the summer their inhabitants suffered from the heat and in the winter from the cold and the humidity that rose from the ground and seeped through the poorly insulated walls. Since the majority of the homes had no electricity in the absence of windows their inhabitants were condemned to a life of perpetual darkness.

Apart from personal memories and journalistic materials, descriptions regarding the form of the *chabolas* and of life within them can be found in many literary works of the epoch. Antonio Ferrés (in his 1959 novel *La Piqueta*) described the *chabolas* of Orcasitas:

> The 'would be' streets twisted smoothly downhill, the walls [of the houses] appeared white or red, according to the light of day. Some stood there, no more than niches, with their brick walls full of holes like honeycombs ... Maruja had put down the water jug right beside the washing board and went down on her knees in-front of a pile of children's cloths. Her mother was already inside, besides a kitchen stove of sorts which stood like a little island with flaks of recently lit flames coming out of it.[8]

Valencia-born novelist Francisco Candel provided a detailed and moving description of the *barracas* of Barcelona in his book *Han matado un hombre, han roto el paisaje*:

> I saw a shanty home of a miniscule size. Its only luxury was the whiteness of the walls, a whiteness that hid the bricks and mud. It was made up of two compartments like all other [*barracas*]. The one inside – if you can qualify its distance from the front-door as an 'inside' – functioned as a bedroom. It was separated [from the rest of the house] by a curtain and included one bed with no more space left around it.
>
> The other compartment – two square meters in size – functioned as the entrance to the house. A small fire place situated on the ground with a tiny chimney, two chairs and two spikes: on the one hung a jacket and on the other – in the most curious way – a mirror. This broken mirror which simply hung there still comes back to me in my nightmares. A mirror that forces you to look at [yourself] in pieces: an eye here, an eye there, and then a mouth[9]

In 1957 (following a decision to proceed with the demolition of certain self-constructed dwellings and to tighten the control over those employing illegal migrants) the authorities in Madrid and Bilbao started to systematically monitor the shantytowns and collect information on their inhabitants. In the case of Orcasitas the files compiled by the Ministry of Housing in 1957–1958 include detailed information on the make-up of the *chabolas*, the number of inhabitants and their declared income. These files (and the expropriation files compiled between the years 1962–1966) provide further evidence regarding the deplorable living conditions in the *barrio*. The following note, for example, refers to a *chabola* constructed in C/ Madrigal no. 13 in 1956. The *chabola* housed a married couple, their three children and their two nephews and was inspected in 1957 and again in 1961. The note read:

> During a routine inspection of this *chabola* and the neighboring one I was able to detect several cracks in the walls and the ceiling. The cracks formed as a result of the heavy rains that flood the house ... In view of the size of the house, and the number of the inhabitants, one notes with preoccupation the fact that young boys and girls of different ages all share the same bedroom.[10]

Figure 3.1 The entrance to a *chabola* with view to the inside
Source: Asociación de Vecinos del Barrio de Orcasitas, Archivo Fotográfico

It is clear from the note that the inspector's greatest preoccupation resulted from the final observation and not from the poor living conditions or the danger of collapsed walls.

A similar description can be found in the file on a *chabola* situated on C/ *Robustiano Gonzalaz* no. 18. The *chabola* housed five persons and was first inspected in 1958. Upon a second inspection in 1963 the report read:

> This single story house is made of bricks and its ceiling is made of curved wood. The house was torn down several times and the rains and the defective construction caused the left wall to separate from the main structure in a way that endangers both this *chabola* and the neighboring one. To this must be added a hole in the ceiling of the bedroom and many other cracks in the surrounding walls.[11]

Despite the deplorable conditions most of the *chabolas* that were constructed throughout the 1950s were larger in size than those constructed a decade later. Félix López Rey (a resident of Orcasitas since 1956 and the former head of the Orcasitas Neighborhood Association) explained:

> The average size of a house in Orcasitas as it was recorded in a 1973 survey was 24 square meters. These houses were used by families of 4–5 members each. The uniform size is easy to explain. The first settlers who came here in the 1950s ... their homes were much larger. But what happened then? As soon as those people could move to other *barrios* they did so. They moved to Usera or Getafe. And then they subdivided their old *chabolas* and leased them.[12]

López Rey's testimony is supported by reposts such as the following one which was filled in Orcasitas in 1959:

> On this parcel of land stands a two-story house. The first floor is divided into three apartments and a small secluded corner where the toilet is found. Each apartment is made up of two rooms and a kitchen. The first apartment is occupied by the owner, his wife and son. The second one is occupied by a couple with their three children and the third by a couple with one child. The upper floor is made up of five apartments. Four of them are made up of one room and a kitchen and the fifth of two rooms and a kitchen. The larger apartment is occupied by a married couple with two children and a mother-in-law. The others are occupied by married couples each with a child.[13]

Documents of the Ministry of Housing indicate that by 1958–9 the parceling off of larger *chabolas* and renting of smaller units had become a profitable business for those who could afford it. In times when the average salary in Orcasitas was 1,300 pesetas, L. F., for example, rented out four *chabolas* in C/ *Del Río*

Figure 3.2 Cooking outdoors in Orcasitas
Source: Asociación de Vecinos del Barrio de Orcasitas, Archivo Fotográfico

earning additional 550 pesetas; A. C. rented out ten *chabolas* in *C/ Villaverde Prado Consejo* for 1,125 pesetas; and E. M. rented out six *chabolas* in *C/ Gines* for 600 pesetas.[14] While those were the more prominent *chabola* owners in the *barrio*, there were many others who simply rented out a single room in order to supplement their earnings. Out of the 1,680 *chabolas* documented in my database, only 544 (32.3 per cent) were owned by the family living it them.

Constructing a *chabola* was clearly more difficult (and at times more expensive) than renting a shared apartment in an established working-class neighborhood. Rented apartments in the center of Madrid or Barcelona enjoyed better infrastructures, transportation and educational services, as well as shopping facilities. Why, then, were self-constructed *barrios* the preferred option of so many migrant families? *Barrios chabolistas* provided their inhabitants with two marked advantages in comparison to other forms of dwelling. In cities with fast-growing industries the shantytowns were constructed in relative proximity to the newly formed industrial complexes that provided work for many migrants. This was the result of the exclusionary spatial practices that pushed both labor and the infrastructure of production into the outer perimeter of the city. For a population deprived of any means of transportation, however, the proximity of home and worked proved a marked advantage.

The *chabolas* as housing units also offered flexibility. The uncertain status of the land enabled the inhabitants to use the perimeter surrounding their home in order to supplement their meager earnings. The ability to grow vegetables and

Appropriating urban space 65

wheat and to raise farm animals was an advantage not found in established working-class neighborhoods. As we shall see, the *chabolas* also provided their dwellers with greater freedom to construct their lived space in accordance with specific needs and notions of what could be considered a "good home."[15] While in the countryside many of young couples shared a house with their extended family, doing so in the city was often perceived as a failure of the migratory project. Having an independent home (even a *chabola*) was the hallmark of a functioning family and of adaptation to city life.

Despite the difference in size the relatively large *chabolas* of the 1950s shared some characteristics with the smaller units constructed in later years. Most of the *chabolas*, for example, were divided into a surprisingly large number of bedrooms. The average *chabola* in Orcasitas comprised three to four sleeping areas separated from one another by a curtain, with some reaching up to seven "bedrooms." While the number of family members might explain the need for more than one bedroom, the decision to construct a large number of rooms within a relatively small space merits some explanation.

As noted earlier, Francoist rhetoric presented close human proximity and the so-called chaotic mixing of men and women of different ages as the hallmarks of the moral deprivation associated with the vanquished of the Civil War.[16] Crowded living conditions were of course an undisputed fact of life in many working-class *barrios* all over Spain. The cultural and moral judgments associated with them, however, were highly subjective. Although physically distant from the more affluent neighborhoods of Madrid, the dwellers of Orcasitas shared many of their values. On the level of spatial representations many of the testimonies I read expressed the belief that keeping men and women of different age groups separated (in sleep and work) was a precondition for maintaining a moral family and a moral community. Consequently the dwellers of Orcasitas worked hard in order to create a living space that would be internally segregated. The result was the construction of several minuscule bedrooms, where not even a bed could fit, all for the sake of separating adults and children of different sexes and ages.

The relatively large number of bedrooms left scarcely any space for the construction of living rooms, but this fact had little bearing on the inhabitants' social lives. In Orcasitas, as in the countryside, socialization mostly took place alongside the unpaved streets. This was the case until the early 1970s, when the construction of high-rise apartment buildings and the increased volume of traffic turned the gathering of children and women in the street into a complicated affair. Most *chabolas* also lacked a specific area assigned for cooking. Due to the lack of light and ventilation, cooking often took place outside the house. The *chabola*'s central space, therefore, functioned as an eating area for the family itself and was only provisionally converted into a cooking or a bathing space.

The precocious structure of the *chabola* allowed for a temporary division of its internal space in accordance with the changing profile of the family that inhabited it. By forming makeshift bedrooms, some the dwellers were able to

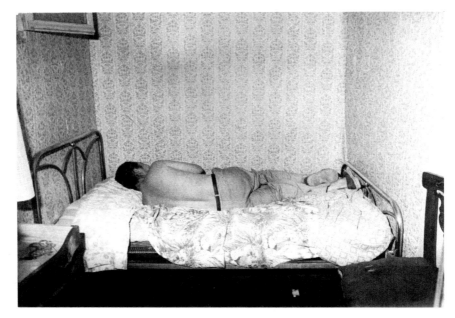

Figure 3.3 A bedroom in one of the *chabolas*
Source: Asociación de Vecinos del Barrio de Orcasitas, Archivo Fotográfico

Figure 3.4 Children playing outside of an open *chabola*
Source: Asociación de Vecinos del Barrio de Orcasitas, Archivo Fotográfico

attain a certain level of coherence between the representations of "adequate" sleeping space (which dictated separation according to age and gender) and their lived (or representational) space. The same level of coherence could not be achieved in relation to hygienic practices, which the *chabola* as a constructed form simply could not contain. Water was a scarce commodity in Orcasitas well into the 1970s. The interviews I conducted make clear the association between running water, modernity and respectability and expose the length to which the inhabitants had to go to in their struggle to maintain personal hygiene. The children of Orcasitas mostly attended school in neighboring Usera, requiring a three-kilometer trip on unpaved roads and along the highly dangerous railway tracks leading to the capital. But the children were not allowed into class if their shoes or clothes were stained with mud. As a result many remember being carried to school on their mothers' backs so that they remain clean.

Years later the neighbors wrote of the dreaded mud:

Figure 3.5 Mothers carrying their children with their school bags on the road leading out of Orcasitas
Source: Asociación de Vecinos del Barrio de Orcasitas, Archivo Fotográfico

68 *Appropriating urban space*

The mud deserves the most extensive chapter in the history of our poor *barrio*. People who work the land are usually happy when the rain comes but here, in Orcasitas, it was the most dreaded phenomenon. The change in our attitude towards the [rain] took place as soon as we got here. When it rained you simply could not leave the house unless it was a case of an emergency.[17]

Under these conditions keeping clean necessitated a tremendous effort. Some of the men who worked in the city took advantage of their time there to bath once a week in one of the public bathhouses at the center of Madrid. For most a proper bath or shower was a rare treat saved for special occasions. Following is a testimony of a 60-year-old man:

When I got married I went into the city in order to take a bath. On the outskirts of Madrid there were several bathhouses ran by the City-Council. The down-side was that in each of them you had to wait in line, sometimes up to three hours. That day I went to one of those places near the *Plaza de Oriente*. I had to pay 5 pesetas, but that was the best bath of my life. What happiness! To feel myself submerged in a bath of hot water and foam! And when I came back home I shouted "mama, smell me! See how good I smell!"[18]

Félix López Rey described the tremendous struggle to bathe privately in a *chabola* that simply could not accommodate the need for privacy:

The custom was that the women who worked here [in Orcasitas], would wash themselves at home when the men and children were absent. They would simply heat water and wash parts of their body. We, teenagers, what could we do? We waited until our sisters and mothers went to bed and did the same. And once we started working we would go to the public baths on Saturdays, after work.[19]

Bathing was one of those mundane activities that helped define one's place within the family, reflecting in one specific moment of the day the appropriate levels of physical intimacy between different members of the household. Women could only bathe in the complete privacy accorded to them in the middle of a working day. Children could take a bath anytime and anywhere until the age they started school, by which time they were no longer considered babies. At that point the girls had to struggle to find those rare times when no one was at home, while the boys had to wait for nightfall. Upon entering the job market (at age 12 or 13 on average) boys were considered to have entered a new life-stage, leaving their childhood behind for good. They then had the doubtful privilege of standing in line for up to three hours on Saturday nights in order to have a decent bath.

The lack of running water, privacy and personal space undermined people's sense of respectability and at times even of humanity.[20] Inés Sáenz Heredia was

Appropriating urban space 69

Figure 3.6 A toddler being bathed outside his home in Orcasitas
Source: Asociación de Vecinos del Barrio de Orcasitas, Archivo Fotográfico

a secular nun, a teacher and one of the few people who lived in Orcasitas out of identification with its inhabitants. In an interview that was later transcribed in a book edited by the Orcasitas Neighborhood Association, Sáenz Heredia reflected on the meaning of a seemingly simple thing like a toilet: "A mother (of one of my students), having moved to a new house with more rooms, came to tell me – 'now we can finally have social relations like other human beings. We can finally have friends and invite them to our house. Finally we have a toilet.'"[21]

It is no accident, perhaps, that during an eight-hour interview in which he told me about his childhood in Orcasitas, Félix López Rey stopped only once to reflect on how the struggle for survival had marked him emotionally. When explaining he constructed his first "proper" bathroom in the late 1970s when he was already a father of three he broke down: "This really marked my life. I really hated those middle-class people who had everything. Hate was unavoidable. Already as kids we had this sensation that the rich were all bad and the poor good."[22]

Such feelings of hate and shame did not generate violence. They did, however, create a situation in which stealing (first construction materials and later on water and electricity) was condoned as part of a new, more equitable division of material goods. Stealing water in Orcasitas was tolerated and even encouraged when it was done at the expense of the few inhabitants who did have running water: the local priest and the doctors who worked in the public clinic. The local priest was accused by many of being a supporter of the dictatorship. The

70   Appropriating urban space

doctors at the clinic "where there was no public toilet, only one toilet saved for the use of the doctors themselves" were also targeted.[23]

In 1972 the building that was to house Orcasitas Neighborhood Association was completed after a year of construction. The association (as will be recounted in the following chapter) was recognized as a legal public entity and the neighbors hoped that its building would be protected from demolition. The final step before opening the association's offices was to construct a public bath and a toilet for the use of all the neighbors. The building, which was open between 8 p.m. and 11 p.m., was guarded by two retired neighbors and some of the younger men set about "stealing" water so that the public bathroom could function. López Rey, who was in charge of finding a way of tapping into the water pipes, recorded:

> One night we set about "stealing" water from the priest. The fascist priest did have running water. We worked at night ... so the Civil Guard guys would not catch us. The street was not yet paved so we tried to tap into his pipe, but it was made of steel so we had to think of something else. There was one *chabola* next door so we told the guy "you go into your house. You did not see anything." We connected to the pipe before the point where the meter was so that the water did not flow into the meter, and everyone was happy. We had water and it was not recorded on any meter.[24]

This revised conception of "good" and "bad" provides an example of agency that counters deprivation by looking for solutions where those could be found. In doing so it laid down the ground for an incipient sense of community that was based on spatial and material divisions: primarily a division between the *barrio* and the city that lay outside its limits, but also a widening definition of "us" versus "them" within the *barrio* itself. Despite the fact that this definition drew heavily on materialistic aspects, it was only partially framed in class terms.

A description of communal life and of the production of public space in Orcasitas would not be complete without referring to a small entrepreneurial group of business owners that lived within the *barrio*. Nearly 6 percent of the heads of households who lived in Orcasitas in 1958 defined themselves as independent businessmen. With the nearest "established" commercial area 3 km away in the *barrio* of Usera and no public transportation at hand, the businesses that formed in Orcasitas catered for a mixed array of needs.

Of the 91 businesses I know of, 12 were bars and taverns. They served mainly men and therefore opened on weekends and weekdays from the early afternoon and well into the night. As indicated by their names some of them functioned as hubs of socialization according to the proprietor's place of origin. Establishments such as *La Andaluza, Soria* and *La Asturiana* (which exist to this day) served traditional dishes and drinks from Andalusia, Asturias and Extremadura, and other primary products acquired during trips to the

Figures 3.7, 3.8 and 3.9 Tavern and self-constructed dancing-hall in Orcasitas. The photos are not dated, but they were taken prior to the first wave of mass demolitions in the 1970s. While the taverns and bars catered during the week almost exclusively for men the dance hall was a meeting place for young men and women from both Orcasitas and the neighboring *barrios*
Source: Asociación de Vecinos del Barrio de Orcasitas, Archivo Fotográfico

Figure 3.9 (Continued)

countryside. Other small businesses included a barbershop, fruit shops, bakeries, butcheries and wine-shops and several shops for the sale of secondhand clothes and fabrics. To these must be added several mobile businesses for the sale of water and carbon. The formation of these businesses constituted an important step in the appropriation of the *barrio* by its inhabitants. By providing for the different needs of the community those businesses bluntly undermined the regime's spatial practices. Some businesses, such as the ones photographed above, also provided the first spaces for communal interaction in Orcasitas.

Gendered spaces and the formation of a community of women

An analysis of the formation of community life and of communal spaces within a *barrio* such as Orcasitas must take into consideration aspects relating to the issue of gender. During the years of the dictatorship working-class women suffered from a double exclusion: they were discriminated against both as women and as individuals who belonged to a marginalized and excluded social group. Working-class women were forced into the sphere of the home where they had to carry the burden of reproduction and of caring for their families in times of immense economic hardship. At the same time many also had to work under dire conditions in order to ensure the survival of their families.

In Orcasitas 5 percent of the households were headed by women. The majority of them were widows and all but three declared themselves to be unemployed. The life history of C. is typical within the group of female heads of households in *barrio*. C. was born in *Villafranca de los Barros* (a town in the province of Badajoz) in 1901. Her husband was arrested by the Francoist authorities following the Civil War.[25] Having spent several years in prison, he

Appropriating urban space 73

was released in poor health and died soon afterwards. C. moved to Madrid in 1957 following the death of her mother, in the hope of improving the occupational chances of her sons. In Orcasitas she shared her home with her four children, her son-in-law and two grandchildren. Although no information exists in the records concerning the employment situation of her children, she herself was employed as a cleaning lady (*ayudante*) on the payroll of Madrid's city council. This final detail made her stand out among the other female heads of households in the *barrio*. C.'s file does not specify her salary, but we do know that she rented a *chabola* for which she paid 250 pesetas a month. Unlike C., the majority of female heads of households in Orcasitas did not register formal earnings of their own; some registered an income resulting from the work of their children or other dependent adults who lived with them and many had additional (undeclared) earnings from temporary work in housekeeping or sewing.

Married women played a significant role in the migratory process and in the process of community formation in squatter settlements. When it came to finding permanent housing in the city women were just as active as the men. In Orcasitas one central hub of information was the water fountain. In his novel *La piquet* Antonio Ferrés provided a detailed reflection on the fountain's centrality:

> The girl walked with the empty pitcher towards the fountain ... One woman was standing at the center of a circle. She did not halt her talking.
> "What is going on?" Maruja asked the woman closest to her.
> "I am not really sure" the other one replied. "They say that the [authorities] are about to pull down the last *chabolas* to be built. They don't want more people to come here from the countryside."
> Maruja looked at the women, trying to read in her face clues for the right answer. She thought to herself that the woman talked like one of those who came from Madrid. She was at loss for words.
> "My father came here to look for a job. In the village he could only find work during the collection of olives" she finally said.
> "Some say that those of the countryside come here in order to steal the bread out of our mouth" replied the woman. She was tall and bony faced, with her hair uncombed.
> Maruja waited her turn silently.[26]

For many women in Orcasitas the public fountain offered a natural opportunity to get acquainted with a larger circle of neighbors. Like the headquarters of the neighborhood association it was another intermediate space which had a specific function (that of drawing water) but was invested with other more elaborated social functions by its users. Even without asking personal questions, simply by listening to the different accents, one was able to locate around the fountain migrants arriving from the same area and get to know others outside her immediate circle. The fountain also functioned as the place where women could catch up with the *barrio*'s latest news. While standing in line for water they exchanged recipes, tips on the cheapest places to shop for food and clothing, information concerning possible job opportunities for their husbands and sons, and on the major events in the life of the *barrio* such as arrests and raids. The fountain functioned as the *barrio*'s billboard. If there was a vacant lot for construction, rooms for lease or a new *chabola* on the market this was the place to find out about it. The information acquired by women often earned their families additional income. Such skills were passed on to other, newly arrived women, in countless encounters all over the *barrio*.

Both men and women played a decisive role in the migration process. But the process of making a new home in the capital was often fractured by contrasting professional, economic and psychological requirements. For most men the

Figure 3.10 A monument in present-day Orcasitas: A woman carrying her pitcher of water down to the fountain
Source: Asociación de Vecinos del Barrio de Orcasitas, Archivo Fotográfico

pressing need was to secure a job. In pursuing this goal many of them entered a hostile and demanding work environment where they had to prove themselves in ways that at times were beyond their skills. In the countryside most women divided their working time between their home and the fields, especially during the more pressing agricultural seasons. In the city, on the other hand, most female migrants found themselves confined to their homes caring for children who did not yet attend school, with significantly reduced help from their extended families. For women the neighborhood was often the most significant spatial unit and they had a different conception of their lived space than men. They understood the distance it was reasonable to expect their children to travel to school; where would be an ideal place to situate a telephone cabin; what could be considered an indispensable shop; what would be a safe and yet reasonable distance between residential areas and the areas where traffic could circulate. This information, as we shall see in the next chapters, would be indispensable for the architects that would assist the neighbors in their struggle for the renovation of Orcasitas in the 1970s.

During the 1950s and 1960s distinct patterns of socialization and different everyday experiences separated the lives of the first generation migrants. The

Figure 3.11 This photo was taken by an inhabitant of Orcasitas prior to the first mass demolition of *chabolas* in the 1970s. The photo is not dated, and while the women clearly came together in order to be photographed, it reflects the fact that during the mornings the *barrio* was almost an exclusively feminine space. The only exceptions were boys under school age and the occasionally unemployed man

Source: Asociación de Vecinos del Barrio de Orcasitas, Archivo Fotográfico

76 *Appropriating urban space*

worlds of home and work were more sharply distinguished in the city, and so were the lives of men and women. At times this gap between husband and wife would only close when they reached their late 60s. Upon retirement, with a relatively secure income and the children no longer at home, many of my female interviewees talked of renewed companionship. Such companionship often centered on the ability to truly enjoy, for the first time, the cultural and educational benefits offered by the city.[27]

***

Going back to Lefebvre it is easy to see how self-construction and different practices of "dwelling" gave rise to new or modified identifications at the level of the individual user of space, the family and the community. On the level of private space it is interesting to compare the make-up of individual self-constructed *chabolas* with that of the social or minimal housing units that were constructed by the regime. Most of the *chabolas* that were documented by the Ministry of Housing included a central space located at the entrance to the house, which functioned as a living-room and was dedicated to socialization and eating. In some of the larger and more established *chabolas* this space also included a permanent kitchen. In most others the kitchen was made up of a makeshift fireplace (which could be situated inside or outside the *chabola* depending on the weather) and several chairs. The same space was converted at night into an additional bedroom.

The social or minimal housing units that were constructed by the regime as part of absorption or controlled suburbs provided their inhabitants with better shelter, with running water and with electricity. In terms of internal design minimal apartments and *chabola*s were often of the same size. Both constructions included multi-functional spaces, although the structure of the new suburbs encouraged socialization within the apartments, while the *chabolas* allowed for minimal socialization to take place indoors. Some of the other functions of everyday life were assigned similar spaces within minimal apartments and the *chabolas*. This was especially the case with permanent sleeping spaces that were situated at the back of the house and separated by a wall or a curtain. A major difference between the two types of dwellings was that minimal housing units were designed to deal with the scarcity of space by designating several alternating functions to the same room. The *chabolas*, on the other hand, had to "expel" certain functions to the outer parameter of the house. Some of those functions were "expelled" from the *chabola* on a temporary basis (as was the case with cooking, eating and studying) and others permanently (bathing, for example).

As could be seen in the first chapter, minimal housing units were constructed using materials of very low quality, which caused rapid deterioration. However, their biggest disadvantage in the eyes of former squatters lay in the fact that they were perceived as suburbs without community life. As such they were constantly compared and contrasted with the old *chabolas*. María (who grew up in Orcasitas) referred to the structure of the *chabolas* and its effect on social life in her interview:

Here we shared everything. The houses were all open. There were no doors, only curtains. You didn't have to knock. You simply entered, and what you saw was there for the taking. It was for everyone – neighbors, friends, family members.[28]

Julio (who moved to Orcasitas from the center of Madrid) also recounted:

There were many shanty homes. Some were made of wood, others of exposed brick. They looked like tiny vacation homes. Life was good then, we all knew each other. Now everything is different, we each live in a closed apartment and it's no longer the same.[29]

The "homely" feeling described above was tied by many of my interviewees to the absence of "transitional spaces." Lefebvre defined transitional spaces or objects (such as doors, windows and threshold) as spaces that direct the movement from the inside to the outside and vice versa, defining the capacity of one space to connect or merge into another.[30] In Orcasitas the open-ended structure of communal and private spaces (most notably exemplified by the lack of doors, fences and thresholds) promoted a sense of intimacy and of coming together.

At the same time it is important to note that the absence of transitional spaces left the *chabolas* "naked" in a sense that could also be very dangerous. It enabled the atmosphere and the happenings on the street quite literally to penetrate the private living space of a family. Lacking in walls and doors some of these homes could not be protected from noises, smells or from the presence of outside intruders. The risk inherent in such penetration was felt most acutely when the neighbors were called to protect their *chabolas* from demolition.

The headquarters of the neighborhood association, the fountain, the bars and shops in Orcasitas all provide examples of popular production and use of intermediate or communal spaces. Their construction reflects a process by which individual squatters, in their capacity as consumers, housewives, parents, etc., identified specific needs that had to be fulfilled. They constructed spaces that could cater for those needs and later on invested them additional functions in accordance with the evolution of community life. The existence of those spaces undermined the spatial strategies promoted by the regime by providing not only services, but also locations for socialization in which (as I show in the following chapter) new subjectivities were formed.

As the current chapter demonstrates communal life and the socio-cultural practices that emerged in Orcasitas throughout the 1960s were encored in concrete spatial arrangements. To what an extent did these arrangements hold a deeper transformative capacity? This is a complex question which the following chapters attempt to answer. Oren Yiftachel, in his work on the formation of illegal Bedouin settlements in Israel, made use of the concept of "gray space" in order to refer to:

developments, enclaves, populations ... positioned between the "lightness" of legality/approval/safety, and the "darkness" of eviction/destruction/death.

78 *Appropriating urban space*

Gray spaces are neither integrated nor eliminated, forming pseudo-permanent margins of today's urban regions.[31]

As Yiftachel noted gray spacing is a process that works simultaneously on two levels: on the one hand it refers to the assignment of specific populations into marginalized spaces where they are doomed to live within the context of illegality. However, through everyday use of space the same populations generate cracks in the working of oppressive power. As the initial phase of community formation in Orcasitas reflects, such cracks are not necessarily the result of comprehensive oppositional strategies. Rather, they are the product of individual and communal acts of appropriation.

Henri Lefebvre speculated regarding the potential of spatial change to bring about political change and vice versa that:

> so long as the only connection between work spaces, leisure spaces and living spaces is supplied by the agencies of political power and their mechanisms of control – so long must the project of 'changing life' remain no more than a political rallying-cry.[32]

In other words as long as no comprehensive challenge was posed to the spatial practices instituted by the dictatorship, the chances for creating viable "counter spaces" were limited. In order for space to be fully appropriated it would have to be produced in a way that makes its full and complete usage possible. In this respect the creative breaking down of boundaries and the processes of appropriation that took place in squatter settlements across Spain during the 1960s were essential pre-conditions for change. However, in order for deep and long-lasting change to take shape, a more extended structure of opportunities had to be created. This structure of opportunities first emerged during the late 1960s when new entities and oppositional practices emerged within Spanish civil society.

Notes

1 Lefebvre, *Writings on Cities*, p. 108.
2 For a definition of deprivation-based squatting and a more elaborated typology of squatting see: H. Pruijt, "Squatting in Europe," in *Squatting in Europe*, pp. 17–60.
3 Lefebvre in Stanek, *Henri Lefebvre on Space*, p. 87.
4 *Normas de Planeamiento para la provincia de Madrid. Documento de Trabajo* 4 *(Programa urgente del suelo)*, COPLACO, Ministerio de Vivienda, Madrid, junio 1977, p. 10.
5 F. A. Burbano Trimiño, "Las migraciones internas durante el franquismo y sus efectos sociales: el caso de Barcelona," doctoral thesis, Universidad Complutense, 2013, p. 110.
6 "A time of tolerance" was a legal term. Any built structure that was constructed within one night and had four walls and a roof by day-break could not be demolished by the Spanish authorities without a due legal process. Montes Mieza, Paredes Grosso and Villanueva Paredes, "Los asentamientos chabolistas en Madrid," p. 161.

Appropriating urban space 79

7 Ibid., p. 172. For further information concerning the district of Villaverde (including family size, housing and infrastructures) see also: COPLACO, *Villaverde*, Madrid: Colección Documentos de Difusión y Debate, 1980.

8 A. Ferrés, *La piqueta*, Madrid: GADIR, 1996, pp. 40, 42.

9 F. Candel, *Han matado un hombre, han roto un paisaje*, Barcelona: La Busca Edicions S.L. 2002, p. 216.

10 Archivo Regional de Madrid, Instituto Nacional de la Vivienda, signatura 216927/2, ficha 2020.

11 Archivo Regional de Madrid, Instituto Nacional de la Vivienda, signatura 219477(1), ficha 1544.

12 Félix López Rey, interview (Orcasitas, Madrid).

13 Archivo Regional de Madrid, Fondo: Instituto Nacional de la Vivienda, signatura216942/1, ficha 1655.

14 The information regarding the owners of the *chabolas* and leasing conditions was processed as part of my database and extracted from the files of the Ministry of Housing.

15 For the role of cultural models in structuring the living environment see the research of the Institute de Sociologie Urbaine in France: H. Raymond, "Habitat, modèles cultureless et architecture," in H. Raymond, J. M. Stébé, and A. Mathieu Fritz (eds.), *Architecture urbanistique et société*, Paris: Éd. L'Harmattan, 1974, pp. 213–229.

16 I. Ofer, "A City of a Thousand Identities: *Vencidos y Vencedores* en Madrid de la Post-Guerra (1939–1945)," presented at The Fifth Woodrow Borah International Colloquium: Rethinking the Spanish Civil War, Tel Aviv University, Tel Aviv, 2007. See also C. Mir and C. Agustí, "Delincuencia patrimonial y justicia penal: una incursión en la marginación social de posguerra (1939–1951)," in C. Mir, C. Agustí and J. Gelonch (eds.), *Pobreza, marginación, delincuencia* y políticas sociales bajo el franquismo, Lleida: Universitat de Lleida, 2008, pp. 69–92.

17 Asociación de vecinos de la Meseta de Orcasitas, *Del Barro al Bario*, p. 70.

18 *Del Barro al Bario*, p. 86.

19 F. López Rey, interview (Orcasitas, Madrid).

20 I. Ofer, "*La Guerra de Agua*: Notions of Morality, Respectability and Community in a Madrid Neighborhood," *Journal of Urban History*, 35(2), 2009, pp. 220–235.

21 *Del Barro al Bario*, 126.

22 F. López Rey, interview (Orcasitas, Madrid).

23 Ibid.

24 Ibid.

25 Archivo Regional de Madrid, Fondo: Instituto Nacional de la Vivienda, signatura 219502 (1), ficha 531.

26 Ferrés, *La piqueta*, p. 26.

27 Many of my interviewees now jointly participate in adult education classes, painting class, cinematic and musical events, and so forth.

28 María, interview (Orcasitas, Madrid).

29 Julio, interview (Orcasitas, Madrid).

30 Lefebvre, *The Production of Space*, p. 209.

31 Yiftachel, "Critical theory and Gray Space," in Brenner, Marcuse and Mayer (eds), *Cities for People not for Profit*, pp. 152–153.

32 Lefebvre, *The Production of Space*, p. 59.

4 Becoming visible

Neighborhood associations under the Franco regime

> In the Greek and Roman antique city, centrality is attached to an empty space, the agora and the forum. It is a place for assembly ... For its part the medieval city soon integrated merchants and commodities and established them in its centre; the marketplace. A commercial centre characterized by the proximity of the church and the exclusion of the enclosure – a heterotopy of territory. The symbolism and the functions of this enclosure are different from that of the oriental or antique city. The territory belongs to the lords, peasants, vagrants and plunderers. Urban centrality welcomes produce and people. It forbids its access to those who threaten its essential and economic function, thus heralding and preparing capitalism.[1]

This chapter analyzes the conditions that led to the formation of neighborhood associations in Spain from the mid 1960s. It focuses specifically on associations that were established within *barrios chabolistas* and other peripheral urban neighborhoods. My contention is that the mass formation of neighborhood associations was a first step in a long-term process of community learning which had potential implications for policy formulation and the political system in Spain. This process fostered new patterns of cooperation (within the community, between the community and professional experts, and across communities), of popular action and of information gathering, processing and sharing. Neighborhood associations, as the current chapter shows, were not necessarily born of a coherent political vision. In the long run, however, they were destined to play a major role in changing the highly restrictive and exclusionary structure of political space in Spain.

The growing literature on the history of neighborhood associations in Spain can be divided into two main interpretive currents: the first centers mostly on the years following 1975 and emphasizes the role of outside actors (such as parties of the democratic opposition; socially minded parish priests and members of the lay organization Acción Católica; and members of the Spanish Workers' Movement) in politicizing the urban question in Spain. According to this view, while neighborhood associations existed from the late 1960s it was outside influence that propelled their members to move from localized protests against poor living conditions and inadequate collective infrastructures to coordinated

Becoming visible   81

mass-mobilizations that called for a more democratic political system.[2] The second interpretive current emphasizes the evolution of neighborhood associations already during the years of the dictatorship. It highlights the presence of members with a double militancy within neighborhood associations and points to their role in aiding their own communities to reframe concrete material demands within the context of a more general debate on the future of Spain's political system.[3]

The current chapter contends that during the final decade of the dictatorship neighborhood associations all across Spain functioned as an interim model between the regime-sponsored associations and the illegal associations of the democratic opposition. On the most basic level the associations functioned as platforms that enabled a growing number of men and women (who lacked prior experience in public activism) to enter into a dialogue with the local authorities and government agencies. This dialogue made explicit in the minds of many people the fact that the relationship between citizens and the state should be reinforced by a set of mutual rights and obligations. Paradoxically perhaps, it was precisely the fact that the right to vote could not be discussed by the associations at that stage, which led their members to focus on other rights, which were just as fundamental for popular participation: the right to information; the right to free expression; the right to culture, and the right to public services. This in its turn led some of the associations to develop a clearer notion of further rights that could not be claimed within the framework of the Francoist political system, rights which Henri Lefebvre defined as essential for claiming the right to the city itself: the right to identity; to equality within an understanding of difference, as well as the right to self-management.

Neighborhood associations all over Spain capitalized on the bonds and alliances that were forged through common experiences and interests, such as the ones described in the previous chapter. Through their work the associations generated a body of knowledge concerning the everyday lived experience of their members. However, the ability to make use of such knowledge as part of an effective dialogue with the authorities depended to a large extent on a structure of opportunities that developed outside the associations' direct realm of action. Between the years 1970 and 1975 it was possible to see in Spain a slow process of rescaling of public and authority, especially apparent in the field of urban planning.[4] Local institutions accepted more responsibility and authority as the state devolved a measure of control from the national level to the local and regional levels. This devolution meant that local governing institutions were increasingly responsible for duties such as economic development, social services and the provision of infrastructure. The limited rescaling of authority in fields that related directly to the concerns of neighborhood associations allowed for a more direct (and at times effective) dialogue with the local authorities.

However, it is important to keep in mind that just as the needs of the communities which gave birth to the associations differed widely, so did the profile of the associations themselves. In some neighborhoods the formation of the association was the result of action taken directly by members of the clandestine

82 *Becoming visible*

opposition. In those cases the activity of the associations was accompanied almost from the start by that of Communist-backed neighborhood commissions (*comisiones del barrio*). Neighborhood commissions were prominent in Barcelona (in the area that would later be called Nou Barris and in neighborhoods such as Carmel, Bon Pastor, Barceloneta, Can Clos and Sant Andreu) and in some *barrios* of Madrid (such as Vallecas).[5] In other cases, however, neighborhood associations emerged out of a complex process of trial and error that was led by men and women who had no prior experience in political activism. Associations such as the one that formed in Orcasitas responded in the initial stages of their existence to concrete situations of acute material crisis. Once they were officially registered they became platforms from which negotiations with the authorities and with a variety of political, professional and economic entities could be carried out.

During the final months of the dictatorship and throughout the early phase of the transition the discourses and the forms of action that were adopted by neighborhood association evolved significantly. During this period neighborhood activists had come to look upon themselves as the representatives of a civic community that had the capacity and the right to take an active part in the decision-making processes that pertained to its future. Neighborhood activists, whatever their background, looked upon the associations as "schools of democracy." The associations provided a space where new practices and capacities (such as public speaking, petitioning, knowledge of the administration and so forth) were acquired. It was this process of organizational and conceptual maturation that enabled neighborhood associations to become one of the driving forces behind the Spanish Citizens' Movement starting in late 1975.

The law under which civic associations formed during the final decade of the dictatorship was approved in 1964. However, its publication did not immediately lead to emergence of neighborhood associations. One of the aims of this chapter is to point to the events that triggered the formation of specific associations: were such events tied primarily to the experience of everyday community life and, if so, how generalized were these experiences? What types of communal spaces and of social networks served the associations during the initial stages of their activity? By focusing on the final years of the dictatorship the current chapter explores the ways in which the experience of collective action prior to the emergence of the Citizens Movement shaped the ways in which ordinary men and women interpreted the socio-economic and political reality around them and worked to change it.

From silence to conditional visibility: Associational life under the Franco regime

The few associational entities that were created in Spain in the decade following the Civil War aimed to carry out the dictatorship's labor and social-aid schemes, while functioning as channels of indoctrination. Under the auspices of the Falange the regime formed labor syndicates, professional colleges and chambers of commerce in which membership was obligatory for workers and employers, professionals of different fields and business owners. The only other entity outside the F.E.T.[6] that could sponsor civic associations during the early years of the dictatorship was the Catholic Church. This state of affairs continued until 1957 when Manuel Fraga Iribarne was appointed as the National Delegate of the F.E.T. in charge of associations. Following the appointment new subventions and other forms of official support became available to association of an academic nature (mostly for students, researchers and teaching staff).

The most significant change in the structure of associational life under the dictatorship came with the publication of the 1964 Law of Associations. The new legislation defined the conditions for the registration and the functioning of an array of new cultural and civic entities. The law decreed that all associations must accept "... the fundamental principles of the [F.E.T] and the organic laws [of the regime]." The associations had to "follow the dictates of the Spanish penal law [and] specifically the legislation relating to issues of morality, public order and the maintenance of the political and social unity of Spain."[7] The new law explicitly forbade the formation of political associations and subjected all of the newly registered entities to a long and complex process of scrutiny by the F.E.T prior to their legalization. At the same time, however, it provided a legal framework for the creation of new entities that were to serve a variety of populations such as neighbors, consumers, housewives and heads of households.

The new Organic Law of the State, which was published in 1967, indicated for the first time the need to explore the conditions under which political associations could be created within the existing structure of the regime.[8] However, it took four more years before the Norms relating to the Right of (Political) Association were published. Despite all hopes, the 1971 law did not view the future political associations as pressure groups of sorts, nor did it acknowledge their right to promote diversified socio-political agendas. Rather the associations were viewed as: "the means for [increasing] the participation of the Spanish people in different forms of collective, political action promoted by the *Movimiento*." Their members were to:

> study and incorporate into the existing social fabric the fundamental principles of the regime ... They were [required] to critically analyze specific government measures and contribute to the formulation of programs oriented towards the service of the national community.[9]

All associations were heavily scrutinized by the authorities, and their members were explicitly forbidden to maintain any working relations with civic entities outside Spain or with members of the democratic opposition within the country.

Judging from the letter of the law it seemed at first sight that the new associations were doomed to operate under similar conditions to those that existed in Spain since 1939. However, those who looked for new avenues for collective action soon seized upon the limited advantages that the law did offer. For

84 Becoming visible

example, under specific conditions members of the newly legalized associations could gather at the headquarters of the association without requesting prior authorization. The new associations had a specific legal standing and as such could petition the authorities on behalf of their members. The impact of the new law was immediately felt and it was reflected by the statistics recorded within the National Register of Associations. The register, which was established in 1964, comprised initially about 2,500 associations. Between the years 1964 and 1974, however, it recorded an increase of about 1,000 new associations per year.[10]

Until late 1975 regime-sponsored Family Associations (*Asociaciones de Cabezas de Familia*) and Associations Representing the Parents of School-Children (*Asociaciones de Padres de Alumnos*) made up the bulk of the registered entities. This did not mean, however, that new entities were not registered under the law. In geographical terms the densest areas of associational activity during the final decade of the dictatorship were Cataluña, the Levant, the Basque region and the Balearic Islands. In all areas accelerated industrialization, diversified patterns of consumption and the growing influence of tourism facilitated the creation of cultural forums as well as associations for consumers, housewives and neighbors.

"Schools of democracy": Neighborhood associations and new practices of citizenship

In his classic essay *The Urban Question* sociologist Manuel Castells proposed a new definition of the urban problem based on the theory of "collective consumption" of goods and services. Based on case studies from the US, Paris, Quebec and Chile, Castells concluded that urban social movements, in the struggle to get their share of those goods and services, become the catalyst of the transformation of social relations. According to Castells those movements, while not necessarily concerned with class or workplace issues, triggered much needed processes of "social readjustment" following periods of rapid urbanization.[11]

In Spain of the 1960s mobilization around issues of collective consumption, and specifically around issues relating to everyday neighborhood life, could be presented as supposedly apolitical in nature, and yet it had far reaching effects on popular notions of citizenship and entitlement. The following quotations, taken from interviews conducted with well-known neighborhood activists in Madrid (Félix López Rey and Antonio Villanueva Agüero) a few months before the dictator's death, reflect this link:

> I can only explain how I see Spain's political future in reference to the concrete experiences in our *barrio* and to the ways in which we went about solving our problems. I hope that the future holds for us a full-scale, complete democracy, with no qualifications ... The most essential rights from my point of view are the right of assembly, the right of expression and the right of association. And direct elections of course.[12]

Becoming visible 85

Faced with the current state of affairs the Spanish citizens are waking up. They know that in order to protect themselves and solve their problems they need to unite in neighborhood associations, housewives associations and so forth. The city-council is an entity ... that does not represent anyone anymore.

We [united within neighborhood associations] constitute truly representative [entities]. We celebrate assemblies that include thousands of neighbors, this is much more than the city-council [of Madrid] ever managed to do.[13]

In their interviews the two activists explained the ways in which the engagement with civic associations shaped people's conception of the required political change in Spain. Through the experiences of everyday public activism, democracy as a concept gained meaning. Pamela Radcliff pointed out that while neighborhood-based associations existed in Spain from the early 1940s, the meaning assigned to the term *vecino* (neighbor) changed over time. During the 1940s this term had a specific juridical meaning closer to "head of household." By the 1960s, however, it evolved so as to mean something similar to the terms "resident" or "neighbor" in English.[14] The latter term clearly implied the existence of some sort of spatially based social relations.

Between the years 1965 and 1975 the growing prominence of neighborhood associations and of their leaders in the public sphere, their cooperation with an array of professionals (journalists, lawyers, architects and educators) and their growing mobilization capacities, meant that they could engage the authorities in a technical and a legal dialogue regarding the latter's obligations. As the following pages make clear, on the eve of the dictator's death many neighborhood activists had come to hold a definition of "democracy" that was equated with a concrete set of rights that would enable citizens to make their voices heard through free association and expression.

Isolated mobilization campaigns of urban dwellers vis-à-vis the local authorities were covered by the Spanish press as early as early as 1960. In March 1960 neighbors in the *barrio* of Son Rapinya in Palma boycotted the public bus company due to the rising prices of transportation. A year later a large-scale protest took place in Madrid when the inhabitants of the Controlled Suburb of Orcasitas were denied entry into the houses, which they themselves helped construct. In 1965 women manifested in Vilanova i la Geltru in the province of Barcelona demanding potable water. However, by 1968 neighborhood associations still made up less than 1 percent of all existing civic associations in Spain. By 1979 this number would increase to 17 per cent. The statistical information regarding the geographical spread of neighborhood associations prior to 1975 is partial at best. The most detailed account relates to the city of Bilbao where, according to Victor Urritia Abaigar, 21 legal associations operated between the years 1966 and 1970; an additional 24 were registered between the years 1971 and 1976; and a further 41 legalized between the years 1977 and 1979.[15]

86   *Becoming visible*

The first neighborhood association to be registered in Bilbao formed in 1965 with the aid of local church members in the *barrio* of Recalde (Rekalde).[16] The Recalde association came to be known for successfully pressuring the regional authorities into publishing the Emergency Education Plan for the Basque Provinces (*Nuevo Plan de Urgencia de Construcciones Escolares para las tres provincias vascas y Canarias*) in 1971. However, the most radicalized association in Bilbao was probably the one formed in the Controlled Suburb of Otxarkoaga in 1968.[17] In Madrid the first neighborhood association was constituted in the *barrio* of *Puerto Chico* in the spring of 1967. *Palomeras Bajas* followed suit in 1968 and *El Pozo del Tío Raimundo* in 1969. The later was the first neighborhood association to stand out in the southern periphery of the capital due to its organizational capacities.[18] In Orcasitas the first association to be registered was that of the *Meseta de Orcasitas* in 1971, followed by the association of *Guetaria* (the Controlled Suburb of Orcasitas) in 1973.

While in the associations that formed in Recalde and El Pozo del Tío Raimundo received financial and organizational aid from the local church, in Otxarkoaga, Palomeras Bajas and Entrevías, the help of the Communist-led Comisiones Obreras (CCOO) was essential to the functioning of the association. In both Orcasitas and Guetaria, on the other hand, the associations were formed by neighbors who had no prior experience in public or political activism. It is important to note that although some of the associations that formed throughout the final decade of the dictatorship operated in middle-class *barrios* the first and the most visible associations operated in neighborhoods of the urban periphery, mostly in former absorption and controlled suburbs and in those with an extensive squatter community. Manuel Castells described the heterogeneous nature of the associations, rooted as they were in the everyday socio-economic reality of urban life:

> In Madrid the movement [of the *barrios*] included [associations] from squatters' settlements ... from middle–class neighborhoods and from neighborhoods situated in the historical center of the city ... It was founded by political activists of different ideological shades and by a multitude of people with no precise ideological inclination, who were willing to fight for better living conditions ... The movement obtained the renovation of underprivileged neighborhoods ... and the construction of urban infrastructures on a scale not seen before. It reanimated popular cultural and street life[19]

The drafting of the associations' statutes was the first step on the way to their legalization. This part of the process allowed neighbors to explore for the first time the limits of a new and a slightly more democratic civic idiom. This, however, was not a conflict-free process. The authorities insisted, for example, on defining as members of the association only those people who resided in the *barrio* and owned property there. This condition (which was the reason for the rejection of the first statutes in the case of Palomeras Bajas) was intended to reduce the influence of "undesired elements" such as members of the clandestine democratic opposition or of the technical experts who were affiliated with it. From the neighbors' point of view the first condition was useful in defining the community of neighbors as the users of a specified spatial unit regardless of their economic and legal status (homeowners, renters, etc.). However, this definition also included all of the landowners who did not necessarily reside in the neighborhood itself.

As long as the associations defined their aims in cultural and moral terms they stood a chance of being legalized. This, for example, was the case of the Recalde association that defined it goal as "... elevating the moral, cultural, social and civic level of the families residing within the territory [defined by the statutes]."[20] The case of Carabanchel Alto in Madrid, on the other hand, provides an example of an attempt to test the limits of the discourse on civic rights and obligations. The association was founded in 1973 but was legally registered only in 1976 due to the neighbors' refusal to modify their original statutes. The 1973 text charged the association with defending the interests of the *barrio*'s community of neighbors and with resolving the problem of *chabolismo*. The neighbors expressed the hope that through collective action they would be able to accelerate the creation of basic infrastructures, schools and medical services in the zone. From a more radical perspective, the association also demanded that the neighbors be allowed to participate in the implementation of new education and urban planning policies "by providing the [authorities] with statistics, information and suggestions." The neighbors demanded that they receive professional counseling "in order to be able to actively take part in the resolution of problems pertaining to the sanitary and cultural conditions in the *barrio*."[21] The authorities did not reject out of hand the notion that the neighbors might have useful information to impart, but they refused to involve them in future planning processes.

Neighborhood associations in Spain were usually propelled into action by what sociologist Igor Ahedo Gurrutxaga defined as a "triggering" event (*detonante*): an event that threatened the wellbeing of the community and focused the attention of the inhabitants on specific manifestations of the unjust reality.[22] It was at that moment that new norms emerged, which defined the existing situation as unjust and provided a justification for action.[23] In the case of associations in both Barcelona and of Madrid the "triggering" event related to the implementation of some of the partial plans that emerged of the Barcelona Metropolitan Plan (1953) and Madrid Regional Plan (1963). In the case of Bilbao the association of Recalde was moved into action by the death of a child, María Teresa Sánchez Rivas, who in November 1970 had been run over by one of the garbage trucks that operated and were parked in the *barrio*. It was this event that drove the neighbors to protest for the first time the use of their *barrio* as a parking lot for the city's garbage clearing companies and the lack of educational and recreational facilities, which led Recalde's children to roam the streets. All triggering events were local in nature. At the same time they all related in one way or another to the deficiencies in collective infrastructures and

88 Becoming visible

services. Those events, therefore, effectively mobilized the community and when recounted in retrospect (as part of the association's *raison d'être*) could also be easily related to the concerns of other communities all over Spain.

Testimonies of the founders of the Orcasitas Neighborhood Association point to the fact that the decision to voice concerns of any kind was accompanied by a strong sense of fear and incompetence:

> In February 1971 we managed to secure for the first time a meeting with José Morán Navalón. He was a member of the Madrid city-council in charge of our district ... None of us had any experience of talking in public and before coming to the meeting we chose the person who would represent us. The hairdresser was a man of confidence. He spent his entire working-day talking to others. So we chose him to [speak] for us. During the interview, however, Félix [López Rey] jumped in and started to explain something. He did it so well that in the following meetings we let him do it again.[24]

In a society where every interaction with the authorities could potentially result in economic or penal sanctions, in neighborhoods where the population was a priori tagged as deviant and troublesome the process of forming, registering and operating a new association intimidated the majority of the men and the women involved in it. To these understandable fears were added the feelings of inadequacy of people who were at best unused to debating and explaining themselves in public, and at the time were unable to even read and fill in the necessary documents for the registration of an association. Nonetheless, the initial stages of public activism flashed out individuals who were better suited to represent others.

The founders of the Orcasitas Neighborhood Association were Félix López Rey and Antonio Circuéndez. López Rey (a goldsmith who worked from home) first took upon himself the responsibility of representing his community in 1970. He responded to the call from *Radio España* of the broadcaster Paco Galindo, went on air and described the living conditions in Orcasitas. Antonio Circuéndez was Orcasitas' hairdresser. He ran his own business where he "trimmed mustaches, cut people's hair and talked of football, the mud and politics."[25] Neither one underwent a process of professional socialization that enabled him to acquire public speaking or negotiating capacities. And yet both possessed important qualities: they were well known and trusted by their neighbors; they worked in the *barrio*, which meant that they had intimate knowledge of its layout and deficiencies; in their professional capacity they came into contact with different populations and were aware of their needs; and perhaps most importantly (as both testified) they had control over their time and were almost always around in cases of emergencies (arrests, unexpected demolition of *chabolas* etc.).

Antonio Egea Gil, a member of the association in Orcasitas, described the process undergone by himself and his friends:

Bit by bit we lost our fear of the administration, and of the agents of law and order with their truncheons and pistols. At the end all that was left was the fear of being afraid ... We learnt how to formulate requests and write down petitions; how to go from one office to another; how to cause surprising and paralyzing traffic jams without being arrested. We learnt how to talk to journalists and guide them through our *barrio*.[26]

Following the registration of the association the neighbors gathered wherever they could (in an empty *chabola*, a bar and at times at the local church). Soon, however, the local priest refused to let them use the church for "association business" and they were forced to construct their own building. The office of the Orcasitas Neighborhood Association functioned to a large extent like the socialist *Casa de Pueblo* of the pre-Civil War years. It housed cultural events, the meetings of the association's directive committee and its general assembly, and it provided free use of a bathroom and the toilets for the inhabitants who did not yet have running water in their homes. The same was true in the case of the associations in *El Pozo del Tío Raimundo* and *San Blas*, where the neighbors (for the first time in their lives) fashioned a space that had a formally recognized function after their own style and needs. Years later some neighbors in Orcasitas recorded:

We started working on the design [of the building]. We had to make sure it included plenty of showers and bathrooms, of the kind we did not have at home ... We singled out an appropriate spot, closed it off and started working. We volunteered our time constructing the place so obviously some spent all their free time there and others were never seen around. And since we were no professionals we simply went on constructing the "natural way."[27]

In an interview given in 2006 Félix López Rey recounted with pride:

This is where the original headquarters of the association stood. We built it with our own bare hands. Later on we convinced the authorities to finance the purchase of a cinema projector and we started screening movies here. There was no other space in the *barrio* for recreational activities ...

We did a really good job building this place. Nobody got paid, but some of the companies that operated nearby would let us unload the leftover cement from the trucks. Each of us came when he could. I lived 100 meters from here so at three o'clock in the afternoon I would come over with my boots and I would go around looking for other neighbors who could help."[28]

The words of López Rey emphasize the way in which the production of a new space enhanced existing communal identifications and generated new ones. This newly created space could be a physical one (the offices of the association,

Figures 4.1 and 4.2 The construction and the opening of the association headquarters, Orcasitas, 1971
Source: Asociación de Vecinos del Barrio de Orcasitas, Archivo Fotográfico

for example) or a symbolic one (such as the one that emerged with the legalization of the association). Either way it was clear that through the final years of the dictatorship neighborhood activists had come to see the *barrio* as a spatial unit that could mediate or cut across differences (between men and women, the young and the elderly, homeowners and renters). In an interview given by Antonio Villanueva, President of the Federation of Neighborhood Associations in Madrid, in 1975 he stated:

> When he returns from the factory the worker turns into a citizen ... A worker leaves the factory and is faced with everyday situations of exploitation in his *barrio*. He gets on a bus and finds that the transportation service is unbearable. He wants to take a walk and realizes there are no green zones. And that is before we even start talking about issues such as the lack of street lights, running water or pavements.[29]

The *barrio* was a space where notions of entitlement and justice were debated and formulated. Neighborhood associations played a central role in this process by attempting to think from a plurality of perspectives and take into consideration the different needs of the neighbor as a worker, a consumer, a head of a household and a parent.

The attempts of neighborhood activists to present the associations as representatives of the "community" were enhanced the position adopted towards them by the Spanish Workers' Movement, and especially by the Communist-led Comisiones Obreras. The CCOO and other Communist organizations across Spain reached the second half of the 1960s while operating within a rigid organizational structure that centered on the link between workers and the workplace. In 1967 Santiago Carrillo (the general secretary of the Spanish Communist Party) published an article titled "Salir a la superficie." In the article he officially embraced a practice termed *"entrismo,"* which encouraged the infiltration of legally recognized entities (such as the Falange's worker and student syndicates) in order to use them as platforms for oppositional strategies.[30] Carrillo encouraged the Spanish Communists to capitalize on the growing disaffection with the regime among diversified sectors of the population by creating new channels for collective protest. This policy proved of critical importance against the background of increased repression. In January 1969 the government decreed a state of emergency for the first time since the end of the Civil War. In 1970, with the commencement of the Burgos Trials, the regime's crackdown on all opposition forces continued. Under these conditions new forms of activism, via supposedly apolitical entities such as neighborhood associations, became indispensable.

Paca Sauquillo was a young lawyer, who completed her studies in Madrid and specialized in labor laws. She joined the Workers Syndical Association (Asociación Sindical de Trabajadores—AST) in the early 1970s and was assigned to assist the neighborhood association in Palomeras Bajas. Years later Sauquillo recounted:

92 *Becoming visible*

Many of us saw clearly the fact that the struggle against the dictatorship could not pass through the factory-floor only. We had to expend it to other spaces. Spaces of reproduction: the [peripheral] *barrios* where people lived in misery. And where with their pathetic salaries they were forced to pay [taxes] that should have been returned to them in the form of services, infrastructures and dignified housing.[31]

Saquillo cooperated with neighborhood associations as an outside adviser. Vicente Llopíz González, the vice president of the neighborhood association in the working-class barrio of *La Concepción* in Madrid, was an activist with a double militancy. He recounted:

"I was tried and sentenced to 16 years in jail for being a member of the opposition *syndical obrera* and of the committee in charge of restructuring the [illegal] Communist Youth Movement. When I got out of jail on probation I could not join any political entity. In La Concepción we had an Association of Heads of Households that was withering away for lack of popular support. It was replaced by a neighborhood association, which committed itself to [activism through] popular participation and I was elected president."[32]

Of course the idea of double militancy—within the workplace and the neighborhood—was not without problems as can be understood from the following report by Gregorio López Raimundo before the third congress of the PSUC (the Unified Socialist Party of Cataluña) in 1973:

In the *barrios*, just as in the workplace and the university, the Workers' Movement can become a mass movement only if it keeps itself open. Open to legal and semi-legal forms of action, open to everyone, not only [diehard] revolutionaries. The revolutionary parties need to extend their activism into the sphere of the *barrio* as well, but they must avoid the mistake ... of creating 'clandestine' mass movements through reunions and organizational structures that are based exclusively on revolutionary [activists].[33]

The contradictions between two forms of mobilization—one popular and led by ordinary citizens, and the other selective by nature and carried out by "professional" revolutionaries—generated continued tensions between the representatives of the clandestine democratic opposition and some neighborhood activists. Many neighborhood activists were not associated with a specific opposition party, nor were members of the clandestine opposition dominant within the founding ranks of most of the associations. While borrowing from the discourse and practices of the Workers' Movement, most neighborhood associations refused to adopt identifiable political labels. Their aim was to turn the neighbors, whatever their socio-political background, into partners in a dialogue with the authorities. The central meaning of this partnership was that despite their lack of formal education, despite their inability to express themselves in legal and professional terms, despite their presumed ignorance in matters of politics and of public financing, the authorities had to acknowledge the fact that the neighbors had valuable information to contribute to the process of policy formulation.

In this respect, neighborhood associations constituted a space where a process of "articulation," in the Gramscian sense, often took place, a process by which class status and socio-cultural practices forged collective identifications through ongoing contestations over power and resources. As one neighbor explained: "If one of us had a piece of information he would share it with everyone and put it to [collective] use. And so little by little our knowledge and confidence increased. So did our demands."[34] The internal structure of the associations directly contributed to this process. The work of the associations was carried out within the assemblies as well as within small, thematic groups (*vocalías*). The *vocalías* collected and processed information regarding specific issues (relating to housing, education, sanitation, etc.) and were in direct contact with the affected populations (such as women, the elderly, heads of households, etc.).

At the heart of associational life, however, was the general assembly. "*Asambleismo*" was a modality of action with a long history (especially within the Workers and Students' Movement). By 1970 assemblies seemed to mushroom everywhere in Spain. In the case of neighborhood associations, as we shall see later on, the assemblies' most distinguished feature lays in the interaction between professionals and ordinary citizens. When a problem arose the association would call all the neighbors together in order to discuss the situation. The neighbors would formulate one or more demands or suggested forms of action vis-à-vis the administration, and they would then deliberate on the matter and try to reach a consensual decision. The neighbors would then proceed to elect a group of representatives who were charged with conveying their demands to the administration or with organizing the collective action decided upon. The assemblies were open assemblies—that is open to all the neighbors who lived in the *barrio*. In times of acute crisis (when forced evictions were carried out in violation of previous agreements, for example, or when neighbors were arrested by the police) the assemblies would become "permanent" ones—that is they would be maintained with a certain level of participation until the crisis was resolved. As one of the neighbors in Orcasitas aptly described it:

> Here there was a general assembly ... hundreds of people sitting down, voting, every single Wednesday for over 9 years. Why Wednesdays? Because all of the matches of the European Cup took place on Wednesdays. Everyone here supported Real Madrid. And one day there was an assembly and no one came. So some of us – full of revolutionary ardor – said: The hell with them! If they want to know what's going on let them come on a Wednesday. That might have been a mistake because the assembly started at 20:30, when most people came back from work. So many would go home first or come with their transistors.[35]

The procedures described above functioned as a model for many neighborhood associations. Most of the associations, however, were faced with alternating

94 *Becoming visible*

periods of great activism in which mobilization of the mass of neighbors proved to be a relatively easy tusk, but other times when the social base for decision-making would shrink, sometimes to the point of including only the association's executive committee. Diani and Della Porta defined the fluctuating levels of participation and the complex interplay between different groups of members as the most problematic features of organizations and of social movements that embrace the grass-root model. According to them:

> Participatory democracy may often reduce the decision-making efficiency of assemblies and lead to very long periods of confusion and incertitude ... In fairness, the concrete realization of the organizational principles of grass-roots democracy has never been a simple matter. Many activists have complained of the *de facto* oligarchies which tend to form and impose their will when collective decision-making becomes difficult. An organized minority can win out in an assembly by wearing down the majority, and forcing them to give up and leave after hours of strenuous discussion. In a few extreme cases physical force has been used by some groups to occupy impor-tant decision-making positions such as the chair of meetings. Even without reaching those excesses, the risks of a "tyranny of emotions," whereby the most committed activists profit from the lack of formal procedures and secure control of decision-making processes, have been pointed out"[36]

As both scholars pointed out, the existence of grass-root organizations (such as neighborhood associations) very much depends on the willingness of their members to maintain a certain level of participation. Participation may be encouraged through a different combination of ideological and united incentives and is oftentimes very local in nature.

In the case of neighborhood associations the assembly encouraged participation by opposing (in theory at least) the patriarchal model that designated leaders who had better access to information and complete influence over the decision-making process. While not all neighbors felt comfortable about expressing their opinions in front of the entire assembly, the great emphasis put on the need to reach a consensus forced those who did speak to try and explain themselves in clear terms and take into consideration the needs of the entire audience—women and men, working people and housewives, youths and the elderly.

Women and the workings of neighborhood associations during the dictatorship

Despite the innovative nature of the associations not all groups within the *barrio* enjoyed an equal level of visibility and influence within them. Women, especially, were liable to be excluded from the assemblies. Historian Pamela Radcliff and anthropologist Britt-Marie Thurén examined the gender dynamics that emerged within neighborhood associations.[37] Their work points to the fact that women's presence within these entities was not matched by an ability to formulate an independent agenda. This is despite the fact that women constituted a majority in most street demonstrations and were engaged with the day-to-day functioning of the association. José Manuel and Emilia lived in Orcasitas since the 1960s. When asked about their involvement in the activities of the association they explained the division between them:

> [José Manuel] Yes, she was very active [within the neighborhood association]. Me? I would go into the restaurant at 9:00 and come out at 23:00 or 24:00. And you know what we are like, waiters. We close down and then stay for one nightcap, and another one, and another one. And you end up coming home at 2:00.
>
> [Emilia, with great pride] But I was here and I was very active.[38]

While women could be rapidly mobilized for ad-hoc action (getting petitions signed and delivered, blocking traffic, demonstrating in front of one of the ministries) they had a harder time participating in the general assemblies. The assemblies took place mostly in the evenings. In a society where most men did not change a diaper or fry an egg for dinner it was obvious from the start who would attend the assembly and who would stay home to put the children to bed. The interviews I conducted with women activists within the Orcasitas Neighborhood Association show that even those women who did attend the assemblies found it hard to express themselves. Pura López, the head of the Women's Association in the *barrio* was very clear on the subject:

> Look, the struggle here was a project built on active cooperation between men and women ... But from the start it was clear that we, women, were second-class citizens. We were invisible. If we had a meeting, everyone together, and a woman wanted to speak someone would always say "shut up you! You have no idea what you are saying."[39]

When not completely excluded, women were often ridiculed into silence. And yet women had a very real power base within the associations. They were not only the driving force behind street demonstrations but also had very concrete and valuable knowledge. Such knowledge became critical in the second half of the 1970s, as the final stage of urban reconstruction started to take place in many barrios around the city. Women had a more intimate understanding of what were the "essentials" of a newly remodeled *barrio*. While that information was not always valued by their male counterparts it was considered essential by the professionals who worked alongside neighborhood association. For many men, the neighborhood consisted first and foremost of their homes, the local bar and of course the transportation networks that would connect them with their place of work. Women, on the other hand, had a more holistic vision of the *barrio* as a social unit. Apart from the perfect location for shops, women knew where each plaza, playground and phone cabinet had to be located. They also knew how far it was reasonable to expect their children to walk in order to

96   *Becoming visible*

reach school and what could be considered a safe street as far as the division between roads and sidewalks was concerned. This crude information was recorded by teams of architects, translated into professional language and incorporated into the remodeling plans that were presented to the authorities by the neighborhood associations.

With the passing of time women also found their own voice within the associations. As was the case with many other public entities, this was often done within separate women's working groups or committees. The need for the existence of specific working groups for women was not something everyone agreed upon. Some felt that the struggle and the goals of neighborhood associations were common to men and women and so should be the organizational structure. Others acknowledged the need for specific working groups that would concentrate on issues relating to the social and political promotion of women.[40] These committees proliferated as women became more aware of their potential contribution to the *barrio* and their right to have a say in the way their living environment would look. As the feminist discourse of the 1970s legitimized the debate over typical "women's issues" (such as the division of labor within the home or family planning) women became acutely aware of the need for a space of their own. In the words of Pura López:

> It was then that we started meeting, a small group of women ... We had reading and writing classes, since some of us did not even know how to sign their own name. Others knew how to write but wanted to improve their skills. Another class we started was related to family planning schemes. And then there were many *charlas* [talks] on how we see our lives as women. We fought shoulder to shoulder men and women, but we, as women, always had this space of our own where we could think. We needed to discuss who we are and who we want to be. We needed a place where we could try and figure out what is our assigned role in society, and whether we agree with it.[41]

García's words testify to the exclusion suffered by women within the associations. At the same time, however, she points to the ways in which women did manage to forge a space of their own via sections or organizations that functioned within the general framework of the associations. When referring to those "islands" of empowerment she in fact points to the conditions that enable space to be fully appropriated. An appropriated space is one in which real differences (in interests, capacities and so forth) can be expressed from an egalitarian perspective. It is a space in which individual and collective progress can be achieved. It is a space from which one can consider the place assigned to one's self within society. Finally, it is a space where one is free to critically consider one's identifications. In their own way (and despite their double exclusion as working-class women) rank-and-file activists did manage to leave their mark some of the most vibrant civic entities during the years of late Francoism and the transition to democracy. By doing so they contributed to forging a space

Becoming visible 97

where the personal was accepted as political. And while this understanding did not always resonate outside the neighborhoods themselves, it marked—as we shall see—the ways in which neighborhood activists experienced and interpreted the process of democratization.

The emergence of a new legal idiom: The petition of the Orcasitas Neighborhood Association before the courts

As indicated previously the *Meseta de Orcasitas* neighborhood association was prompted into full action by the publication of the *Partial Plan for the Reconstruction of the Municipal Area of Orcasitas* in April 1971. The declared goal of the plan was to clear all *infraviviendas* from the area. At the same time it was clear from the detailed documents that the plan rested on a new conceptualization of the capital's southern periphery. The future Orcasitas was to be very different from the old *barrio*. The area covered by the new plan included the three barrios of Orcasitas (Meseta, Poblado Dirigido and Poblado Agricola / Mínimo). Of the entire sector, only the Controlled Suburb (which included temporary high-rise apartment buildings) was to be left as it was. The new *barrio* was divided into seven sections with mixed functions: housing, recreational areas, green spaces, educational and shopping facilities, religious and cultural spaces.

The neighbors learnt of the Plan from the local press. Despite their confusion, for a brief time it seemed that they were finally going to receive the neighborhood that they were entitled to a well-defined spatial unit that would include not only permanent housing units and infrastructures, but also communal and commercial spaces. The preamble to the Plan stated:

> The specific characteristics of the area, and the existence of over 600 shanty houses, call for a progressive action. Such an action should enable us to expropriate some of the land and then proceed with construction on that land ... thereby avoiding temporary resettlement.[42]

The neighbors took the statement to mean that their right to remain "on the land" was guaranteed. However, they were soon to learn that the administration did not view the preamble to the plan to be a legally binding document. The reconstruction plan was to be carried out in cooperation with private developers. And while the authorities intended to reserve some of the housing units in the new *barrio* for the original inhabitants (the number was never made explicit; one can only guess that the 600 *chabolas* indicated in the preamble constituted the base-line for any future calculation) the majority of the housing units were destined to be sold by the construction companies to new comers. The "New Orcasitas" was destined for a new population. Faced with forced eviction and complete uncertainty concerning their future the neighbors started exploring the possibility of resistance.

In the final months of 1971 two additional concerns emerged: the neighbors found out that the largest landowner in the area, María Orcasitas, was

98 Becoming visible

promised a much higher rate of compensation for her lands. Despite the fact that her lands housed only 150 families, María Orcasitas was to receive 32.4 percent of the new housing units (1,444 apartments). The neighbors also contested the number of *chabolas* indicated in the preamble. By 1971 the *Meseta* alone housed over 1,500, *chabolas* and 500 additional *chabolas* were scattered on the road connecting Orcasitas with neighboring Usera. To those were to be added 500 families that had to be evacuated from the temporary high-rise apartment buildings in the Controlled Suburb. The 3,300 housing units planned as part of the first phase of construction could provide a solution for all 2,500 families, but not if the Orcasitas family was to receive 1,444 apartments.

The neighbors recorded their frustration:

> We saw the largest landowner in the area was to be freed from the entire process of expropriation and handed the most desirable sector of the neighborhood. We understood immediately that this decision compromised the rights of smaller landowners. Worse than that, it turned the preamble of the plan into an irrelevant text. If a single landowner was to be allocated a major part of the new housing units where were we supposed to go to?[43]

The initial reaction of the Orcasitas Neighborhood Association was to petition the Planning Committee of the City of Madrid and demand that the plan be changed in line with the promises indicated in the preamble. The petition was rejected in 1972 and all the neighborhood associations across Spain were informed that the preambles to the urban reconstruction plans were not considered to be legally binding documents. By April 1973 the Planning Committee of the City of Madrid made clear that it was not going to consider the concerns raised by the neighbors in Orcasitas. At this point the association in the *Meseta* held a general assembly in which it was decided to petition the Territorial Tribunal of Madrid (*Audiencia Territorial de Madrid*).

This first general assembly was a major turning point in the history of the *barrio*. The police authorized the assembly under the condition that a petition to the courts would not be discussed. In order to ensure this, agents of the feared Socio-Political Brigade accompanied Félix López Rey from his house to the association's headquarters and monitored the meeting. When the assembled neighbors were asked what they wanted to do next a unanimous cry arose from the crowd "to the Supreme Court."[44]

From that moment on, neighborhood associations all over Spain started to follow the events that took place in Orcasitas. The weekly *Sábado Gráfico* declared in May 1973: "The Issue of Orcasitas goes before the Supreme Court."[45] The Catholic periodical *YA* followed suit by asking:

> What can be achieved by petitioning the tribunals? One can only hope that the administration makes explicit its commitment to maintain the [social fabric] that has emerged out of a life lived together. Furthermore, we urge

the authorities to execute the [reconstruction] plan by following a process of expropriation that is based on an exact census of the houses that are located in this sector.[46]

Three months later the weekly *Informaciones* told its readers that the neighbors in Orcasitas had carried out their own independent census and were now demanding that all of the 3,600 new housing units be reserved for the existing inhabitants.[47]

While neighborhood associations all over the country were waiting to see what would happen in Orcasitas the situation in the *barrio* itself was deteriorating rapidly. The authorities stopped all garbage collection services to the area, and an epidemic of typhus spread across the *chabolas*. As if by coincidence the Chrysler automobile company decided to reclaim some of the lands it owned on the eastern outskirts of Orcasitas at precisely the same time and demanded the immediate evacuation of all the inhabitants. Finally, the authorities (under the pretext of conducting a new survey in the area) attempted to pressure individual families into signing expropriation agreements. The journal *Nuevo Diario* reported in mid 1973:

> The neighbors [we spoke to] – about 100 families all in all – are complaining that in the past several days representatives of the authorities visited the *barrio* and attempted to manipulate them into signing a certain agreement. The representatives walk around with pieces of paper lacking an official caption and refuse to show identification of any sort. The papers only say that an apartment has been assigned to the person signed bellow by the Ministry of Housing. No house number, no street name, only a general indication that the apartment is situated in the *barrio* of *Entrevías*. The document empowers the authorities to tear down the house of the person who signs it without mentioning compensation of any sort. Neighbors who have 40,000 pesetas to pay upon entry, and further 850 pesetas monthly, are sent to *Entrevías*. Those who do not have that sum pay 40 pesetas and are sent to temporary housing projects [UVA]. What a fascinating way to conduct a survey.[48]

In the meantime, the high-rise apartment buildings of the Controlled Suburb of Orcasitas started to show major defects, from uneven floors to serious cracks in the walls and ceilings. The authorities offered to fortify the buildings with external cement beams. The neighbors found the solution provisory and insufficient, and the newly founded neighborhood association of the Controlled Suburb managed to carry out several mass demonstrations outside the offices of the Madrid Planning Committee before it was threatened with the suspension of its activities.[49] From that moment on it was clear to both the association of the *Meseta* and that of the Controlled Suburb that they would need to coordinate their actions in order to reach a solution that would be satisfactory and include the entire population of Orcasitas.

100 *Becoming visible*

Through 1973 the neighbors in Orcasitas moved from a purely defensive position to a more critical one. In December 1973 they demanded that the processes of expropriation and of construction should be conducted at the same time, so as to shorten the time left for them to live in the existing *chabolas*. They also asked for the construction of street-lights, water fountains, and the creation of transportation services prior to completion of the reconstruction process. But most important was the demand that surfaced in mid 1973—to take an active part in the process that was to have a long-lasting effect on their lives:

> The local authorities have no choice but to pay attention to us when we come to complain about things that are taking place in our neighborhood. We ask that they tell us exactly what is going on, even if there is no solution to the problem, and not make false promises. We want to take part in the reconstruction process ... we want them to explain what exactly is going to happen: Who has to leave? Who can stay and under what conditions?
>
> We want our representatives to be present in the meetings in which decisions are made regarding our future. This is essential so that things can later be related to the neighbors without delay. We ask to take part in the surveys that are being conducted in order to record and evaluate our homes. This is of great importance in a situation where many of us lack official documents that testify to what is ours and what is not.
>
> We ask that all plans and documents pertaining to the reconstruction process be deposited at the association's headquarters, so that we can study them and respond in time.[50]

The above quotation points to the fact that in the time that passed between the presentation of their petition to the Territorial Tribunal and its discussion the neighbors had become aware of their ability to take part in producing the space which they inhabit. In order to do so successfully they demanded transparency and information from the authorities.

Through their petition to the Territorial Tribunal the neighbors of Orcasitas also laid the groundwork for a new legal discourse. In formulating their petition they were aided for the first time by a professional living outside the *barrio*: a professor of civil law, Eduardo García de Enterría. García de Enterría was one of the many professionals that assisted neighborhood associations during the final years of the dictatorship. Manuel Castells wrote of these professionals:

> They had a major role in the development of the Citizens' Movement. They agreed to work shoulder to shoulder with the neighbors and promoted their participation in joint projects, teaching them and being taught by them in a highly productive and innovative process.
>
> They also provided the movement with much-needed social and professional legitimization. They were respected by their colleagues in the administration and won several of the legal battles simply because they understood and worked with the existing urban and administrative

legislation better than many of the bureaucrats who faced them. This synthesis between a professional social movement and an urban social movement is what turned the Madrid movement into a historical precedence.[51]

Experts such as García de Enterría had a double commitment: politically most wished to see a change in the administrative structures of the regime. As lawyers and architects many also embraced the concept of "advocacy planning," which encouraged experts to identify with the citizens (in their capacity as neighbors, consumers and parents) instead of the authorities as the beneficiaries of their work.[52]

In the concluding chapter of *The Production of Space* Henri Lefebvre defined the essential difference between "city planning" and "advocacy planning." According to Lefebvre:

> Faced with the city's complexity and intelligibility ... some in the United States were inspired to take the practical and theoretical initiative of creating specialists responsible for disentangling the web of problems and explaining them, though without necessarily proposing solutions ... The notion was that in this way 'users' and 'inhabitants,' as a group, would secure the services of someone competent, capable of speaking and communicating ... who would negotiate for them with political or financial entities.[53]

This position of the engaged professionals in their capacity as translators who took upon themselves to "frame" the knowledge, arguments and demands of the neighbors into a formally recognized legal and technical idiom was especially apparent in the case of Orcasitas. The legal exchange that took place between the neighbors and the administrators following the 1973 law suit centered upon two issues specifically: García de Enterría's main argument was that ownership in itself could not take precedence over actual use of the land. By living "on the land" for over 20 years and leaving their mark on it the neighbors had elevated its value. They were therefore entitled to be resettled on it. This claim acknowledged two distinct sets of rights: those of landowners (*propietarios*), who did not necessarily reside in Orcasitas, and those of the neighbors (*vecinos*). Since over half of the *barrio*'s population consisted of renters, the neighborhood association also demanded that all forms of lease (with or without a contract, subletting and/or sharing) should be acknowledged by law so as to render the entire "community of neighbors" eligible for resettlement in the renovated *barrio*.

The way in which the Orcasitas Neighborhood Association used the term *vecindario / comunidad de vecinos* in its appeal before the Territorial Tribunal conferred on it a collective status over time. This meant that the neighbors had a common history, and that the authorities had the obligation to provide for their common future. Antonio Egea Gil explained in simple words the process by which a "community of neighbors" emerged:

102   *Becoming visible*

> Orcasitas [started off] as a transit station, the last one on our journey to Madrid ... But we never attained our goal. We were left there – in that final transit station ...
>
> ... And when we finally won, when the dream became a reality, we were surprised to find out that we did not actually want to move to the center of Madrid, perhaps we never did ... Men of the land as we were our roots had grown deep and we no longer longed for the shining city. We wanted to remain loyal to the space that gave rise to our battle.[54]

Going back to our earlier discussion regarding the meaning of spatial appropriation, this citation adds an important component to the definition which emerged from the words of Pura López. A sense of belonging and identification with one's lived space did not necessarily imply the ability to control and shape that space. In the case of Orcasitas it is clear that identification with the old *barrio* resulted from the formation of strong community ties. Those ties, in their turn, constituted a powerful motivation for individual neighbors to join forces in the struggle to make their "final transit station" truly theirs. Those who accompanied García de Enterría to the courthouse recorded with emotion that day:

> We filled the courthouse, few times in the past, if at all, did people see something such as this: Women with their shopping baskets, the elderly with their caskets and walking sticks. Full of emotion we listened to the brilliant speech of Professor García de Enterría. He asked who had more of a right to enjoy a new [neighborhood] than the people whose patience and suffering had revalorized it?[55]

Throughout the 1960s several aspects of Francoist legislation were being re-evaluated by the regime's formal institutions. This was especially apparent in the fields of family and labor law. Only a few, however, stopped to reconsider the status of private property. This was first done in when the Territorial Tribunal rendered its verdict concerning the Orcasitas Reconstruction Plan in 1973. The verdict supported the neighbors' demand to be resettled in the renovated *barrio* and further declared the preambles of all Reconstruction Plans legally binding, thereby preparing the way for numerous law suits all across Spain.

How can one explain this change in policy? One possible answer has to do with the overwhelming reality of squatting. Despite the regime's attempts to combat the phenomenon of illegal self-construction through the mechanisms of eviction and alternative planning it failed miserably. The reformed Land Law of 1975 constituted an attempt to change the face of urban planning in Spain, while taking into consideration simultaneously the needs of the construction industry and the increasing popular pressure. The new Land Law essentially it allowed for more flexibility at the level of municipal planning, which in its turn made the authorities more susceptible to popular pressure and better disposed towards the incorporation of citizens into the process of urban planning. In the decade following the publication of the Land Law it was implemented through constant contestations between citizens and private capital. Despite a more coherent planning vision reality on the ground still depended more on the balance of power between those two forces than on the nature of the new regional plans. In the case of Orcasitas both the Madrid Planning Committee and the construction companies refused at first to hand control over the remodeling project. During the final months of the dictatorship, therefore, the inhabitants of Orcasitas rejected a second Reconstruction Plan. The new plan allocated more housing units within the renovated *barrio* to the neighbors but did not offer a solution to the problems of the Controlled Suburb. Nor did it incorporate the association's representatives into the planning process.

✳✳✳

The struggle to find adequate solutions to the problem of *chabolismo* all over Spain continued throughout the years of the democratic transition and beyond. So did the process of contested urban reconstruction. In this respect, Spain followed a pattern similar to other Western European countries in the wake of the 1968 mobilizations and the crisis of Fordism. Margit Mayer characterized this phase of urban opposition in the following words:

> A struggle around housing, rent strikes, campaigns against urban renewal … against what the German psychoanalyst Alexander Mitscherlich back then aptly called 'the inhospitality of our cities' … and struggles for youth and community centers were all politicized in a progressive manner by the wider 'threat context' which the student, ant-war, and leftist mobilization of the 1960s and early 1970s had created and by the political openings which governments (generally in the mold of social democratic compromise) allowed at that time.[56]

While the context of urban struggle in Spain was different from that of countries such as France and Italy, there is no doubt that neighborhood associations in general, and the community in Orcasitas specifically, entered the years of the transition to democracy with a new sense of political purpose and of civic empowerment. The legal precedent set by the Territorial Tribunal acknowledged the right of use (of land and of infrastructures) as an essential component on the way to attaining other rights. *Assembleismo* was well established as a deliberative decision-making procedure that was adopted by many civil communities across Spain. While it was not yet elaborated into a more extended model of self-management outside the work place and the *barrio*, many citizens came to view it as an essential component of political life. The cooperation between neighbors and committed professionals was extended to include various communities in Cataluña, Andalusia, the Basque region and Valencia. Neighbors

104 *Becoming visible*

were gaining professional knowledge and the ability to analyze their everyday experiences in more generalized terms. By the time of the death of the dictator in November 1975 communities of neighbors all over Spain had come to accept the fact that a permanent and a sustainable change in their living conditions would entail a major change in the existing political system. It was clear that transparency, access to information and consensual decision-making processes were essential components of any new political system. However, the death of General Franco in no way signaled a smooth move towards democracy. Rather, it was the starting point of a process of democratization that was not as secure or as irreversible as the hegemonic political discourse of the 1990s would have us believe. Within this shifting socio-political context, communities of neighbors would have to negotiate their specific democratic visions, which rested to a large extent on their past experiences.

Notes

1 Lefebvre, *Writings on Cities*, p. 169.
2 J. Borja, *Por unos municipios democráticos. Diez años de reflexión política y movimiento ciudadano*, Madrid: Instituto de Estudios de Administración Local, 1986; J. Borja, *Luces y sombras del urbanismo de Barcelona*, Barcelona: Colección Gestión de la Ciudad, 2010; C. Molinero and P. Ysàs (eds.), *Construint la ciutat democràtica: El moviment vecinal durant el tardofranquisme i al transició*, Barcelona: Icaria Editorial, 2010.
3 For this position see: Castells, *City and the Grassroots*; V. Urritia Abaigar, *El movimiento vecinal en el área metropolitana de Bilbao*, Bilbao: Instituto Vasco de Administración Pública, 1985; M. Castells, 'La formación de un movimientos social urbano: el Movimiento Ciudadano de Madrid hacia el final de la era franquista," in *La ciudad y las masas. Sociología de los movimientos sociales urbanos*, Madrid: Alianza Editorial, 1986; R. G. Fadiño Pérez, *Historia del movimiento ciudadano e historia local: el ejemplo del barrio de Yagüe en Logroño (1948–1975)*, Logroño: Instituto de Estudios Riojanos, 2003; C. Gonzalo Morell, "Una visión global de movimiento asociativo vecinal regional durante la Transición: 1970–1986," *Estudios Humanísticos. Historia*, 9, 2010, pp. 195–220; Radcliff, *Making Democratic Citizens in Spain*.
4 See the discussion in the first chapter concerning the 1975 Land Law and the evolving role of the local administration in matters of local and regional planning.
5 Bordetas Jiménez, *Nosotros somos los que hemos hecho esta ciudad*, p. 362.
6 F.E.T.— Falange Española Tradicionalista y de las Juntas de Ofensiva Nacional Sindicalista or F.E.T y de las J.O.N.S.
7 Ley 191/1964 de 24 de diciembre, de Asociaciones, BOE 28 diciembre de 1964, artículo primero.
8 Ley Orgánica del Estado, http://www.cervantesvirtual.com/servlet/SirveObras/ 12159641912327174198846/p0000001.htm#I_1.
9 *MAYO-JUNIO 1971. Anteproyecto: Normas sobre asociacionismo*, available at http://www.march.es/ceacs/biblioteca/proyectos/linz/documento.asp?reg=r-4992.
10 See Radcliff, *The Making Democratic Citizens in Spain*, pp. 91–92. For more limited statistics, based solely on the information provided by the National Delegation of the F.E.T in charge of Associations see: E. Maza Zorria, *Asociacionismo en la España Franquista. Aproximación Histórica*, Valladolid: Universidad de Valladolid, 2011, pp. 102–103.

Becoming visible 105

11 M. Castells, *The Urban Question: A Marxist Approach*, Cambridge, MA: MIT Press, 1979.
12 Interview with Félix López Rey, *Mundo Social*, Junio 1975.
13 Interview with Antonio Villanueva Agüero, "La Democracia de los Vecinos," *Doblón*, 22.3.1975.
14 Radcliff, *Making Democratic Citizens in Spain*, pp. 39–41.
15 V. Urrutia Abaigar, "La ciudad de los ciudadanos," *Actas del VI Symposium: Movimientos ciudadanos y sociales en Bilbao*, p. 18.
16 The *barrio* of Recalde, much like that of Orcasitas in Madrid, was made up of a community divided between those living in *chabolas* (mainly in the area of Uretamendi), in single-story family homes and in high-rise apartment buildings.
17 On the *barrio* of Otxarkoaga, see: J. M. Paredes, "Otxarkoaga," in M. Toral, J. del Vigo, J. Eguiraun, J.M. Paredes and A. Izarzelaia, "Movimientos ciudadanos en Bilbao: Rekaldeberri, Otxarkoaga, S. Francisco," *Revista Bidebarrieta*, 10, 2001, pp. 229–248.
18 For more on the history of the *barrio* El Pozo del Tío Raimundo, see: J. L. González Balado, *Padre Llanos: Un Jesuita En El Suburbio*, Madrid: Temas de Hoy, 1991.
19 M. Castells, "Productores de ciudad: el movimiento ciudadano de Madrid," in V. Pérez Quintana and P. Sánchez León (eds.), *Memoria Ciudadana y movimiento vecinal. Madrid 1968–2008*, Madrid: Catarata, 2009, p. 21.
20 J. del Vigo, J. Eguiraun, Recalde, in *Movimientos ciudadanos en Bilbao*, pp. 232–233.
21 Carabanchel Alto, *Historia*, available at https://aavvcarabanchelalto.wordpress.com/historia-de-la-asociacion/.
22 I. Ahedo Gurrutxaga, "Bilbao y frontera interna: integración comunitaria desde la exclusión urbana. El caso de Rekaldeberri," *Bidebarrieta: Revista de humanidades y ciencias sociales de Bilbao*, 23 (2012), p. 109.
23 D. Della Porta and M. Diani, *Social Movements an Introduction*, Oxford: Blackwell, 2006, p. 12.
24 Asociación de Vecinos de Orcasitas, *Del Barro al Barrio*, p. 131.
25 Ibid., p. 53.
26 Ibid., pp. 45–46.
27 Ibid., p. 143.
28 Félix López Rey, interview (Orcasitas, Madrid).
29 Interview with Ernesto Garrido Treviño, *Doblón*, 7.6.1975.
30 S. Carrillo, "Salir a la superficie," *Nuestra Bandera*, 65(3), 1966, pp. 15–16.
31 P. Sauquillo, "El movimiento madrileño en la conquista de las libertades," *Memoria ciudadana y movimiento vicinal. Madrid 1968–2008*, Madrid: Catarata, 2009, p. 140.
32 "Así son los lideres de Madrid," *El País*, 4 de mayo 1976.
33 G. López Raimundo in G. Pala, "El Partido y la Ciudad. Modelos de Organización y Militancia del PSUC Clandestino (1963–1975)," *Historia Contemporánea*, 50, 2015, pp. 209–210.
34 Asociación de Vecinos de Orcasitas, *Del Barro al Barrio*, p. 144.
35 Antonio, interview (Orcasitas, Madrid).
36 Diani and Della Portela, *Social Movements: An Introduction*, pp. 147–8.
37 P. Radcliff, "Ciudadanas: las mujeres de Las Asociaciones de Vecinos y la identidad de género en los sesenta," in Pérez Quintana and Sánchez León (eds.), *Memoria Ciudadana*, pp. 54–78; B. M. Thurén, *Mujeres en la casa, hombres en la calle?* Madrid: Biblioteca Básica Vecinal, 1977.
38 José Manuel and Emilia, Interview (Orcasitas, Madrid).
39 Pura López, Interview (Orcasitas, Madrid).
40 For more on this debate see: T. Magro Huertas and Z. Muxí Martínez, "La mujeres constructoras de ciudad desde los movimientos sociales urbanos," available at http://fundacion.arquia.es/files/public/media/-ldRvoIlT6wOReeX4yM2e2hs8Sw/MjIyODg/MA/f_pdf.pdf/.

106 *Becoming visible*

41 Ibid.
42 The number of shanty homes cited in the document was based on a partial survey of the neighborhood that was conducted in 1961 and covered only about 20 percent of the *barrio*'s area. It was later contested by the Orcasitas Neighborhood Association. See Gerencia Municipal de Urbanismo, *Plan parcial de ordenación de Orcasitas*, Madrid, noviembre 1971.
43 *Del Barro al Barrio*, p. 156.
44 *De Barro al Barrio*, p. 170.
45 M. Muñoz and M. Frias, "El tema de Orcasitas va al Supremo," *Sábado Grafico* (12.5.1973).
46 "Los problemas del barrio madrileño de Orcasitas," *YA* (24.8.1973).
47 M. Luz Nachón, *Informaciones* (8 de abril 1973).
48 M. Quintero, "Cara y Cruz. Un censo ciertamente singular," *Nuevo Diario* (Madrid, 11.5.1973).
49 Asociación de Vecinos Guetaria, "Apuntas sobre la Historia del Poblado Dirigido de Orcasitas," p. 10, available at http://es.scribd.com/doc/28561435/Historia-de-ORCA SITAS#scribd.
50 "Orcasitas quiere algo mas que ser escuchados," *Los Barrios* (diciembre, 1973).
51 Castells, "Productores de Ciudad: el Movimiento Ciudadano de Madrid," in *Memoria Ciudadana y Movimiento Vecinal*, p. 29.
52 P. Davidoff, "Advocacy and Pluralism in Planning," *Journal of the American Institute of Planners*, 31, 1965, pp. 186–197. For more on engaged professionals during the Spanish transition to democracy, see: T. Groves, *Teachers and the Struggle for Democracy in Spain 1970–1985*, Basingstoke: Palgrave Macmillan, 2014, chapters 4–6.
53 Lefebvre, *The Production of Space*, p. 364.
54 *Del Barro al Barrio*, pp. 46–48.
55 Ibid., pp. 171–172.
56 M. Mayer, "The 'Right to the City' in Urban Social Movements," in N. Brenner, P. Marcuse and M. Mayer (eds.), *Cities for People not for Profit: Critical Urban Theory and the Right to the City*, London: Routledge, 2012, p. 65.

5 Alternative visions of democracy
Urban space and the Spanish transition

> The state cannot coexist peacefully with radicalised and generalised *autogestion*, as it must be put under the democratic control "of the base." The state *of autogestion*, that is to say a State in which an internalised *autogestion* gains power, could only be a State that is withering away. The party *of autogestion* could therefore only be that the party which leads politics towards its conclusion and the end of politics, beyond political democracy.[1]

During the years 1968–1975 individual neighborhood associations across Spain started to establish mechanisms of cooperation and of information-sharing while expressing similar goals in relation to specific projects of urban renovation within their respective *barrios*. Prior to 1975, however, most forms of cooperation took place in a provisional way and on a local level. The Barcelona area constitutes a singular example, where a Federation of Neighborhood Associations was founded as early as 1972. It was followed in 1976 by Federation of Neighborhood Associations in Madrid and only later by other cities such as Bilbao, Valencia and Valladolid. During the initial stages of their existence individual neighborhood associations carried out important work through which new social and political sensibilities emerged. Their most significant contribution to the general processes of socio-cultural change that took place in Spain prior to November 1975 lay in igniting a debate regarding the nature of citizenship on a sub-national scale. The associations responded to situations, which the dictatorship acknowledged as problematic but attempted to present as unrelated and local in nature. Neighborhood associations (on the other hand) claimed that such situations emerged out of generalized conditions: the limited representational capacity of local and regional institutions, and the unequal distribution of resources on all levels of governance.

Some of the more militant associations put forth concrete plans of action in order to rectify the situation prior to 1975. Apart from Orcasitas another case in point is that of Recalde in Bilbao. In 1968 Recalde Neighborhood Association conducted a survey which indicated that the *barrio* included a population of 8,333 children under the age of 14. Of those, 1,928 children received some sort of formal instruction in temporary classes constructed in the neighborhood and a further 947 had school placements in other areas of Bilbao; 2,850 children

108 *Alternative visions of democracy*

had no access to formal education. Following the death of María Teresa Sánchez Rivas in 1970 six neighborhood associations of the Bilbao area (headed by representatives from Recalde) demanded a meeting with the Minister of Education and the Minister of Housing. The meeting took place in May 1971 and was followed in September by the publication of the Emergency Education Plan for the Basque Provinces. However, by early 1975 the plan had not been implemented. At that stage the pressure from 12 neighborhood associations forced the mayor of Bilbao, Pilar Careaga, to resign.[2]

In Barcelona the struggle against the implementation of several partial plans between the years 1973 and 1976 led to creation of a new district named "Nou Barris." The nine neighborhoods which made up the district upon formation included a significant migrant population divided between zones of mass social housing and areas of self-constructed *barraques*. The new district, while lacking a coherent communal identity such as the one that emerged in Orcasitas, proved to be a major force in the struggle to modify the General Metropolitan Plan of 1976 in ways that met the housing and the cultural needs of the *barrios'* inhabitants.

Through the initial phases of their activism neighborhood associations defined new organizational goals and constituted a space within which new public leaders emerged and were trained. Prior to November 1975, however, the actions of most of the associations could be described more in terms of subversion rather than explicit resistance to the dictatorship.[3] Only in 1976, when individual neighborhood associations merged into a Citizens' Movement, were dispersed projects of consensual self-management gradually reframed in relation to a larger political project—that of direct/radical democracy.

The concept of direct democracy gained prominence throughout Europe during the 1960s and the emergence of a variety of new social movements. In Germany, France and Italy students, workers, feminist activists, neighbors and consumers combined different cultural projects, based on their everyday experiences with a widespread critique of the existing power relations. The varied projects that were grouped under the heading of direct or radical democracy advocated the use of deliberative procedures (such as the ones adopted within the general assembly) at most of the levels of policy formulation.[4] They highlighted the diversity of human experience, while at the same time striving to surpass the social fragmentation that characterized life in late-capitalist societies. They did so by calling for unity of action across differences, and by encouraging people to critically examine the relationship between existing social categories and identifications.

At the heart of the project of direct democracy during the Spanish transition was the concept of self-management (*autogestión*). The Greek philosopher and psychoanalyst Cornelius Castoriadis defined a self-managed society as:

> a society in which all the decisions are taken by the collective that is directly concerned by these decisions. A society in which all those who are engaged with achieving a certain goal decide collectively what it is that they

wish to do, and how they wish to do it ... Self-management requires cooperation between those who possess knowledge, or a specific competence, and those who perform the productive process itself.[5]

Castoriadis believed that there were two preconditions to the successful functioning of a self-managed society. The first was full access to information on the part of those who are to take part in decision-making processes. The second was flexibility in the assignment and/or redistribution of resources (both natural and produced) so that decisions, once reached, could be effectively implemented. Henri Lefebvre provided a more extended definition of the concept in 1966:

> *Autogestion* is defined as knowledge of and control (at the limit) by a group – a company, a locality, an area or a region – over the conditions governing its existence and its survival through change. Through *autogestion*, these social groups are able to influence their own reality. The right to *autogestion*, like the right to representation, can be proclaimed as a citizen's right, with the ways in which it is applied being spelled out later. Action and initiative by the rank-and-file are always desirable. But have we to wait until the practice is working before espousing the principle? The growth of democracy goes like this: either democracy declines – or the right to *autogestion* is brought into the definition of citizenship[6]

Lefebvre's definition complements that of Castoriadis by specifically adding the notion of scale. Autogestion, according to him, has to be applied and thought of at both the level of the unit of production (the firm or enterprise) and the territorial level of government (local communities, towns or regions). Although spontaneity is a crucial element of self-management, it needs to be prepared for theoretically as it would dissolve the relations between the rulers and the ruled, the active and passive, subjects and objects.

I would like to suggest that the concept of self-management, thus understood, posits deliberation and action as two constitutive elements of participatory democracy. By accentuating the *productive*, not simply distributive, side of politics, it highlights people's capacities, and their need to work collectively across differences to build and sustain a democratic life together.

In Spain, as we saw in the previous chapter, many neighborhood associations adopted certain forms of deliberation and decision-making that were associated with the idea of self-management. Such practices were "imported" from more ideologically oriented oppositional entities such as the Students' Movement and the Spanish Workers' Movement.[7] In the early stages of their development, however, neighborhood associations did not always adopt practices of self-management with a clear ideological vision in mind. In many cases such practices were assimilated first because they enabled activists to mobilize large segments of the population in their *barrios*. Through their cooperation with different

110   *Alternative visions of democracy*

professionals the neighbors learnt where to seek and how to process information concerning their living and working environment. They became more proficient in expressing their needs and in navigating the existing political system in search of solutions. Self-management, then, was an effective mechanism in the everyday struggle for better living condition.

By their very nature, however, practices of self-management were destined to have empowering effects on both individuals and the community at large. Following the death of the dictator many neighborhood associations allied with those entities that called for a complete rupture with the existing political system. The process of a political transition clearly opened the way for a second phase in their development: Faced with an expanding structure of opportunities many associations turned to mass public mobilization in order to demand the implementation of unfulfilled agreements. Against this backdrop some activists had come to see a possibility of broadening their "right to the city." Throughout the initial stages of the transition, however, most neighborhood activists did not adhere to a coherent discourse that rejected the model of a liberal democracy in favor of a deliberative political system.

Between the years 1976 and 1977 even the most radical associations in Spain were still struggling to define their role within the emerging political system. By early 1978, however, a shift could be sensed in the discourse and actions of many neighborhood associations: 1977 saw the first democratic elections since 1936; in 1978 the new constitution was approved. In 1979 the local elections brought into power in Madrid a socialist-led coalition under the leadership of Enrique Tierno Galván, in Barcelona the socialist Narcís Serra i Serra and in Bilbao Jon Castañares Larreategui of the Basque Nationalist Party (PNV). At precisely the moment in time in which democracy started to take shape in Spain, however, some neighborhood activists felt that they were becoming increasingly isolated. The repercussions of the second petroleum crisis greatly limited the implementation of previously agreed upon remodeling plans throughout the country. On a deeper level the new constitution and the laws that regulated the workings of Spain's local administration did not accord the associations a formal status, nor define their role within the newly formed political system.

My contention is that during this period many neighborhood activists, who were increasingly frustrated with the direction which the democratic project had taken, started to manifest a deeper and more revolutionary understanding of Lefebvre's concept of "right to the city": rights not to an existing city as they knew it, but rather to a future urban space that would be more pluralistic and democratic in nature.[8] In order to analyze this process the current chapter is divided into three sections. The first section briefly explores the political and economic turning points of the Spanish transition. The second section analyzes the evolution of neighborhood associations during the transition by concentrating on the case of Orcasitas and examining three central issues: the call for consumers' protection and control programs, the implementation of new educational and cultural policies, and the execution of urban renovation plans. By focusing on the solutions offered by the associations to these issues I wish to highlight the deepening understanding of their members regarding the potential of self-management as an extended form of governance. The final section of the chapter examines the progressive exclusion and the limitation of the role of neighborhood associations following the publication of the democratic constitution and the local elections of 1979.

Times of change: Political and economic turning points of the transition

General Francisco Franco died on November 20, 1975. His death signaled the end of a 36-year dictatorship and constituted one of the most important turning points in the history of twentieth-century Spain. When I first came across the book *Del Barro al Barrio* (which was edited by the Orcasitas Neighborhood Association in order to document the story of the neighbors' struggle), I remember how surprised I was to discover that there was only one reference to the dictator's death in the entire text. While the term transition was mentioned several times it seemed as if the major political events that shook the country provided no more than a background setting to the struggle in Orcasitas. This impression, of course, is not true. The process of political transition affected the lives of all Spaniards in ways that are beyond the scope of analysis offered by this book. However, this impression highlights an obvious fact: in many cases the transition was experienced and analyzed through the prism of everyday life. In the case of neighborhood activists this meant that events on a national level were recorded and explained in relation to their effect on the local struggle in which they were engaged.

It was for this reason that I included in each of the interviews conducted in Orcasitas a question, which encouraged the interviewees to share with me how they remembered the dictator's death and the weeks that followed. Two were too young according to their own admission; one had a clear memory of the great feelings of joy that swept over her and her husband as they visited their family outside Madrid; and another interviewee remembered the Spanish TV following the thousands of people who came to the capital in order to pay their last respects to the dead dictator.

Following, however, are some of the more interesting responses I received. José Luis turned 17 in 1975. He recorded:

> The day Franco died? Yes, I remember it. At that age I had a certain understanding of what was going on. My older brother used to talk to me about things that happened in our country. So I knew a little bit about the man, of the way he treated the Spanish people. We were happy, but I can not tell you exactly why. I guess I thought or hoped that his death would mean something positive for us. I remember thinking: Something will have to change in the lives of simple, poor people like us. We went on with our lives in our poor little homes, but I remember the day.[9]

112 *Alternative visions of democracy*

María, another one of my interviewees recorded:

> Yes ... I do remember. I remember feeling the fear around me. People did not know what was going to happen, what awaited us ... this is what I record most of those days, fear of the unknown. My mother was a far-sighted woman ... and I remember she always made plans 'just in case' before each and every strike and demonstration.[10]

Another woman added:

> Yes I do remember. The fear ... how scared I was. Everyone was talking about the fact that something was about to happen, something, but we did not know what. My husband called me by telephone and told me: 'don't you dare leave the house! Franco just passed away.' And I thought straight away of another civil war – the rich against the poor. I did not understand politics, but we all knew that they were keeping him [Franco] alive, and that something was going to happen. It was all for the best the nothing did.[11]

The above quotations reflect the fact that the majority of Spanish citizens had no idea of what was going to take place following the dictator's death. Many of the people I interviewed did not have a clear vision of the political and social reality they wished to see around them. The transition, therefore, was not only a period of complex structural changes, but also a period during which ordinary men and women had to consider what political future they wished to see for themselves. How did they define their status as active citizens? How did they view their relationships vis-à-vis the state and its different institutions? Who could be considered as legitimate partners in any future political dialogue?

Immediately following the death of General Franco the forces of the democratic opposition in Spain were divided into two entities: *La Plataforma de Convergencia Democrática* (formed around the Spanish Socialist Party and the Democratic, Christian Left party) and *La Junta Democrática* (dominated by the Spanish Communist Party, PCE). The central reasoning behind the formation of the *Plataforma* was to provide a space of cooperation for those political groups that recoiled from direct collaboration with the PCE. On January 17, 1976 the General Secretary of the Spanish Socialist Party (PSOE), Felipe Gonzalez, outlined the agenda of the *Plataforma* vis-à-vis Carlos Arias Navarro's government. In the name of his political partners he demanded an amnesty for all political prisoners, the annulment of all anti-democratic legislation, freedom of expression, strike and assembly and free and democratic elections.

One point especially stands out in this very preliminary list: civic liberties were perceived by all members of the *Plataforma* to be directly linked to the exercise of the vote, to the free expression of political opinion and to the creation of democratic labor unions. On January 20, in preparation for a joint demonstration that was held by *Junta* and the *Plataforma* in Madrid, both organizations expressed themselves in some more detail. A week later the PCE published an independent press release in which it outlined its own vision of what could be considered "a democratic rapture." These texts make clear the fact that all of the forces of the democratic opposition were concerned with two central issues during the first months of the transition. The most pressing issue at hand was the demand for an amnesty for all political and labor activists. Furthermore the rights of assembly, strike and free public demonstrations were perceived as universal rights, essential for the formation of an effective political opposition and a functioning labor movement.

On March 17 the leaders of the *Junta* and of the *Plataforma* published a much-awaited document announcing their unification into the *Coordinación Democrática* (CD). The founding document of the CD included seven demands: full amnesty for all labor and political prisoners; the return of all those exiled under the dictatorship and the full restitution of their rights; the full and efficient exercise of all human rights and of the political rights acknowledged internationally; freedom of association and the dismantling of all state-sponsored syndicates; the granting of political and cultural autonomy to the different regions that make up the Spanish state; the formation of a single, independent and democratic judiciary; and the initiation of a process of popular consultation based on universal suffrage.[12]

On July 3, 1976 (before any meaningful negotiations could take place between the existing government and the opposition forces) Carlos Arias Navarro was relieved of his position as Spain's Prime Minister by King Juan Carlos. He was replaced by the relatively unknown Adolfo Suárez, who was to hold this position until February 1981. From the start it was clear that Suárez' government was willing to carry the process of political transition much further than that of his predecessor. However, by mid 1976 the political tensions were compounded by the worsening economic situation.

During the final year of the Franco regime the Spanish economy was hit by the effects of the first petroleum crisis. Faced with the fear of growing inflation the dictatorship decided to push forward its plans for the liberalization of the Spanish market by further opening it to foreign investments and by suppressing many of the existing protectionist and regulatory policies. During the first year of the transition the fear of a growing recession and the uncertain political situation led the government to further loosen the existing monetary controls in an attempt to encourage economic growth. Such measures led to increased levels of inflation and could no longer protect the majority of the Spanish population from the worse effects of unemployment.

The June 1977 general elections brought into power the *Union of Democratic Center* (UCD): a coalition made up of Christian democrats, liberals and social democrats headed by Adolfo Suárez himself. From the start the new government stated that mutual concessions were needed from all of the democratic forces in order to prevent the economic crisis from destabilizing the fragile political system. Out of this understanding were born the *Moncloa Pacts* of October 1977. The Pacts were signed by all the major political parties, including the recently legalized PCE. In the economic realm the pacts strove to reduce

114   *Alternative visions of democracy*

inflation by getting public spending under strict control. On the labor front the pacts limited the increase in salaries, while at the same time setting the limit for labor cuts at 5 percent of the total working force of an individual business. The Pacts also included a reference to the obligation of businesses to guarantee their employees freedom of union and the need to improve the existing system of social security.[13]

Laura Dessfor Edles noted that "… the Moncloa meetings were not designed for symbolic purposes … Yet from the beginning [they] contained vital symbolic dimensions." The idea of an "all-party meeting" was not simply the rational response to the developing economic crisis. In fact, the pacts constituted a response to the June elections in which all of the parties on the extreme Left and Right of the political spectrum were defeated. It was this defeat, which signaled the will of the electors and had given the impetus to the notion of *"convivencia"* or "national reconciliation."[14]

The 1978 constitution was the political expression of the spirit of national reconciliation. Its first article declared Spain to be "parliamentary monarchy," which constituted a major compromise on the part of those who had come to see republicanism and democracy as synonymous terms. In terms of the structure of the Spanish state the constitution presented a paradox that was never resolved: defending simultaneously a unitary national structure and regional decentralization. Finally, it consolidated the economic direction that was agreed upon in the Moncloa negotiations by introducing a mixed economic structure. While article 38 noted that the free enterprise system is recognized within the framework of a market economy, other articles reserved for the government and for the public sector important regulatory and distributive functions.

By 1979 Spain was hit by the second petroleum crisis. Unlike the first, the second crisis had a severe impact on the Spanish industry. Between the years 1978 and 1985 inflation was accompanied by increased unemployment not only in the agrarian sector, but also in the construction and the service sectors that previously enjoyed sustained growth. Against this backdrop the debate escalated between those who called for a more radical socio-economic reform and those who feared that such a reform will endanger the existing political order. The debate engaged politicians, labor union representatives and members of the business community, the Spanish media and most importantly ordinary citizens. However, as the following pages demonstrate, this debate was carried out within a pre-defined political framework: one committed to a liberal economy and a representative form of democracy.

The quest to define democracy: Neighborhood associations and the Citizens' Movement

In his study of the mobilizations that took place in Madrid from 1975 and onwards sociologist Ramon Adell concluded that over 70 percent of all the demonstrations in the capital between the years and 1982 were initiated by the Citizens Movements.[15] The extensive press coverage of those demonstrations

Alternative visions of democracy   115

reflects the fact that during the final months of the dictatorship the repertoires of action that were adopted by neighborhood associations changed significantly. The general assembly continued to be the main mobilizing framework within the *barrios*, but the forms of action which the assemblies initiated, became more varied in nature. In cities all across Spain neighborhood activists moved from requesting meetings with municipal functionaries and presenting petitions to mass demonstrations, as well as collective sit-downs and lock-downs.

Paca Sauquillo (a lawyer attached to the Workers Syndical Association and assigned to assist the neighborhood association in Palomeras Bajas) reflected on the nature of the cooperation which took place between professionals and neighbors in the early phases of the transition:

> Our activities were in no way the result of a decision taken by the [association's] executive committee. Those were not acts carried single-handedly by a highly conscious and active minority. Our actions were the result of a continued process of debate and consensual decision-making. We conducted house visits. To those were added what we called "arm-chair reunions" (*mesas camilla*) – informal meetings that were called in order to discuss the neighbors' problems. Later on we transmitted the information to the authorities. This was the only form of action that was open to us in a time when we did not have yet a truly democratic local administration.[16]

For the purpose of this chapter I analyzed 40 street demonstrations that were promoted by neighborhood associations in the Madrid area between the years 1975 and 1979.[17] Of these the majority were initiated in order to protest a set of varied demands. Small-scale, single-issue demonstrations were often sparked by the opposition to land expropriation or in response to the authorities' inability to carry out the plans of urban remodeling within a reasonable timeframe. Large-scale demonstrations were often initiated for specific reasons (such as the call for amnesty or in order to protest the rising cost of living), but were often used by individuals and groups in order to raise further demands. A demonstration that took place in Moratalaz in September 1976, for example, included over 100,000 participants— men, women and children. The demonstration was called to demand that the government curtail rising prices. At the same time many participants also held banners, which read: "democratic city-councils," "No more prohibitions! No more repression!" and "Legalization of all democratic associations."[18]

The change in tactics following November 1975 had clear spatial implications: it shifted the associations' sphere of action from the neighborhoods of the periphery into the center of the capital. Large-scale demonstrations literally occupied (even if for a short time) the streets of Madrid. Collective sit-downs, on the other hand, were usually staged in front of government ministries and of municipal buildings, while lock-downs usually occupied community buildings of an intermediate scale (such as local churches, schools and at times market places). Those acts of occupation centered on fixed protest sites, but they did so

116   *Alternative visions of democracy*

while employing a range of mobile and flexible spatial strategies. Lock-downs were most often carried out in sites that were part of the community's everyday lives. While not entirely improvised they were organized within short timeframes and made use of the inhabitants of the *barrio* that were most available—women and children. Sit-downs often took place outside the *barrio* in sites that symbolized the interaction between the demonstrators and the authorities. Demonstrations were more mobile in nature, often time producing interactions between groups of protesting citizens, sympathetic crowds, indifferent observers and the forces of law and order.

Sit-downs and lock-downs were often unauthorized acts. Large-scale demonstrations, on the other hand, had to be approved by the authorities beforehand. In such cases a process of contestation often took place: the associations would request that the demonstrations take place in one of the plazas at the center of Madrid. The ability to temporarily take over a space such as the *Plaza de Colón* or *Plaza de Cibeles*, which were not open to popular public demonstrations during the years of the dictatorship, had clear symbolic implications. For this reason precisely the requests were often denied by the authorities during the initial stages of the transition. In the days prior to the massive demonstration that took place in Moratalaz in September 1976, for example, the organizers asked to occupy *Plaza de Cibeles* and were denied.[19] Instead the demonstration was re-routed to the streets of the working-class neighborhood of Moratalaz. While the plaza was not conquered, the demonstrators' visibility and their ability to block the circulation of traffic leading to the center of the capital were probably just as impactful.

The negotiations that took place prior to the event reflect the fact that both the neighbors and the authorities were concerned with the physical impact of the demonstration (on traffic for example), with issues of accessibility, and with the allocated venue's ability to accommodate the demonstrators. Both sides were also highly aware of the symbolic weight of the chosen location. In an interview that was given by Cristina Sobrino (the vice president of the Madrid Federation of Neighborhood Associations) to the daily newspaper *Arriba* in November 1976, she declared in this regard:

> Our first step is always to try and establish a dialogue with the Mayor by means of a petition or a visit, but no one pays attention to us. My personal impression is that the authorities see in us enemies instead of allies ... The administration refuses to enter into a dialogue with us. It's as simple as that. Otherwise how can you explain the fact that instead of drawing us closer they act against us?[20]

Sobrino's choice of adjectives was intentional. Her words reflected the feelings of many activists that not much has changed in the months following the death of the dictator. The *barrios* were still thought of as "periphery" in the worst sense of the term: as something to be feared, to be kept at arm's length. While this was true it would be misleading to view the attempts to isolated political

Alternative visions of democracy 117

mobilization as a tactic aimed exclusively at neighborhood association of the periphery. As Stuart Elden rightly notes once the streets become political places the stress on the location of the struggle becomes doubly important:

> because not only are spatial relations – marginalization and centrality, uneven development, ghettoization and so on – political in themselves, politics is played in a spatial field. What is important in the movement being on the streets is that groups who are normally kept apart – such as students and workers – are able to meet.[21]

By 1976 the regime was clearly losing its capacity to keep different urban populations segregated from one another. Neighborhood associations could no longer be contained within the periphery of the capital and their interactions with other oppositional entities became more sustained. During the first year of the transition neighborhood associations initiated 22.1 percent of the 145 demonstrations and public gatherings that took place in the capital. They managed to mobilize 208,000 people. Labor unions affiliated with parties of the democratic opposition initiated 43.1 percent of the acts that took place that year, but mobilized only 79,000 people.[22] These numbers point to the fact that neighborhood associations were a moving force behind large-scale popular mobilizations. While fully embracing the call of other oppositional forces for an amnesty to all political prisoners and for the complete restoration of all democratic liberties they had further demands on their agendas. The ability to bridge the gap between local and more universal experiences of the struggle were crucial to their ability to interact with and mobilize other entities within the Citizens' Movement.

Diani and Della Porta defined the dynamics of new social movements in the following terms:

> We have a social movement dynamic going on when single episodes of collective action are perceived as components of a longer-lasting action, rather than discrete events; and when those who are engaged in them feel linked by ties of solidarity and of ideal communion with protagonists of other analogous mobilizations.[23]

I find the above definition useful for the analysis of the relationship between core organizations which made up the Citizens' Movement. Neighborhood associations had agenda of their own and functioned as independent entities in order to realize them. At the same time their members saw themselves as part of a large-scale dialogue with the authorities around a series of core issues common to other civic entities. Throughout the first year of the transition they developed what Mark Granovetter defined as networks of "weak-tie relations" in relation to other entities of the democratic opposition.[24] These networks connected neighborhood activists with the wider political field. They allowed for the circulation of information and pooling of resources. They also provided

118   *Alternative visions of democracy*

activists with the collective know-how that enhanced their own position vis-à-vis the authorities and allowed them to act within multi-actor campaigns.

In the following pages I analyze the role of neighborhood associations in the context of the transition to democracy and their position within the Citizens' Movement. In doing so I wish to focus on several questions. How did neighborhood association develop a sense of a collective "We" in relation to other entities within the Citizens Movement and who were defined as part of that collective? How were specific problems relating to issues of housing and collective services framed as objects of collective action? And finally how did resistance and political protest produce space in terms of both the geographical ground upon which conflict takes place and the representations through which collective action is understood and interpreted?

Consumption in transition

The first campaign that called for sustained cooperation on the part of neighborhood associations in Madrid started off three months prior to the death of the dictator. In the summer of 1975 the neighbors of Orcasitas and en El Pozo del Tío Raimundo discovered that the two most popular loaves of bread sold to them (*barra familiar* and *las pistolas*) that were supposed to weigh 500 grams and 260 grams respectively, did not reach 500 grams jointly. It was calculated that millions of Spaniards were robbed by the bread industry of thousands of pesetas each year. Félix López Rey of Orcasitas later wrote of what would become known as the "Bread War":

> Some of us were aware of the fact that the [Franco] regime had robbed us of our liberty, but none of us had imagined that the regime was also stealing the bread out of our very mouths. This was too much! We were not going to take it quietly.[25]

The initial stage of the "Bread War" coincided with the formation of the Madrid Federation of Neighborhood Associations. The Federation soon proved the value of coordinated action. It collected information about the extent of the fraud and synchronized local protests against specific bakeries. The Federation also published an open letter to all of the associations in Madrid in which it encouraged them to examine the bread sold in their neighborhoods. In early 1976 the local authorities were flooded with letters of complaint. The campaign was reinforced by the local and national media, but the local authorities claimed in response that the problem lay in the structure of the bread manufacturing industry and therefore could only be resolved by the government.[26]

At this stage the Madrid Federation was split between those who felt that the associations could do no more than denounce the fraud and those who felt that the associations had the responsibility to prove that cheap, quality bread could indeed be manufactured. The latter group demanded the creation of a mixed working commission (made up of consumers, legislators and members of the bread manufacturing industry) that would propose a comprehensive reform of the industry.

In July 1976 the associations of Orcasitas and El Pozo del Tío Raimundo started to sell self-manufactured bread in order to prove that it was possible to bring down the prices. The associations demanded the dismantling of the existing bread consortium and an increase in the number of licenses accorded to independent bakeries. Throughout the summer the associations proved that regulated bread could indeed be manufactured more cheaply (6–7 pesetas less than the previous price). After a sustained effort of almost a year the authorities agreed to regulate the price and weight of bread across the country and in 1977 the Consortium of Bread Manufacturers that existed since 1939 was dismantled, thereby opening the market for new manufacturers.

The most important achievement of the "Bread War," however, lay in the fact that for the first time since 1939 ordinary citizens were involved in the process of manufacturing and determining the price of a basic commodity. On a deeper level the production of bread within the *barrios*, by the neighbors and for the neighbors, shattered not only the distinction between producers and consumers but also between the space of production and that of consumption. By bringing the production process into the *barrio* and under the control of the association the neighbors created an intermediate space of experimentation: a flexible space where different solutions to the problem at hand could be tried out and assessed.

Figures 5.1 and 5.2 The selling of self-manufactured bread in Ocasitas
Source: Asociación de Vecinos del Barrio de Orcasitas, Archivo Fotográfico

120   *Alternative visions of democracy*

During the second half of 1976 neighborhood associations developed firmer working relations with other civic entities such as Housewives Associations. Simultaneously, the appointment of Adolfo Suárez raised the expectations for a faster political transition backed by economic reforms. On the street these expectations were translated into a growing number of mass demonstrations. One of the biggest demonstrations of neighbors and housewives in Madrid took place in Aranjuez on May 16: 2,000 activists and their families responded to a call by the Federation of Neighborhood Associations and came to spend a day that was a mix of family fun and political activities. The gathering ended with the reading of a document that specified the Federation's goals: the implementation of all existing remodeling plans; the institution of price controls for basic commodities and services; and the legalization of all existing neighborhood associations. At this point Civil Guard forces attempted to disperse the assembled crowd by opening fire. Consequently several demonstrators and journalists (from *El País* and *YA*) were injured and detained. A spokesman for the security forces informed the press a week later that the actions were "inevitable" due the insistence of the "inexistent Federation of Neighborhood Associations to carry out an illegal demonstration."[27] The dismissive words of the spokesman for one of the major law and order forces reflected the shakiness of the Federation's formal standing.

The Madrid neighborhood associations refused to give in. In June they launched a "Civic Week" (*semana ciudadana*) under the suggestive heading "Madrid is Ours." The week included a variety of public acts in different *barrios* and culminated in an authorized demonstration that took place along *C/ Preciados* on July 22. The authorities authorized a short demonstration (20:00–21:00) for housewives only. By 20:15, however, over 50,000 demonstrators already crowded the street. They carried a mix of banners that denounced the chaotic state of the schools in the periphery; the great deficiencies in transportation and sanitary infrastructures; the rising cost of living; the lack of cultural programs for children and youth, for the elderly and for populations with special needs; and the refusal of the authorities to legalize many of the existing civic associations. The demonstration was a show of unity and proved that the new and diverse civic entities that gathered under the banner of the Citizens' Movement could come together and generate a common socio-political agenda.

Throughout 1976–1977 neighborhood associations in Madrid proved their growing ability to process concrete material demands into a more comprehensive political vision. In a series of demonstrations and press releases they stated that they wished to see a city where the centralized and corrupt tendencies of the local bureaucracy were suppressed; they called for the democratically elected mayor, accountable before the citizens for policy and budgetary issues; they asked for technical experts who will work with, and be supervised by, the citizens; finally they demanded that authorities divide the perimeter of the capital into smaller districts with independent budgets. This last demand grew out of an understanding that self-management would be better practiced within smaller spatial units.

Neighborhood activists were fully aware of the fact that they were part of a process of political maturation. José Luis Lorca Palencia, president of the Neighborhood Association in La Paz, Entrevías, explained:

> The neighbors come together in order to decide on the [solutions] that are most convenient in their view. The association arranges for street lights but it also promotes cultural activities, dialogue with the authorities and active participation, as far as we are allowed to [participate].[28]

Félix López Rey of Orcasitas was even more explicit:

> If our people were politicized from the start, with a defined ideology, it would not have taken us 25 years to solve our problems. The existing level of political consciousness today is not the result of the adhesion to one ideology or another, [neighbors] and workers are not following today an ideology that has been imposed on them. Rather they are responding in an honest and a [consistent] way to the injustices that surround them.[29]

The above quotations highlight two points: local identity and shared everyday experiences generated a sense of belonging and a shared fate which functioned as an important incentive for mobilization over time. Both middle-class and working-class associations cooperated in order to promote the identity of neighbors as collective consumers (of goods, infrastructures and services) and as individuals capable of contributing to policy formation. At the same time neighborhood associations that worked in peripheral *barrios* highlighted the role of unequal distribution of assets in the creation of peripheral spaces within the city. Within both the Madrid and the Barcelona Federations these associations constituted a majority. However, the fulfillment of their demands (if carried to their logical conclusion) would have come at the expanse of those raised by other associations situated in more the more affluent zones of the city.

Educational initiatives and youth delinquency

Another issue that generated much frustration amongst neighborhood activists had to do with the rising crime rates across the southern periphery of Madrid. From mid 1976 the local press reflected the growing preoccupation of many *barrios* with increased youth delinquency. Sporadic police incursions into the neighborhoods only worsened the situation and neighborhood activists were convinced that only long-term prevention programs could solve the problem. They blamed the lack of adequate educational facilities and the fact that most adolescents were unable to find constructive ways to spend their days. Poor performance in schools and the lack of centers for professional training doomed the children in *barrios chabolistas* to a future of unemployment.

The Orcasitas Neighborhood Association attempted to attract the *barrio*'s children and adolescents to its activities by scheduling talks and film projections

122 *Alternative visions of democracy*

especially for them. Lacking in equipment and funds, members of the association's Committee for Youth and Culture toured the municipal centers and the embassies in the capital looking for used equipment that would be donated.[30] In June 1977 the problem of youth delinquency exploded publicly when the police arrested eight men in the *Poblado Agricola de Orcasitas*. The men were caught patrolling the neighborhood armed with an assortment of rubber hoses, hammers and other working tools. The press reported that they were part of an armed guard, which the community mounted in order to protect itself following the abduction and rape of a 16-year-old girl by a street gang that controlled the area.

The following day the entire *Poblado* (numbering around 900 households) shut down in protest. The school and shops were all closed down and the neighbors demonstrated in front of the local police station. To a journalist of the weekly *Diario 16* they explained that solutions offered to them by the authorities were insufficient:

> This guy came and presented himself as a 'supposed' expert on the issue of youth delinquency, but in reality he was no expert at all. We asked for an interview with him. We wanted to talk about the most urgent issues: about prevention, about ways of stopping this wave [of violence] before it becomes contentious. And all he had to say was that his job is to arrest those already caught in [violent acts]. He wasn't concerned with prevention.

The neighbors clearly expected something quite different from the authorities:

> We thought that as citizens we had the obligation of cooperating with the police in order to help maintain the peace. We do not understand what is going on here. The neighbors will decide if we go on patrolling the streets today or not. But one thing is clear: we will employ all of the legal measures at our disposal in order to bring about the release of those arrested. We intend to sit in a permanent assembly [until they are released].[31]

The authorities presented youth delinquency as an isolated problem that needed to be handled by means of supervision and repression if needed. Neighborhood associations, on the other hand, attempted to explain the complexity of the issue: on the one hand the neighbors were called to patrol the *barrio* in order to protect themselves. On the other hand, the *barrio*'s adolescent population were presented as victims of an economic and a social situation that pushed them into a life of crime. Violence was their way to leave their mark on the social fabric of Orcasitas. The association wished to equip them with other, more constructive, options.

In 1980 (almost two years after the municipal elections that brought into power a left-wing government in Madrid) the neighbors in Orcasitas despaired of seeing effective action on the part of the municipal authorities. They therefore published their own anti-delinquency program. Similarly to the case of

Recalde a decade earlier the neighbors pointed to the long-term social and personal costs of neglect in the field of education and professional instruction. They warned that the low quality of primary education in Orcasitas prevented most of the children from even considering the option of full matriculation. They identified the lack of opportunities for professional training between the ages of 14 and 18 as a major problem in the *barrio*. The association claimed that due to the socio-cultural profile of the neighborhood the teachers and the social workers who worked in Orcasitas needed special training and support. This was especially important since the neighbors viewed the ability of the educational staff to carry out its work over long periods of time as an important component in the creation of preventive infrastructures. Dedicated educators, who got to know their students over time, were more likely to understand their immediate environment and keep in touch with them and with their families. The Ministry of Education was asked to shoulder the cost of the teachers' training and to provide them with a supportive working environment. The municipality was required to set a permanent crew of psychologists that would work with the association. The Ministry of Labor was asked to provide professional training schemes for the age groups 14–16 and 16–20. In order for these programs to be effective they had to take into account the existing qualifications of youngsters and the demands of the job market in the capital.[32]

The program was elaborated in cooperation between educators and social workers who interviewed parents, and children in the *barrio*, as well as some of the teachers who worked in Orcasitas. With the help of the association they then processed the information that was obtained from the interviews into a program that was officially adopted by the Civil Governor of Madrid and the Mayor, Juan Francisco Pla, in 1983. The neighbors proved that theirs was a global vision: it focused on the need for cooperation between of different administrative entities. But it was also global in its assessment of the problem: despite the advanced stage of its remodeling plan, Orcasitas of the early 1980s was still a deprived *barrio*.

The authorities tried to fragment the situation into seemingly unrelated problems in the fields of consumption, housing, education and transportation, each with its concrete solution. The association, on the other hand, was persistently attempting to tie them together: to explain that deprivation was the result of the existing power relations and these power relations had not changed.[33] In a meeting that took place between the neighbors and members of the collective CODEMAR (*Colectivo de defense del marginado*) on March 19, 1982 the position of the association was stated clearly: "In the past youth delinquency was defined and understood in relation to an individual who commits a crime. Today we understand delinquency as an all encompassing situation. It is the culmination of situations and processes that promote crime."[34]

The anti-delinquency plan was adopted by a PSOE-led city council; however, the lack of funds and cooperation between the different ministries and municipal entities prevented its full implementation. There is no doubt that a

124   *Alternative visions of democracy*

democratically elected city council was more willing to allocate funds to *barrios* such as Orcasitas, and its discourse was more egalitarian and compassionate towards the population in these neighborhoods. But five years following the death of the dictator the spatial practices that defined these *barrios* as a periphery did not change. The young men and women of the periphery were still seen as a problem or as a threat. They were not viewed as part of a thinking, active community that needed economic support and social recognition in order to change its own reality.

Finally making space truly ours? Urban remodeling and the transition

In late 1975 the Orcasitas Neighborhood Association rejected a second remodeling plan that was presented by the City Planning Commission. In rejecting the plan the neighbors were reinforced by a parallel struggle that took place in the city of Barcelona. In the Catalan capital just as in Madrid the implementation of partial plans increased densities without a corresponding provision of public facilities, at times taking over spaces dedicated to the development of precisely such facilities. Throughout the long administration of Mayor Josep María de Porcioles (1957–1973) land speculation soared due to "increases in permitted construction levels ... without any preliminary partial planning."[35]

In late 1973 a confrontation took place in Barcelona's city hall during a debate regarding the implementation of several partial plans on the northern side of the city. Before the meeting began municipal functionaries occupied the seats usually reserved for the public to preclude the participation of protesting citizens. In response neighborhood associations occupied city hall. When the events were publicized the resulting scandal forced the central government in Madrid to replace the mayor Porcioles. The partial plans under debate were frozen and the neighborhoods involved came together to form an association called *Nou Barris* (named after the nine neighborhoods involved). This episode, as Calavita and Ferrer indicate, reflected the weakening grip of the dictatorship and greatly influenced the direction taken by the General Metropolitan Plan of Barcelona.

In the case of Orcasitas a third and final partial plan was finally approved in 1976. This plan was formulated jointly by the neighbors, the technical experts that assisted them (the architects José Manuel Bringas, Eduardo Leira, Ignacio Solana and Javier Vega) and the authorities. Some neighbors recorded the first meeting in which they felt that their voices were being heard. It took place following the 1977 elections in the offices of the new Minister for Public Works and Urbanism Juaquín Garrigues Walker:

> It was Garrigues who finally aided us in making real progress ... He asked us to give him 'classes' – as he called it modestly – in urban planning and remodeling. And during two long evenings we went to his office. There we met all the men in charge and we gave them some practical [planning] lessons with ideology to boot.[36]

The working relations which the neighbors established with Garrigues' administration were based on more mutual respect and trust than with previous administrations. It was, no doubt, this working environment which produced the third and final remodeling plan. The plan was structured in three phases. the first phase incorporated the 824 apartments completed in 1974, which were built much after the style of the old dormitory suburbs. The second phase included the construction of 1,516 apartments, which were completed in 1980. This phase already reflected a new vision of *barrio* as a complex spatial unit that had social, communal and commercial functions. The third phase of construction started in 1980. After many delays it was completed in 1986 and included an additional 760 housing units.

Just like the anti-delinquency plan the new remodeling plan, too, was formulated by the neighbors and their technical advisers. The neighbors determined both the internal structure of their apartments and the structure of the entire *barrio*. How was this done? In 1976 the architects that worked with the association carried a survey that was intended to verify the priorities of the future dwellers. They entered the existing *chabolas*, interviewed the neighbors and then recorded and analyzed the information. One set of questions was intended to collect information on the socio-economic profile of the family (the family's joint income, the number of people living in the house, whether the family owned a car etc.). The second set included questions that were meant to give the architects an idea about the ways in which each family used its living space. People were asked if they wished to live in a house of a single or multiple floors and whether they preferred to live in a four-story building without an elevator or a seven-story building with one. They were also asked how far away from the house they were willing to park their cars in order to allow for the safe circulation of pedestrians.

The preamble to the new plan stated accordingly:

> We wish to reproduce the [atmosphere] experienced by the neighbors of Orcasitas, who at the moment live in a *barrio* made up of a single-story houses, and in which the street is used and valued in its original form ... We wish to mix housing spaces with other spaces intended for commerce ... We want to reduce to a minimum the height of the buildings. This is the preference expressed by all of the neighbors, who indicated they did not want to live in high-rise apartments nor be surrounded by high buildings.[37]

The neighbors were further asked to decide on to two issues that generated much debate in the architectural world: the desired relationship in each of the model apartments between the kitchen and eating space, as well as the standing of the living room. Of the people interviewed, 94 percent indicated that if the kitchen was large enough they would like it to incorporate the cooking and eating functions. They viewed the living room as the most important area in the house; 56 percent responded that if allowed to enlarge a room they would

126 *Alternative visions of democracy*

enlarge the living room regardless of its original size. It was the one room which everyone insisted would have to include windows facing the outside, and when asked what defect would cause them most concern in an apartment 42 percent answered that is would be a small living room (compared to 36 percent who were concerned with the size of the bedrooms and 22 percent with the size of the kitchen).[38]

The architects processed the information and constructed sets of three-dimensional model apartments, which they presented to the neighbors. The three model apartments that were finally chosen were structured around a living room that was indeed large and well lit (all the apartments had a terrace coming out of the living room). However, due to economic constraints the kitchens in all three apartments were small and the eating space was therefore incorporated into the living room instead. In all three models the bedrooms were separated from the main space dedicated for social interaction by a corridor.[39]

The new *barrio* was divided into six residential nuclei (which included a mix of four-, eight- and ten-story buildings) and structured around a Civic Center (which to this day serves as the heart of community life in Orcasitas and housed the neighborhood association). Each nucleus was made up of eight to ten apartment buildings that were arranged around a small courtyard and a commercial space. The ground floor of each apartment building included a nursery and a playroom for the children. The aim was to create multi-scalar spaces for socialization—from the playrooms in each building, to the courtyard that united several buildings and up to the Civic Center and its large plaza.

José Manuel Bringas, who was the first architect to join the technical advisory team in Orcasitas, wrote about the process of informed election that culminated in a plan for the new *barrio*:

> there are those who talk negatively of the architects [turned] activists. I did not infiltrate the association under the pretext of advising the people in order to agitate and propel them into a struggle against those in power. Anyone who knows the story of the struggle in Orcasitas personally would burst out laughing when hearing these accusations. In the *Mesta* no one had to agitate, no one! not the president [of the association], not the members of the directive committee, not the technical advisors. The entire *Meseta* agitated if the people were made aware that something threatened **their** remodeling project ... In this type of work the 'technical advisor,' in his capacity to offer technical or academic solutions, can not be replaced by a neighbor. At the same time it is important that he or she understand that their job is to accompany the neighbors in managing [and assessing] the solutions that are being offered to them. No more and no less than that.[40]

The approval of the remodeling plan constituted a turning point in the life of Orcasitas. But its implementation was long and torturous. As the process got

Figure 5.3 A list presenting before the neighbors the advantages and disadvantages of living in high-rise towers
Source: Asociación de Vecinos del Barrio de Orcasitas, Archivo Fotográfico

Figure 5.4 The election process of the windows in the apartments.
Source: Asociación de Vecinos del Barrio de Orcasitas, Archivo Fotográfico

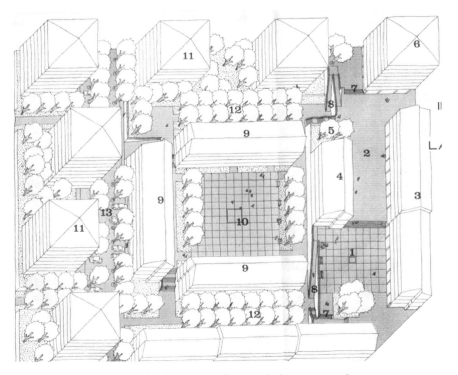

Figure 5.5 The structure of a housing nucleus (including towers, four-story apartment buildings and commercial and recreational spaces)[41]

underway new problems arose. The most urgent one put to a test the very fabric of the community: who would receive priority to the first apartments? And what would be done in order to prevent new squatters from moving into the empty *chabolas* in the time that passed between their eviction and demolition?

The first question was decided upon in a general assembly that took place in Orcasitas in early 1977. While some suggested that priority should be given to those who lived in the worst conditions, the majority agreed that the first to be resettled should be those whose *chabolas* would leave the most space for effective construction.[42] The problem of second wave squatters was harder to solve. On the one hand there was much sympathy amongst members of the association towards those who suffered under similar economic hardship. On the other hand the neighbors demanded the eviction (forcefully if need be) of those who occupied the empty *chabolas* and thereby slowed the process of construction.[43]

On January 16, 1979 the government published new legislation regarding the construction of protected housing units. Faced with the total lack of interest on the part of private investors in shouldering the burden of construction, the government attempted to boost social housing programs by readjusting the price and size of the apartments.[44] The publication of the decree generated a wave of demonstrations by neighborhood associations that were already engaged in a remodeling process. The neighbors protested the fact that the new decree limited the size of the apartments, increased their price and worsened the conditions of payment. Neighborhood activists were especially outraged to learn that the decree was approved with no objection on the part of any of the political parties. On January 19 the Orcasitas Neighborhood Association launched a 15-km march that passed through all the *barrios* on the southern periphery of Madrid. In each *barrio* members of the local association called the neighbors to an open assembly in which they explained the disadvantages of the new decree.[45] On each stop along the way the neighbors were asked to join the human chain that made its way to the *Plaza de la Villa* in the center of Madrid and later on to the Ministry of Public Works.[46]

At this point in time, again, the struggle in Madrid was enhanced by the state of affairs in other cities. In Barcelona, for example, neighborhood activists took to the streets as early as 1976, demanding the elimination of roads that cut through their neighborhoods. They also called for the re-designation to public spaces that had been transformed and allocate for private use (such as the *Espana Industrial*—a huge complex of textile factories). While the thorough-fares were eliminated, many of the associations' other objections were not met when the Metropolitan Plan was approved by Mayor Joaquim Viola in the summer of 1976. The Barcelona associations realized that they had no chance of success with Viola in power and turned their energies toward eliminating him from the scene. They demanded his resignation from the King, the Minister of Internal Affairs and the governor of Barcelona. In December 1976 Viola resigned and a new "conciliatory" mayor (Josep María Socias) took over.

Figures 5.6 and 5.7 The green march. Neighbors walking to the Ministry of Housing.
Source: Asociación de Vecinos del Barrio de Orcasitas, Archivo Fotográfico

Alternative visions of democracy   131

However, the struggle to change certain elements within the Metropolitan Plan continued in the streets and the courts until the early 1980s.

In 1980 the Ministry of Housing announced that neighborhoods that were already in the middle of a remodeling process that was based on an approved partial plan would be excluded from the new decree on protected housing units. However, by 1982 the cut-downs in the budgets of the municipalities all across Spain generated corresponding cut-downs in the budgets allocated for remodeling. This in its turn sparked another wave of protest, but this time to no avail. The remodeling process in Orcasitas, for example, was delayed by two years and the keys to the new apartments were only handed over to the neighbors in 1986.

***

In 1986 the neighbors of Orcasitas celebrated the inauguration of the new _barrio_ with an exposition on 15 years of struggle, housed in the new headquarters of the neighborhood association. In a final act, which perhaps best symbolized the control they gained over their renovated living space, the neighbors named their streets. The action of naming symbolized a move from the stage of an active struggle to the stage of memory conservation. _Calle de la Remodelación_ (remodeling), _calle de los Encierros_ (lock-downs), _Plaza del Movimiento Ciudadano_ (Citizens' Movement), _Plaza de la Memoria Vinculada_ are some of the more interesting street names in present-day Orcasitas. The neighbors recorded this process with great pride:

> Let us talk for a moment of the plaza, which is named today _Plaza de la Memoria Vinculada_. It commemorates the decision of the courts to hold the preamble of the first Partial Plan as legally binding. This is not a common name, no other plaza or street are so named. In the classical center of Madrid there are streets whose names are repeated: streets named after lords and generals.
>
> Who decides on those names? In Orcasitas we named our own streets. We are the ones who live here. We get our mail delivered to those addresses. There is no greater testimony of our sovereignty.[47]

Street names did not just passively testify to struggles of the past. They prompt questions by visitors and by the _barrio_'s younger population, which in their turn allow the story of Orcasitas to be told and retold. The act of naming space invests it with meaning, which in some cases had the potential of outliving the people who produced it. The generation of new representations of space took different forms within different associations: the production of temporary exhibits; collective conservation of personal photos and newspaper clippings testifying to the transformation of the _barrios_; the publication of neighborhood newspapers or collectively written and edited books (such as _Del Barro al Barrio_ in Orcasitas or _el Libro Negro de Rekaldeberri_ in Recalde). Through all these means different communities worked in order to situate their neighborhoods and their respective histories at the center of a much larger narrrative – that of

Figures 5.8, 5.9 and 5.10 Plaza de la Memoria Vinculante, calle de la Remodelación and Plaza de la Asociación in present-day Orcasitas
Source: Asociación de Vecinos del Barrio de Orcasitas, Archivo Fotográfico

Alternative visions of democracy 133

Figure 5.10 (Continued)

Spain's transition to democracy. They attempted to turn their own (individual and communal) narratives into a reference point for future generations. In doing so they exemplified a crucial aspect in the contribution of new social movements to changes in the environments that surrounded them. In the words of Mario Diani, some of the greatest stakes in the struggles which new social movements take upon themselves have to do with:

> the control of resources which produce meaning, and which allow actors to intervene not only on their own environment but also on the personal sphere, and above all on the link between these two levels. Rather than economic or political power, contemporary social conflict has, according to this view, more to do with the production and circulation of information; social conditions for production and the use of scientific knowledge; and the creation of symbols and cultural models concerned with the definition of individual and collective identities.[48]

Figures 5.11 and 5.12 The 1986 exposition on the history of the struggle in Orcasitas
Source: Asociación de Vecinos del Barrio de Orcasitas, Archivo Fotográfico

An additional question that emerges out of the history of neighborhood associations has to do not only with the conservation of collective memory, but also with scale of change over time. In the decade following 1986 trucks of neighbors from Orcasitas would still occasionally pour into Madrid's central Plaza. Men, women and children protested crowded classes, lack of transportation services, the administration's failure to deal with increased unemployment and drug-related problems. But this was in no way the "radical democracy" neighborhood activists had in mind during the years of the transition. The ability to protest urban policies, once those were established, differed greatly from the ability to take part in their formulation. In that respect the levels of participation, achieved by the neighborhood associations during the later phases of the transition were not seen again.

This state of affairs characterized the final phase in the existence of the Citizens' Movement in general. Jesús Mari Paredes (who wrote about the history of the Otxarkoaga neighborhood association in Bilbao) described this phase in the association's history:

> From that moment onwards [1978] the movement of the neighborhoods, which originally emerged around specific vindications relating to [the management] of urban space languished due to the lack of immediate and concrete objectives ... Many neighbors continued to work together towards achieving goals that were previously considered as second in rank: those associated with sports, culture and leisure. During the first half of the 1980s the neighbors progresses from being identified principally with neighborhood association to other forms of association identified with concerns relating to issues of ecology, feminism, [Basque] nationalism.[49]

Sociologist Jordi Borja (who cooperated closely with different entities of the Citizens' Movement in Cataluña) reflected as early as 1976 on the desired standing of neighborhood associations within a democratic system:

> What does it really mean when we say that the associations have a role to play in promoting a participative local democracy? That means that the

neighbors should have two ways of controlling the local administration: through elections and the functioning of the existing political parties, and through the associations. Via the first channel the neighbors exercise their right to elect the administration, via the second channel they participate in controlling the budget [and the policies] which the elected authorities implement.[50]

However, neighborhood associations were not mentioned within the new democratic constitution that was published in 1978, nor in the Law of Local Administration (Ley regulador de las bases del régimen local) that was published in 1985. In April 1980 the Federation of Madrid's Neighborhood Associations published a press release. The text reflected the great disappointment its leaders felt with the newly elected administration. Despite the clarity of their proposals and the intensity of their activism it seemed that the democratic vision of the neighborhoods had left little impression on the new system:

> There are clear distinctions between the different city-councils. Unfortunately commonalities include: Little participation by the neighbors; Lack of public information concerning the functioning of the administration ... General apathy of the neighbors resulting from the fact that very little has really changed ... We therefore declare that it is the right of all citizens to take part in municipal life, not just on a formal level but in a truly open manner.[51]

At almost the same time the president of the Federació d'Asociaciones de Vecinos Barcelona, Carles Prieto, told a reporter that "the political parties of the governing coalition have abandoned the neighborhood associations."[52]

In February 1983 (four months after the 1982 elections which brought into power the Socialist government led by Felipe González) Juan Manuel López Rubio, a member of the PCE district committee in Villaverde, wrote in the bulletin of the Orcasitas Neighborhood Association:

> People do not live off ethics alone, especially when the ethical [system] is falling apart. It's not ethical to buy airplanes overseas when they can be produced here, nor is it ethical to leave untouched the men who ran all the big businesses under the previous government ... Worst of all in our view is the fact that the national radio and television channel – RTVE – being the most important cultural medium in this country – does not reflect the fact that there is a socialist government in power. It seems that Felipe is less concerned with the country than he is with his number two political partner [Manuel] Fraga"[53]

The words of López Rubio sparked a debate within the pages of the bulletin regarding the priorities of the new political system, the nature of participatory democracy and the fact that it was not achieved within the Spanish context.

136   *Alternative visions of democracy*

The new democratically elected administration clearly brought about change. In Madrid, Barcelona and Bilbao the local authorities spent a large percentage of their budgets on the extension of public infrastructures. Peripheral neighborhoods were finally brought into contact with the city through the construction of an extended system of roads, electricity and water provision facilities. Green areas and recreational facilities were expanded all throughout the city. Regeneration plans for the classical center in Barcelona and Madrid were progressively implemented. And yet the dream of some neighborhood associations of a more participatory form of government has not materialized. Those activists who strove to achieve higher levels of civic participation felt excluded from the beating heart of the local and the national administration. The willingness of democratic authorities to allow the "community" to take an active part in designing and regulating its living-environment was limited. Within the framework of a liberal democracy the Spanish state guaranteed an extended list of essential rights (such as housing, education, health and so forth). Continued civic participation at all levels of governance, however, was never perceived as one of those rights. But it was precisely the right for active, innovative and creative participation which lay at the heart of the Orcasitas success. Without it, as most neighborhood activists understood, the ability of ordinary citizens to shape their lived-in space could not be sustained over time.

There was never a specific moment in time in which the Spanish Citizens' Movement declared its own work done. Like many other social movements it was never formally "disbanded." Many of the organizations that made up the heart of the movement continue to exist to this day; however, for reasons which I analyze in the following chapter, most found it difficult to maintain constant levels of civic participation once their most urgent goals were achieved. With the consolidation of democracy the opportunities for action seemed more modest, and maintaining the type of cooperation that previously existed between the different "command centers" of the Citizens' Movement seemed less urgent. The core organizations, which made up the movement, managed to secure a level of continued collective action by redirecting their energies and focusing on specific goals in relation to issues of cultural production and education. But only when massive economic crisis hit Spanish society once again in 2008 were the levels of civic mobilization experienced during the transition duplicated.

Notes

1 H. Lefebvre, "Problemes theoriques de l'autogestion," *Autogestion*, December, 1966, p. 69.
2 Ahedo Gurrutxaga, "Bilbao y frontera interna," pp. 108–110.
3 For more on the difference between subversion and resistance in the context of social struggles see: K. N. Rankin, "The Praxis of Planning and the conditions of Critical Development Studies," in *Cities for People not for Profit*, pp. 109–110.
4 See for example: J. Abelson, P. G. Forest, J. Eyles, P. Smith, E. Martin and F. P. Gauvin, "Deliberations about Deliberative Methods: Issues in the Design and Evaluation of Public Participation Processes," *Social Science and Medicine*, 57, 2003,

Alternative visions of democracy   137

pp. 239–251; R. Abers, *Inventing Local Democracy: Grassroots Politics in Brazil*, Boulder, CO: Lynne Reinner, 2000, Introduction; G. Baiocchi, "Participation, Activism, and Politics: The Porto Alegre Experiment," in A. Fung and E. O. Wright (eds.), *Deepening Democracy: Institutional Innovations in Empowered Participatory Governance*, London: Verso, 2003, pp. 45–76; A. Fung, "Associations and Democracy: Between Theories, Hopes, and Realities,"*Annual Review of Sociology*, 29, 2003, pp. 515–539.

5 C. Castoriadis, "Autogestion et Hièrarchie," in *Le Contenu du Socialisme*, Paris: Union générale d'éditions, 1979, p. 2.

6 Lefebvre, *Key Writings*, pp. 252–253.

7 R. Vega García, "Radical Unionism and the Workers' Struggle in Spain," *Latin American Perspectives*, 27(5), 2000, pp. 111–133; F. Fernández Buey and J. Mir García "Apropiación del futuro: revuelta estudiantil y autogestión durante el tardo-franquismo y la Transición," *Desacuerdos*, 6, 2011, pp. 161–168.

8 For a discussion on the concept of "right to the city" in the writings of Lefebvre and its later applications, see: P. Marcuse, "Whose Right(s) to What City?" in Brenner, Marcuse and Mayer (eds.), *Cities for People not for Profit*, pp. 34–35.

9 José Luis, Interview (Orcasitas, Madrid).

10 María, interview (Orcasitas, Madrid).

11 María, interview (Orcasitas, Madrid).

12 J. Rodríguez Cortezo, *Desde la calle. La Transición cómo se vivió*, Madrid: Visión Net, 2007, p. 264.

13 On the Moncloa Pacts, see: L. Dessfor Edles, *Symbol and Ritual in the New Spain: The Transition to Democracy after Franco*, Cambridge: Cambridge University Press, 1998, pp. 81–88; O. G. Encarnación, *Spanish Politics: Democracy after Dictatorship*, Cambridge: Cambridge University Press, 2008, pp. 39–41.

14 Dessor Edles, *Symbol and Ritual in the New Spain*, pp. 83–4.

15 R. Adell, "El estudio del contexto político a través de la protesta colectiva. La transición política en la calle," in J. M. Funes and R. Adell (eds.), *Movimientos sociales: cambio social y participación*, Madrid: UNED, 2003, p. 77.

16 Suaquillo was joined by other lawyers such as Mariano Gamo in Moratalaz, José Capa in Orcasitas and Carlos Jiménez de Parga in Palomeras Alto. P. Sauquillo, "El movimiento madrileño en la conquista de las libertades," *Memoria ciudadana y movimiento vecinal*, pp. 141–142.

17 My analysis is based on the information collected from the sections of local news in the following newspapers: *YA, Pueblo, El País, Gaceta Ilustrada, Informaciones, Diario 16, Mundo Obrero, ABC, Nuevo Diario, Ciudadano, Doblón, Mundo Social, Boletín HOAC, Arriba, La Tribuna Libre*.

18 "La concentración de Moratalaz," *El País* (septiembre, 1976).

19 "Una espectacular concentración en Moratalaz. Decenas de millares de personas protestan por la carestía de la vida," *El País* (20.12.1976).

20 C. Sobrino, "Le tienen miedo a la periferia," *Arriba* (17.11.1976).

21 S. Elden, *Understanding Henri Lefebvre: Theory and the Possible*, London: Continuum, 2004, p. 156.

22 Adell, "*El estudio del contexto político a través de la protesta colectiva. La transición política en la calle*," pp. 78–79.

23 Diani and Della Porta, *Social Movements: An Introduction*, p. 23.

24 M. S. Granovetter, "The Strength of Weak Ties," *The American Journal of Sociology*, 78(6), 1973, pp. 1360–1380.

25 F. López Rey, "Las protestas por la pan en los comienzos de la transición y el movimiento ciudadano," in *Memoria ciudadana*, p. 133.

26 For more information on the "Bread War," see: J.L. Martin Palacin, *Movimiento ciudadano y defensa del consumidor: La batalla del pan en Madrid*, Madrid: Ciudad y sociedad, 1978.

138 *Alternative visions of democracy*

27 See: "La Guardia Civil disuelve una concentración de 'vecinos,' en Aranjuez," *El País* (18.5.1976); "Procesado y multado por la concentración de Aranjuez," *El País* (21.5.1976); "Nueva nota de la Dirección General de Seguridad sobre los sucesos de Aranjuez," *El País* (22.5.1976).

28 J. L. Lorca Palencia, "Así son los lideres de Madrid," *El País* (4.5.1976).

29 F. López Rey, ibid.

30 *Informaciones de Madrid* (30.6.1976).

31 "Detenido un piquete armado de defensa contra la delincuencia," *Diario 16* (Madrid, 20.6.1977).

32 For information on the plan, see: "Delincuencia: Paz en el Barrio," Meseta de Orcasitas, *Boletín Informativo*, no. 6 (Febrero, 1983), pp. 14–15. See also: M. Botin, "Aceptado el plan anti-delincuencia elaborada por los vecinos," *El País* (no date, 1983); A. del Río, "El gobernador civil acepta el plan de los vecinos para erradicar la delincuencia," *YA*, Los barrios de Madrid (28.1.1983).

33 A similar claim was raised by Monica Threlfall in her research into the activism of women's organizations during the Transition. See: M. Threlfall, "Gendering the Transition to Democracy: Reassessing the Impact of Women's Activism," in M. Threlfall, M. Cousins, and C. Valiente (eds.), *Gendering Spanish Democracy*, New York: Routledge, 2005, p. 46.

34 "Debates en el barrio," Meseta de Orcasitas, *Boletín Informativo*, no. 1 (abril 1982), p. 11.

35 N. Calavita and A. Ferrer, "Behind Barcelona's Success Story: Citizen Movements and Planners' Power," *Journal of Urban History*, 26(6), 2000, p. 798.

36 *Del Barro al Barrio*, p. 182.

37 Polígono Meseta de Orcasitas, Hoja Informativa no. 3—La manzana, editada por el equipo de técnicos de la asociación de vecinos.

38 For information on the results of the survey see: "Los 'Tecnicos': una encuesta histórica," Meseta de Orcasitas, *Boletín Informativo*, no. 6 (abril 1983), pp. 6–7.

39 Polígono Meseta de Orcasitas, Hoja informativa no. 3—la Vivienda, edita el equipo de técnicos de la asociación de vecinos.

40 J. Manuel Bringas, "El técnico de los vecinos," Meseta de Orcasitas, *Boletín Informativo*, no. 1 (abril 1982), pp. 7–8.

41 Ibid.

42 *Del Barro al Barrio*, pp. 193–4.

43 In this regard see for example the reports about a mass demonstration that took place in San Blas and Orcasitas in October 1977: "El tema de la ocupación de pisos. Un punto muerto," *El País* (9 de octubre 1977).

44 A new decree on the subject was published in 1976, but by late 1977 not a single Social Housing-unit was constructed in the Madrid area. For the first decree, see: https://www.boe.es/buscar/doc.php?id=BOE-A-1976-26183. For the second decree, see: http://igvs.xunta.es/normativa/2_REAIS%20DECRETOS/RD%203148-78.pdf/.

45 The price of the apartments in Orcasitas, for example, rose from 1,400,000 pesetas (with a monthly return of 4,000 pesetas spread over 35 years) to 2,450,000 pesetas (with a monthly return of 9,600 pesetas spread over 25 years). Widows and retired persons were no longer allowed to spread the payments over 50 years. No discount was given to those neighbors that were qualified and willing to take part in the construction processes.

46 "Marcha verde de los vecinos sobre el ministerio de OBRAS Publicas," *Informaciones*, Madrid (19.2.79); A. Yañez," Vecinos de Orcasitas protestan por el encarecimiento de las viviendas protegidas," *ABC*, 20 de febrero 1979.

47 *Del Barro al Barrio*, p. 37.

48 Diani and Della Porta, *New Social Movements: An Introduction*, p. 53.

49 J. Mari Paredes, "Otxarkoaga," in *Movimientos ciudadanos en Bilbao: Rekaldeberri, Otxarkoaga, S. Francisco*, p. 244.

50 J. Borja, "Los nuevos movimientos urbanos están construyendo un nuevo marco político social," *Jano Arquitectura. Revista de Arquitectura, interiorismo y diseño* (diciembre, 1979), p. 39.

51 Federación de Vecinos de Madrid, "Queremos participar activamente," *Pueblo* (30 de abril, 1980), p. 170.

52 Quoted in Calvita and Ferrer, "Behind Barcelona's Success Story," p. 803.

53 J. M. López Rubio, "Opinión—Gobierno socialista. Cambio pero poco," in Asociación de vecinos meseta de Orcasitas, *Boletín informativo numero 6*, p. 9.

Conclusion
Some thoughts on civic participation, the production of urban space and the meaning of the right to the city

The evolution of the Citizens' Movement in Spain reflects a process by which dispersed struggles for improved living conditions, for gender equality and for increased professional autonomy merged in order to create a new actor in the public sphere. Despite its heterogenic nature and wide geographic spread, the Citizens Movement was primarily an urban movement. Neighbors, consumers, housewives and youth made up the backbone of this movement. They were joined by teachers, priests, lawyers, architects and social workers who mobilized both as individual members of the communities in which they lived and worked, as well as in their professional capacity as advocates of those same communities.

The present book does not pretend to provide an exhaustive account of the development and workings of the Citizens' Movement. Such an account still needs to be written, and will depend to a large extent on future research into the history of individual entities and associations that made up the movement. In following pages I wish to present a tentative analysis of certain characteristics and capacities which this movement developed throughout Spain's transition to democracy, as well as of the constraints under which it operated from the angle of my own research into the role of neighborhood associations. My aim is to signal additional directions for research and relate the history of Orcasitas and of other neighborhood associations that were founded within squatter settlements to the process of democratization undergone by Spanish society.

Manuel Castells defined "urban social movements" as movements that share three central characteristics: they share concerns relating to issues of collective consumption, particularly around the provision of use values; they conceive territory, particularly the neighborhood, as the basis for creating common collective identities; and they view the local state as the principal target of collective mobilizations, with the primary goal of achieving decentralized, territorially based mechanisms of self-management.[1] This formulation not only posits distinct goals for urban social movements but also suggests that urban movements are constituted in ways that differentiate them from other social movements. Both Castells and David Harvey argued that the very thing that makes these movements urban is also their fatal flaw: their "urban" basis predisposes them towards defensive struggles to protect their particular places.

Conclusion   141

According to Castells it is the inherent particularism of such urban movements that narrows the political visions and relationships of their members rather than opening them up to broader political struggles.[2]

Movements that are thus constituted are liable to experience a more acute disjuncture between what Byron Miller defines as the "geographies of life-worlds" and the "geographies of systems." As Miller explains:

> On the one hand, most major political grievances derive from processes that are systemic in nature; they stem from the functioning (or dysfunctioning) of the economy or the state. On the other hand, social movements mobilize around shared life-world identities and values that have their own geographies, usually different from those of systemic processes.[3]

Miller and Nicholls, who analyzed the relationship between recent anti-systematic social movements and the city, proved more flexible in defining the capacity of urban social movements to bridge the gap between knowledge derived from everyday life in the city, and knowledge of broader systemic processes and obstacles. They too, however, pointed to several factors that may condition the route taken by movements in this respect. Among them is the fact that "... local actors may fail to see, or strive to build, connections to other activists and organizations." They further explain that:

> beyond the difficult task of finding a common motivating frame, are two critical and related questions: (1) what is the diagnosis of the actual problem, i.e. what is the diagnostic framing; (2) what actions should the movement take, i.e. what is the prognostic framing? The answers provided to these questions frequently represent the Achilles' heel of urban social movements. The very strength of urban social movements – the fact that they emerge from a shared and largely localized socio-spatial life-world; that the networks of information-sharing, resource-sharing, and trust are based in the city; that oppression and discrimination are experienced in the city – often gives rise to diagnoses and prognoses that locate the source of grievances, and strategies for addressing those grievances, in the city.[4]

As this book has shown, the political vision of neighborhood associations emerged out of local experiences but was not necessarily a narrow one. Throughout the initial stages of the transition this vision did not limit the associations' capacity for cooperation with other civic and political entities. When this capacity diminished it was not due to the local or particular nature of their concerns, but rather because their political vision itself came into conflict with other, universal visions of democracy.

Without necessarily coming to know the work of Henri Lefebvre, many neighborhood activists adopted the distinction Lefebvre himself made between "the city" and "urban society." Thinking beyond the notion of the city or the neighborhood as a bounded category they focused on the processes that "run

142 Conclusion

through" and shape the social relations of cities. They opposed processes which they identified as potentially harming, processes that could lead to the creation of a society based on highly structured power relations and defined in terms of a single center and multiple peripheries. Instead, they embraced a socio-political vision that strove to produce multiple hubs of knowledge, resources and decision-making processes.

That is not to say that neighborhood associations rejected the notion of scales of governance. As we saw in the previous chapter, the associations negotiated flexibly and skillfully by identifying those issues that should be most effectively addressed at the scale of the neighborhood (the internal structure of the neighborhood itself, the design of private and communal spaces); those issues that had to be dealt with at the scale of the city (determining the density and quality of collective services); and those that could only be addressed on a national scale (such as the regulation of consumption). When the debate regarding the nature of democratic citizenship erupted, the Federation of Neighborhood Associations both in Madrid and in Barcelona went a step further by questioning the relationship between democratization and different scales of citizenship.

In Francoist Spain the structures of political participation were linked to the status of formal citizenship within the nationalist state. The access to all representative entities was conditioned upon ideological and / or economic support of the regime (or at the very least upon its passive acceptance). Citizens had some institutionalized say in the decisions that the state took, but were enfranchised through a limited set of municipal and regional institutions, as well as through the syndicates to which they belonged in their professional capacity. The top-down structure of state power meant that a limited number of those enfranchised through sub-national institutions could have a formal say in the running of industries or municipalities other than their own. Furthermore, the access to those institutions which enabled political representation was not open to all members of the national community. Women and political opponents of the regime in particular were denied access.

While all the entities that opposed the dictatorship supported the institution of a democratic regime, most viewed democratic enfranchisement as arranged in a hierarchical manner, with the national scale being hegemonic. All neighborhood associations shared the assumption that one must be a citizen of the nation state in order to take part in political participation on other, sub-national, scales. However, those who supported the institution of a participatory democracy (based on the notion of self-management) did not view the national scale as the hegemonic scale within which political and economic decision-making processes should take place. Nor did they view the national community as a whole as the unique source of political legitimacy.

The Bread War, for example, revealed a situation in which neighborhood associations were forced to deal with the state, in its capacity as legislator, as their exclusive addressee. However, it was at the sub-national scale (of the neighborhood and the city) that information regarding the extent of corruption was collected, and experimentation was carried out in order to offer the legislator proof of the ability to manufacture cheap, high-quality bread. In the field of education both the Orcasitas Anti-Delinquency Program and the Emergency Education Plan for the Basque Provinces reflected a different route: in both these cases the community was not only a source for professional information, but also the designer of future policy and a driving force behind a demand for the redistribution of resources.

As I noted earlier, most neighborhood activists in Spain of the 1970s were probably not aware of Henri Lefebvre's work. However, it was precisely their experiences at the urban grassroots level that made them think in terms of Lefebvre's *Right to the City*. Mark Purcell recently pointed out that much research is still needed in order to fully comprehend the meaning of Lefebvre's battle cry:

> Unfortunately, however, few in or out of academia have offered a detailed exposition of just what the right to the city would entail, and they have not developed what benefits or detriments it might have for the enfranchisement of urban residents. To be clear, [current] work is innovative, stimulating, and welcome. However, it falls short of a careful exposition and evaluation of the right to the city idea. We lack a comprehensive explanation of what the right to the city is or how it would challenge, compliment, or replace current rights. And we are left without a good sense of how the right to the city might address the specific enfranchisement problems associated with urban neo-liberalism.[5]

The history of neighborhood associations that emerged out of community life in shantytowns such as Orcasitas is greatly enhanced by a thorough reflection on the meaning and nature of Lefebvre's the right to the city. According to Lefebvre the right to the city is defined by two interrelated concepts: appropriation and inhabitance. Appropriation, as mentioned earlier, refers not only to the right to occupy already-produced urban space, but also the right to produce urban space so that it meets the needs of inhabitants. Because appropriation gives inhabitants the right to "full and complete usage" of urban space in the course of everyday life, space must be produced in a way that makes that full and complete usage possible.[6]

The community of squatters that formed in Orcasitas throughout the 1950s was made up of distinct social groups that were divided by age and gender, as well as by their original geographic affiliation. Social alienation, the harsh living conditions, and the similar personal and professional challenges with which the population faced soon generated intimate relationships. These relationships were based on internal hierarchies (between different migrant communities, between men and women, between small landowners, home owners and tenants, etc.) but also on varied ties of mutual help. By the late 1960s the community that formed in Orcasitas was characterized by relatively high levels of solidarity and resourcefulness that compensated, whenever possible, for the

144 *Conclusion*

harsh living conditions. The newly formed community produced its lived space within the economic and material constraints imposed on it by the dictatorship. It did not appropriate space in the full Lefebvrian sense, but rather imbued it with meaning and functions which at times undermined the logic and spatial practices advocated by the regime. This hybrid, communal space played an important role in carrying the process of spatial appropriation a step further: it was precisely within intermediate spaces produced by the community (in the form of taverns, a barbershop, the headquarters of the association) that people came to think for the first time of the need to challenge the existing political arrangements.

As this book has shown, however, the ability of most neighborhood activists to conceive a more permanent and far-reaching transformation of urban space was not born simply of the harsh reality of everyday life. The first steps towards organization and mobilization were taken following specific events, which triggered the understanding that life could not go on as it did. In the case of both Barcelona and Madrid the trigger was related to the implementation of partial plans, which constituted part of the metropolitan plans decided upon in the 1960s and early 1970s. In both cities neighborhood associations moved throughout the first half of the 1970s from an attempt to modify the existing partial plans to focusing on additional issues relating to education, transportation and medical services. In the case of Bilbao, as we have seen, the early triggering issue had to do with education infrastructures and only later did the associations expand their critique so as to include other issues.

This process of "becoming conscious" (as it was described by many activists) meant that during the first half of the 1970s neighborhood associations had come to define a series of core issues, which they felt were within their sphere of intervention (such as housing, education, consumption and transportation). Thinking about the issues at hand had a direct impact on the process of identity formation. The definition of a community of neighbors (to which I referred in Chapter 4) was related to the concept of "inhabitance." A neighbor was described as person who dwelled, interacted and made use of specific services and infrastructures common to all others who resided within the same spatial unit.

During the final years of Francoism and throughout the transition to democracy the insights that were gained during the initial phases of the struggle in Orcasitas and in other peripheral *barrios* were further developed. Through constant dialogue with the professionals that assisted them and with other entities within the Citizens Movement neighborhood associations had come to see the concept of "periphery" as a constructed one. Consequently they learned to identify the conditions that led to the creation of spatial peripheries and suggest ways in which the use of space could empower rather than weaken their communities. The community was the moving force behind this struggle but lawyers, architects and journalists assisted the neighbors in translating their insights regarding urban space into the more universal language of urban planning and political programs. Prior to 1978 (when the form of Spain's future democracy was still negotiated on the ground) some neighborhood activists held the hope that the future system would be rescaled in ways that went beyond the mere expansion of existing civic and political rights.

In the case of Orcasitas it is tempting to equate the inhabitants' critical engagement with three reconstruction plans with an incipient process of rescaling. The struggle in the *barrio* highlighted the difference between productive and non-productive ways of using space and turned the neighbors into active producers of their own living environment. The third and final renovation plan ensured that the new Orcasitas would be constructed in accordance with the needs of its future users. This was manifested on both the private and the intermediate levels: in the structure of the apartments, of the recreational and commercial spaces, transportation routes, educational facilities and the spaces designated for social interaction and civic activism (such as the civic center, a sporting complex, and the headquarters of the association). For a short period, during the transition itself, the inhabitants of Orcasitas were also successful in taking over some of the more "global" spaces designated for political interaction and deliberation (such as Madrid's city hall, the courts, Plaza de la Villa, etc.).

The structures for political and civic participation, however, were never truly rescaled. Present-day Spanish cities clearly present a more heterogeneous profile in terms of planning, architecture and demographics. They meet the complex and multiple needs of their inhabitants to a larger extent than in previous decades. It is enough, however, to look at present-day Orcasitas in order to understand the limitations of change. The new *barrio* of Orcasitas was constructed as a neighborhood unto itself. It might have been conceived as a perfectly formed *barrio* on the inside, but throughout the 1980s and 1990s it had few sustainable ties with the city around it. On a practical level this is best manifested by the fact that Orcasitas directly connected to the Madrid Metro line only in 2008. More disquieting, however, is the fact that in the decades following the renovation the *barrio* was referred to in the Madrid press either in relation to its successful past struggle or as a current hotbed of criminal activity and of drug trafficking. While the neighbors and the association struggled to combat drug consumption within the community, many outsiders still view drug trafficking as one of the characteristics of the *barrio* itself. In other words, the empowering struggle and the consequent remodeling process changed some of the existing spatial practices and the structure of representational space within the *barrio*. But they did not bring about a lasting change in the representations of that space as a marginalized periphery in the eyes of those outside the *barrio*.

A study, published by the Autonomous Community of Madrid in late 1985 indicated that the renovated *barrio* of Orcasitas included 12,384 inhabitants. Just as in the 1960s it was still a relatively young neighborhood: 57 percent of the inhabitants were under the age of 30. However, just like in the 1960s it was also a neighborhood with exceptionally high levels of unemployment (37.5 percent of the adult population) and exceptionally low levels of professional qualification: 32 percent of the employed population comprised of unqualified laborers in the service sector and 32.3 percent of unqualified laborers in the industrial sector (32.3 per cent). Qualified laborers were mostly found in the construction

146 *Conclusion*

sector.[7] These statistics point to the fact a decade after the death of the dictator there was no significant change in the socio-economic profile of the population.

The difficulty of changing in a meaningful and lasting way the peripheral status of a neighborhood such as Orcasitas had much to do, in my view, with the issue of popular participation. For a short time during the first phase of the transition, it seemed as if the Citizens' Movement in general (and neighborhood associations in particular) might have sufficient mobilizing capacities in order to bring about a lasting change in the existing power relations between the community, the authorities and the economic forces that affected the structure of urban life. By mid 1977, however, the impact of labor unions on street mobilizations in the capital increased drastically, while that of neighborhood, housewives and consumers associations decreased. Throughout 1977 the CCOO and other syndicates initiated 29.5 percent of the 170 demonstrations that were recorded in Madrid, mobilizing some 643,000 people. Neighborhood associations, on the other hand, managed to mobilize only 24,000 people that were spread across some 55 public acts and gatherings. These numbers reflect the retreat of neighborhood associations into smaller events with a decreased number of participants.

Following the signing of the Mocloa Pacts in late 1978, the image of the CCOO and of the Socialist-led labor union UGT as crucial political actors, who could shape the direction of the transition to democracy, was enhanced. Neighborhood associations, on the other hand, could not reconstruct the mobilizing capacities which they demonstrated in 1976. This situation clearly affected their ability to increase their sphere of action and consolidate their legal standing within the new political system. A consolidation of the associations' status as political actors would have provided neighborhood activists with the opportunity to regulate their public work. As representatives of their *barrios* most of their work had to be carried out vis-à-vis government agencies in times that took them away from their workplace. If their work had been acknowledged, as was the case with syndical representatives, for example, they would have been economically compensated for that time.[8] Legal acknowledgment would have constituted a clear statement on the part of the authorities that the neighbors did, indeed, possess information and understanding essential to urban governance. Finally, the presence of neighborhood activists within the different municipal organs (especially the District Boards) would have ensured continued flow of information to the neighbors at large. The dream of neighborhood associations for a more participatory form of government has not materialized. Those citizens who strove for higher levels of participation felt excluded from the beating heart of both the local and the national administration. The willingness of democratic authorities to allow the "community" to take an active part in designing and regulating its living environment was limited. Continued civic participation at all levels of governance was not perceived as an essential characteristic of the new democratic system that emerged out of the Spanish transition. But it was precisely the right for active, innovative and creative participation which lay at the heart of the Orcasitas success. Without it, as

Conclusion 147

most neighborhood activists understood, the ability of ordinary citizens to shape their lived-in space could not be sustained over time.

Notes

1 Castells, *The City and the Grassroots.*
2 M. Castells, *The Rise of the Network Society: The Information Age,* Oxford: Blackwell, 1996; D. Harvey, *The Condition of Post-Modernity: An Enquiry into the Origins of Cultural Change,* Cambridge, MA: Blackwell, 1991.
3 B. Miller, *Geography and Social Movements: Comparing Antinuclear Activism in the Boston Area,* Minneapolis, MN: Minnesota University Press, 2000, p. 67.
4 B. Miller and W. Nicholls, "Social Movements in Urban Society: The City as a Space of Politicization," *Urban Geography,* 34(4), pp. 461–465.
5 Purcell, "Excavating Lefebvre: The Right to the City and its Urban Politics of the Inhabitant," p. 101.
6 Lefebvre, *The Production of Space,* p. 179.
7 *Del Barro al Barrio,* p. 211.
8 For more in that regard see: "Los directivos de las asociaciones de vecinos pierdan tiempo y dinero en sus gestiones," *ABC* (13.11.78); F. López Rey, "La lucha en el movimiento ciudadano me ha envejecido," *Diario 16,* Madrid (24–12–79).

Bibliography

Primary sources

Archive sources

- Archivo Fotográfico, Asociación de Vecinos Meseta de Orcasitas, Madrid.
- Archivo de Prensa, Asociación de Vecinos Meseta de Orcasitas, Madrid. Including materials that were published in: *Mundo Social, Doblón, Nuestra Bandera, El País, Sábado Grafico, YA, Informaciones, Nuevo Diario, Gaceta Ilustrada, Diario 16, Mundo Obrero, ABC, Ciudadano, Boletín HOAC, Arriba, La Tribuna Libre*.
- Archivo Juan Linz de La Transición Española, Fundación Juan March: Artículos, "Semana Política."
- Archivo Regional de Madrid, Fondo: Instituto Nacional de la Vivienda, Signaturas 137087–137627 and 216861–219599.

Interviews

- María, Orcasitas, Madrid.
- Felicitas, Orcasitas, Madrid.
- Cristobal, Orcasitas, Madrid.
- Antonio, Orcasitas, Madrid.
- Cristian, Usera, Madrid.
- Gregorio, Orcasitas, Madrid.
- María, Orcasitas, Madrid.
- José Luis, Orcasitas, Madrid.
- Ángela, Orcasitas, Madrid.
- Pura López (head of the Women's Organization, the Orcasitas Neighborhood Association) Orcasitas, Madrid.
- Félix López Rey (former head of the Orcasitas Neighborhood Association) Orcasitas, Madrid.
- Antonio, Orcasitas, Madrid.
- Miguel Ángel, Orcasitas, Madrid.
- Ángel, Orcasitas, Madrid.
- María López, Orcasitas, Madrid.
- José Manuel and Emilia, Orcasitas, Madrid.
- Mariano, Orcasitas, Madrid.
- Daniel, Orcasitas, Madrid.
- Jesús, Orcasitas, Madrid.

Bibliography 149

Other primary sources

Asociación de Vecinos Guetaria, "Apuntas sobre la Historia del Poblado Dirigido de Orcasitas," p. 10, available at *http://es.scribd.com/doc/28561435/Historia-de-ORCASITAS#scribd/*.

Asociación de vecinos de la Meseta de Orcasitas, *Del barro al barrio. La Meseta de Orcasitas*, Madrid, 1986.

BOE Presidencia del Gobierno, "Decreto de 12 de diciembre de 1958 por el que se crea una Comisión Interministerial para estudiar y proponer los núcleos urbanos de descongestión de Madrid y demás comarcas de inmigración interna."

Carabanchel Alto, Historia, available at https://aavvcarabanchelalto.wordpress.com/historia-de-la-asociacion/.

COPLACO, Villaverde, Madrid: Colección Documentos de Difusión y Debate, 1980.

Le Corbusier, *The Athens Charter* (translated by A. Eardely) New York: Grossman Publishers, 1973.

D'Ors, V., "Estudios de Teoría de la Arquitectura, I. Sobre el Ábaco y el equino," in *Revista Nacional de Arquitectura*, 70–71, 1947.

FOESSA – Cáritas Diocesa de Madrid. *Informe sociológico sobre la situación social en Madrid*. Madrid: Euramèrica, 1967.

Gerencia Municipal de Urbanismo, *Plan parcial de ordenación de Orcasitas*, Madrid, noviembre 1971.

Ley 191/1964 de 24 de diciembre, de Asociaciones, BOE 28 diciembre de 1964, articulo primero.

Ley Orgánica del Estado, available at http://www.cervantesvirtual.com/servlet/SirveObras/12159641912327174198846/p0000001.htm#I_1/.

Anteproyecto: Normas sobre asociacionismo, MAYO-JUNIO 1971, available at http://www.march.es/ceacs/biblioteca/proyectos/linz/documento.asp?reg=r-4992/.

Ministerio de Vivienda, *Reforma de la ley del Suelo y Ordenación Urbana*, Madrid, 1975, available at https://www.boe.es/diario_boe/txt.php?id=BOE-A-1976-11506/.

Meseta de Orcasitas, *Boletín Informativo* (1978–1985).

Normas de Planeamiento para la provincia de Madrid. Documento de Trabajo 4 (Programa urgente del suelo), COPLACO, Ministerio de Vivienda, Madrid, junio 1977.

Poligono Meseta de Orcasitas, Hoja Informativa no. 3 – La manzana, editada por el equipo de técnicos de la asociación de vecinos.

Sauquillo, P., "El movimiento madrileño en la conquista de las libertades," in V. Pérez Quintana, and P. Sánchez León (eds.), *Memoria Ciudadana y movimiento vecinal. Madrid 1968–2008*, Madrid: Catarata, 2009, pp. 138–147.

Sambricio, C., *Plan Bidagor 1941–1946*, Madrid: Nerea, 2003.

Terán, A., *Planeamiento urbano de la España contemporánea. Historia de un proceso imposible*, Barcelona: Alianza, 1982.

Vivienda Social, available at https://www.boe.es/buscar/doc.php?id=BOE-A-1976-26183; http://igvs.xunta.es/normativa/2_REAIS%20DECRETOS/RD%203148-78.pdf/.

Literary sources

Candel, F., *Han matado un hombre, han roto un paisaje*, Barcelona: La Busca Edicions S.L., 2002.

Ferrés, A., *La piqueta*, Madrid: GADIR, 1996.

150 Bibliography

Secondary sources

Abelson, J., Forest, P. G., Eyles, J., Smith, P., Martin, E. and Gauvin, F. P., "Deliberations about Deliberative Methods: Issues in the Design and Evaluation of Public Participation Processes," *Social Science and Medicine*, 57, 2003, pp. 239–251.

Abers, R., *Inventing Local Democracy: Grassroots Politics in Brazil*, Boulder, CO: Lynne Reinner, 2000.

Adell, R., "El estudio del contexto político a través de la protesta colectiva. La transición política en la calle," in J. M. Funes and R. Adell (eds.), *Movimientos sociales: cambio social y participación*, Madrid: UNED, 2003.

Aguilera, T. and Smart, A., "Squatting, North, South and Turnabout: A Dialogue Comparing Illegal Housing Research," in F. Anders and A. Sedlmaier (eds.), *Public Goods versus Economic Interests: Global Perspectives on the History of Squatting*, London: Routledge (forthcoming).

Ahedo Gurrutxaga, I., "Bilbao y frontera interna: integración comunitaria desde la exclusión urbana. El caso de Rekaldeberri," *Bidebarrieta: Revista de humanidades y ciencias sociales de Bilbao*, 23, 2012, pp. 103–113.

Alonso Hinojal, I., *Algunos aspectos sociológicos de un barrio Madrileño de incorporación*, Madrid: Conferencias, Discursos y Estudios Monográficos, 1969.

Alsina Oliva, R., "La estrategia de desarrollo plantificada en España 1964–1975," doctoral thesis, Facultad de Ciencias Económicas y Empresariales, Universidad de Barcelona, 1987.

Azagra Ros, J., Chorén Rodríguez, P., Goerlich Gisbert, F. J. and Mas, M. (eds.), *La localización de la población Española sobre el territorio. Un siglo de cambios*, Bilbao: BBVA, 2006.

Babiano, J. M., *Emigrantes, Crónometros y huelgas. Un estudio sobre el trabajo y los trabajadores durante el Franquismo (Madrid 1951–1977)*, Madrid: Siglo XXI, 1998.

Baiocchi, G., "Participation, Activism, and Politics: The Porto Alegre Experiment," in A. Fung and E. O. Wright (eds.), *Deepening Democracy: Institutional Innovations in Empowered Participatory Governance*, London: Verso, 2003, pp. 45–76.

Balfour, S., *La dictadura, los trabajadores y la ciudad. El movimiento obrero en el área metropolitana de Barcelona (1939–1988)*, Valencia: Generalitat Valencia, 1994.

Barciela, C. (ed.), *Autarquía y Mercado Negro. El Fracaso Económico del Primer Franquismo 1939–1959*, Barcelona: Critica, 2003.

Barranquero, E. E. and Prieto, L., *Así Sobrevivimos el Hambre: Estrategias de Supervivencia de las Mujeres de la Posguerra Española*, Málaga: Diputación Provincial de Málaga, 2003.

Beascoechea Gangoiti, J. M. and Martínez Rueda, F., "La creación del 'Gran Bilbao' en el franquismo y el alcalde Joaquín Zuazagoitia (1942–1959)," *Bidebarrieta: Revista de humanidades y ciencias sociales de Bilbao*, 22, 2011, pp. 79–92.

Benson, M., "The Movement beyond (Lifestyle) Migration: Mobile Practices and the Constitution of a Better Way of Life," *Mobilities*, 6(2), 2011, pp. 221–235.

Bidagor, P., "Primeras problemas de la Reconstrucción de Madrid," in C. Sambricio (ed.), *Madrid, vivienda y urbanismo: 1900–1960*, Madrid: AKAL, 2004, p. 309.

Bilbao Larrondo, L., *El poblado dirigido de Otxarkoaga: Del plan de urgencia social al primer plan de desarrollo (La vivienda en Bilbao 1959–1964)*, Bilbao: UDALA Ayuntamiento, 2008.

Blain, C., "Team 10, the French Context," presented at the International Conference Team 10 – between Modernity and the Everyday, organized by the Faculty of Architecture TU Delft, Chair of Architecture and Housing, June 5–6, 2003.

Blasco Herranz, I., *Armas femeninas para la contrarrevolución. La Sección Femenina en Aragón (1936–1950)*, Málaga: Universidad de Málaga, 1999.

Borderías, C., "Emigración y trayectorias sociales femeninas," *Historia Social*, 17, 1993, pp. 75–94.

Bordetas Jiménez, I., "Nosotros somos los que hemos hecho esta ciudad. Autoorganización y movilización vecinal durante el tardofranquismo y el proceso de cambio político," doctoral thesis, Universidad Autónoma de Barcelona, 2012.

Borja, J., *Por unos municipios democráticos. Diez años de reflexión política y movimiento ciudadano*, Madrid: Instituto de Estudios de Administración Local, 1986.

Borja, J., *Luces y sombras del urbanismo de Barcelona*, Barcelona: Colección Gestión de la Ciudad, 2010.

Box Varela, Z., "La fundación de un régimen. La construcción simbólica del franquismo," doctoral thesis, Universidad Complutense de Madrid, 2008.

Brenner, N. and Elden, S., "Henri Lefebvre on State Space and Territory," *International Political Sociology*, 3(4), 2009, pp. 353–377.

Brenner, N., Marcuse, P. and Mayer, M. (eds.), *Cities for People not for Profit: Critical Urban Theory and the Right to the City*, London: Routledge, 2012.

Burbano Trimiño, F. A., "Las migraciones internas durante el franquismo y sus efectos sociales: el caso de Barcelona," doctoral thesis, Universidad Complutense, 2013.

Bustillo Merino, V. E., "Bilbao 1940–1975: del auge al inicio del declive. Un estudio histórico demográfico," doctoral thesis, Universidad del País Vasco, 2005.

Cabo Alonso, A., "Valor de la inmigración Madrileña," *Estudios Geográficos*, 22 (85),1961, pp. 353–374.

Calavita, N. and Ferrer, A., "Behind Barcelona's Success Story: Citizen Movement and Planners' Power," *Journal of Urban History*, 26(6), 2000, pp. 793–807.

Capel Sáez, H., "Las Migraciones Interiores Definitivas en España," *Estudios Geográficos*, 24, 1962, pp. 600–602.

Castells, M., *The Urban Question: A Marxist Approach*, Cambridge, MA: MIT Press, 1979.

Castells, M., *The City and the Grassroots: A Cross-Cultural Theory of Urban Social Movements*, Berkeley, CA: University of California Press, 1983.

Castells, M., "La formación de un movimientos social urbano: el Movimiento Ciudadano de Madrid hacia el final de la era franquista," in *La ciudad y las masas. Sociología de los movimientos sociales urbanos*, Madrid: Alianza Editorial, 1986.

Castells, M., "Productores de ciudad: el movimiento ciudadano de Madrid," in V. Pérez Quintana and P. Sánchez León (eds.), *Memoria Ciudadana y movimiento vecinal. Madrid 1968–2008*, Madrid: Catarata, 2009, pp. 21–32.

Castells, M., *Networks of Outrage and Hope: Social Movements in the Internet Age*, Cambridge: Cambridge University Press, 2012.

Castoriadis, C., "Autogestion et Hièrarchie," in *Le Contenu du Socialisme*, Paris: Union générale d'éditions, 1979.

Cid Fernández, X. M., Domínguez Alberte, X. C. and Soutelo Vázquez, R. (eds.), *Migracions na Galicia contemporanea: desafíos para a sociedades actual*, Santiago de Compostela: Sotelo Blanco, 2008.

Coudroy de Lille, L., Vaz, C. and Vorms, C. (eds.), *L'urbanisme espagnol depuis les années 1970*, Rennes: Presses Universitaires de Rennes, 2013.

Cresswell, C., "Towards a Politics of Mobility," *Environment and Planning D: Society and Space*, 28(1), 2007, pp. 17–31.

Davidoff, P., "Advocacy and Pluralism in Planning," *Journal of the American Institute of Planners*, 31(4), 1965, pp. 186–197.

152 Bibliography

De la Torre, J. and Sanz Lafuente, G., *Migración y Coyuntura Económica del Franquismo a la Democracia*, Zaragoza: PUZ, 2008.

del Arco Blanco, M. A., *Hambre de Siglos. Mundo Rural y Apoyos Sociales del Franquismo en Andalucía Oriental (1936–1951)*, Granada: Comares, 2007.

Del Vigo, J., Eguiraun, J., Recalde, J., Toral, M., Paredes, J. M. and Izarzelaia, A., "Movimientos ciudadanos en Bilbao: Rekaldeberri, Otxarkoaga, S. Francisco," *Revista Bidebarrieta*, 10, 2001, pp. 229–248.

Della Porta, D. and Diani, M., *Social Movements: An Introduction*, Oxford: Blackwell, 2006.

Della Porta, D. and Mattoni, A. (eds.), *Spreading Protest: Social Movements in Times of Crisis*, Colchester: ECPR Press, 2014.

Dessfor Edles, L., *Symbol and Ritual in the New Spain: The Transition to Democracy after Franco*, Cambridge: Cambridge University Press, 1998.

Doménech, X., *Clase Obrera, Antifranquismo y Cambio Político. Pequeños Grandes Cambios, 1956–1969*, Madrid: Catarata, 2008.

Elden, S., *Understanding Henri Lefebvre: Theory and the Possible*, London: Continuum, 2004.

Encarnación, O. G., *Spanish Politics: Democracy after Dictatorship*, Cambridge: Cambridge University Press, 2008.

Esteban Maluenda, A. M., "La vivienda social española en la década de los 50: Un paseo por los poblados dirigidos de Madrid," *Cuaderno de Notas*, 7, 1999, pp. 55–80.

Evans, G. (ed.), *The End of Class Politics? Class Voting in Comparative Context*, Oxford: Oxford University Press, 1999.

Fadiño Pérez, R. G., *Historia del movimiento ciudadano e historia local: el ejemplo del barrio de Yagüe en Logroño (1948–1975)*, Logroño: Instituto de Estudios Riojanos, 2003.

Fernández Buey, F. and Mir García, J., "Apropiación del futuro: revuelta estudiantil y autogestión durante el tardo-franquismo y la Transición," *Desacuerdos*, 6, 2011, pp. 161–168.

Fernández Galiano, L., *La quimera moderna. Los Poblados Dirigidos de Madrid*, Madrid: Hermann Blume, 1989.

Fernández Gómez, J. A., *Buscando el pan del trabajo. Sobre la industrialización Franquista y sus costes sociales en Villaverde (Madrid 1940–1965)*, Madrid: Miños y Davila Editores, 2007.

Flesher Fominaya, C., *Social Movements and Globalization: How Protests, Occupations and Uprisings Are Changing the World*, London: Palgrave Macmillan, 2014.

Foweraker, J., *Making Democracy in Spain: Grass-Roots Struggle in the South 1955–1975*, Cambridge: Cambridge University Press, 2003.

Fung, A., "Associations and Democracy: Between Theories, Hopes, and Realities," *Annual Review of Sociology*, 29, 2003, pp. 515–539.

Gallego Méndez, M. T., *Mujer, Falange y Franquismo*, Madrid: Taurus Ediciones, 1983.

García Barbancho, A., "Los Movimientos Migratorios en España," *Revista de Estudios Agrosociales*, 33, 1960, pp. 7–84.

García Barbancho, A., *Las migraciones interiores españolas en 1961–1970*, Madrid: Instituto de Estudios Económicos, 1974.

García Fernández, J., "La atracción demográfica de Madrid," *Estudios Geográficos*, 1957, pp. 87–91.

Gigosos, P. and Saravia, M., "Relectura del Planeamiento Español de los Años 80: Generación de Planes, Generación de Urbanistas," *Ciudades*, 1, 1993, pp. 36–52.

Bibliography   153

González Balado, J. L., *Padre Llanos: Un Jesuita En El Suburbio*, Madrid: Temas de Hoy, 1991.

González Madrid, D. A. (ed.), *El franquismo, y la Transición en España. Desmitificación y reconstrucción de la memoria de una época*, Madrid: Catarata, 2008.

Gonzalo Morell, C., "Una visión global de movimiento asociativo vecinal regional durante la Transición: 1970–1986", *Estudios Humanísticos. Historia*, 9, 2010, pp. 195–220.

Groves, T., *Teachers and the Struggle for Democracy in Spain 1970–1985*, Basingstoke: Palgrave Macmillan, 2015.

Harding, S. F., *Remaking Ibieca: Rural Life in Aragon under Franco*, Chapel Hill, NC: University of North California Press, 1984.

Harvey, D., *The Condition of Post-Modernity: An Enquiry into the Origins of Cultural Change*, Cambridge, MA: Blackwell, 1991.

Highmor, B., "Between Modernity and the Everyday: Team 10," presented at the International Conference Team 10 – between Modernity and the Everyday, organized by the Faculty of Architecture TU Delft, Chair of Architecture and Housing, June 5–6, 2003.

Higueras Arnal, A., *La Emigración Interior en España*, Madrid: Ediciones Mundo del Trabajo, 1967.

Hoskyns, T., *The Empty Place: Democracy and Public Space*, London: Routledge, 2014.

Kalir, B., "Moving Subjects, Stagnant Paradigms: Can the 'Mobilities Paradigm' Transcend Methodological Nationalism?" *Journal of Ethnic and Migration Studies*, 39(2), 2013, pp. 311–327.

Kaufmann, V., Bergman, M. and Joye, D., "Motility: Mobility as Capital," *International Journal of Urban and Regional Research*, 28(4), 2004, pp. 745–756.

Kitschelt, H., *The Transformation of European Social Democracy*, Cambridge: Cambridge University Press, 1994.

Kriesi, H., Koopmans, R., Willem Duyvendak, J. and Giugni, M.G., *New Social Movements in Western Europe: A Comparative Analysis*, Minneapolis, MN: University of Minnesota Press, 1995.

Laraña, E., Johnston, H. and Gusfield, J. R., *New Social Movements: From Ideology to Identity*, Philadelphia, PA: Temple University Press, 1994.

Lefebvre, H., "Problemes theoriques de l'autogestion," *Autogestion*, 1, 1966, pp. 59–70.

Lefebvre, H., *The Survival of Capitalism* (Reproduction of the Relations of Production, translated by F. Bryant), New York: St. Martin's Press, 1976.

Lefebvre, H., *De l'État*, Paris: UGE, 1976–1978, vol. 4.

Lefebvre, H., *The Production of Space* (translated by D. Nicholson-Smith), Oxford: Blackwell, 1991.

Lefebvre, H., *Critique of Everyday Life* (translated by John Moore), London: Verso, 1991

Lefebvre, H., *Writings on Cities* (translated and introduced by E. Kofman and E. Lebas), Oxford: Blackwell, 1996.

Lefebvre, H., *Key Writings*, edited by Stuart Elden, Elizabeth Lebas and Eleonore Kofman, London: Continuum, 2003.

Lefebvre, H., *The Urban Revolution* (translated by R. Bonnano), Minneapolis, MN: University of Minnesota Press, 2003.

Leontidou, L., "Urban Social Movements in 'Weak' Civil Societies: The Right to the City and Cosmopolitan Activism in Southern Europe," *Urban Studies*, 47, 2010, pp. 1179–1203.

López Díaz, J., "Vivienda Social y Falange: Ideario y Construcciones en la Década de los 40," *Scripta Nova*, 8(146) 2003, available at http://www.ub.es/geocrit/sn/sn-146(024).htm/.

154 Bibliography

Lorenzi, E., "Aportaciones de los nuevos pobladores a la cultura local," in P. Cirujano and A. Lucena Gíl (eds.), *Vallecas. Cultura de Vallecas 1950–2005. La Creación Compartida*, Madrid: Distrito de Villa de Vallecas, 2007, pp. 257–284.

Magro Huertas, T. and Muxí Martínez, Z., "La mujeres constructoras de ciudad desde los movimientos sociales urbanos," available at *http://fundacion.arquia.es/files/p ublic/media/-ldRvollT6wOReeX4yM2e2hs8Sw/MjIyODg/MA/f_pdf.pdf/*.

Marcuse, P., "Whose Right(s) to What City?" in N. Brenner, P. Marcuse and M. Mayer (eds.), *Cities for People not for Profit: Critical Urban Theory and the Right to the City*, London: Routledge, 2012, pp. 34–35.

Martin Palacin, J. L., *Movimiento ciudadano y defensa del consumidor: La batalla del pan en Madrid*, Madrid: Ciudad y sociedad, 1978.

Martínez López, M. A., "The Squatters' Movement in Spain: A Local and Global Cycle of Urban Protests," in Squatting Europe Kollective (eds.), *Squatting in Europe: Radical Spaces, Urban Struggles*, New York: Minor Compositions, 2013, pp. 113–138.

Martínez López, F. and Gomez Oliver, M., "Political Responsibilities in Franco's Spain: Recovering the Memory of Economic Repression and Social Control in Andalusia 1936–1945," in A. G. Morcillo (ed.), *Memory and Cultural History of the Spanish Civil War: Realms of Oblivion*, Leiden: Brill, 2014, pp. 111–145.

Mas Serra, E., "El urbanismo del período desarrollista en las capitales vascas," *Rev. int. estud. vascos*, 50(2), 2005, pp. 443–491.

Mayer, M., "The 'Right to the City' in Urban Social Movements," in N. Brenner, P. Marcuse and M. Mayer (eds.), *Cities for People not for Profit: Critical Urban Theory and the Right to the City*, London: Routledge, 2012, pp. 63–85.

Mayer, M., "Preface," in Squatting Europe Kollective (eds.), *Squatting in Europe: Radical Spaces, Urban Struggles*, New York: Minor Compositions, 2013, pp. 1–11.

Maza Zorria, E., *Asociacionismo en la España Franquista. Aproximación Histórica*, Valladolid: Universidad de Valladolid, 2011.

Miller, B., and Nicholls, W., "Social Movements in Urban Society: The City as a Space of Politicization," *Urban Geography*, 34(4), 2013, pp. 452–473.

Miller, G., *Geography and Social Movements: Comparing Antinuclear Activism in the Boston Area*, Minneapolis, MN: Minnesota University Press, 2000.

Milward, A. S., *The Reconstruction of Western Europe 1945–1951*, Berkeley, CA: University of California Press, 1984.

Mir, C. and Agustí, C., "Delincuencia patrimonial y justicia penal: una incursión en la marginación social de posguerra (1939–1951)," in C. Mir, C. Agustí and J. Gelonch (eds.), *Pobreza, marginación, delincuencia y políticas sociales bajo el franquismo*, Lleida: Universitat de Lleida, 2008, pp. 69–92.

Molinero, M. (ed.), *La Transición treinta años después. De la dictadura a la instauración y consolidación de la democracia*, Barcelona: Atalaya, 2006.

Molinero, C. and Ysàs, P. (eds.), *Construint la ciutat democràtica: El moviment veinal durant el tardofranquisme i al transició*, Barcelona: Icaria Editorial, 2010.

Moneo, R., *"El Desarrollo Urbano de Madrid en los años Sesenta"* in *Ayuntamiento de Madrid, Madrid: cuarenta años de desarrollo urbano (1940–1980)*, Madrid: Temas Urbanos, 1981.

Montes Mieza, J., Paredes Grosso, M. and Villanueva Paredes, A., "Los asentamientos chabolistas en Madrid," *Ciudad y Territorio. Revista de ciencia urbana*, 2–3, 1976, pp. 159–172.

Muguruza, P. and Gutiérrez Soto, L., "Un reto para la vivienda social en España: el hogar sin pasillo," in A. Santas Torres (ed.), *Actas del congreso internacional Los años 50: La arquitectura española y su compromiso con la historia*, Pamplona: T6 Ediciones, 2000, pp. 171–180.

Ofer, I., "A City of a Thousand Identities: Vencidos y Vencedores en Madrid de la Post-Guerra (1939–1945)," presented at the 5th Woodrow Borah International Colloquium: Rethinking the Spanish Civil War, Tel Aviv University, Tel Aviv, 2007.

Ofer, I., *Señoritas in Blue: The Making of a Female Political Elite in Franco's Spain: The National Leadership of the Sección Femenina de la Falange (1936–1977)*, Brighton: Sussex University Press, 2009.

Ofer, I., "La Guerra de Agua: Notions of Morality, Respectability and Community in a Madrid Neighborhood," *Journal of Urban History*, 35(2), 2009, pp. 220–235.

Ofer, I., "The Concept of Mobility in Migration Processes: The Subjectivity of Moving towards a 'Better Life'," in M. Fernández Montes and M. C. La Barbera (eds.), *Negotiating Identity in Migration Processes*, Dordrecht: Springer, 2014.

Ortiz Heras, M. (ed.), *Los movimientos sociales en la crisis de la dictadura y la Transición*, Ciudad Real: Almud Ediciones, 2008.

Pala, G., "El Partido y la Ciudad. Modelos de Organización y Militancia del PSUC Clandestino (1963–1975)," *Historia Contemporánea*, 50, 2015, pp. 195–222.

Paredes, J. M., "Otxarkoaga," in M. Toral, J. del Vigo, J. Eguiraun, J. M. Paredes and A. Izarzelaia (eds.), "Movimientos ciudadanos en Bilbao: Rekaldeberri, Otxarkoaga, S. Francisco" *Bidebarrieta*, 2011, pp. 229–248.

Parejo Alfonso, L., "L'évolition du cadre juridique de la production de la ville depuis 1956," in L. Coudroy de Lille, C. Vaz, C. Vorms and L. Parejo Alfonso (eds.), *L'urbanisme español depuis les années, 1970. La ville, la démocratie et le marché*, Rennes: Presses Universitaires de Rennes, 2013, pp. 28–31.

Pérez Díaz, V. M., "Nota sobre migraciones rurales internas y disparidades regionales en el medio rural," *Revista de Estudios Agrosociales*, 58, 1967, pp. 73–83.

Pérez-Escolano, V., "Arquitectura y política en España a través del Boletín de la Dirección General de Arquitectura (1946–1957)," *Revista de Arquitectura*, 15, 2013, pp. 35–46.

Pérez Pérez, J. A. "La configuración de nuevos espacios de sociabilidad en el ámbito del gran Bilbao de los años 60," *Studia historica. Historia contemporánea*, 18, 2000, pp. 117–147.

Pinto, P. R., "Housing and Citizenship: Building Social Rights in Twentieth Century Portugal," *Contemporary European History*, 18(2), 2009, pp.199–215.

Piven, F. and Cloward, R., *Poor People's Movements: Why They Succeed, How They Fail*, New York: Vintage Books, 1977.

Prados de la Escosura, L., Rosés, J. R. and Sanz-Villarroya, I., "Economic Reforms and Growth in Franco's Spain," Working Papers in Economic History, *Universidad Carlos III de Madrid*, 2011.

Preston, P., *The Spanish Holocaust: Inquisition and Extermination in Twentieth-Century Spain*, London: Harper Press, 2012.

Pruijt, H., "Squatting in Europe," in Squatting Europe Kollective (eds.), *Squatting in Europe: Radical Spaces, Urban Struggles*, New York: Minor Compositions, 2013, pp. 17–60.

Puig i Valls, A., "De Granada a Sabadell: la emigración una experiencia vivida," *Historia y Fuentes Orales: Memoria y sociedad en la España Contemporánea: actas III Jornadas*, 5, 1996, pp. 275–284.

Purcell, M., "Excavating Lefebvre: The Right to the City and Urban Politics of the Inhabitants," *GeoJournal*, 58, 2002, pp. 99–108.

Quirosa-Cheyrouze, R. (ed.), *Historia de la Transición Española. Los inicios del proceso democratizador*, Madrid: Biblioteca Nueva, 2007.

156 Bibliography

Radcliff, P., "Ciudadanas: las mujeres de Las Asociaciones de Vecinos y la identidad de género en los sesenta," in V. Pérez Quintana and P. Sánchez León (eds.), *Memoria Ciudadana y movimiento vecinal. Madrid 1968–2008*, Madrid: Catarata, 2009, pp. 54–78.

Radcliff, P., *Making Democratic Citizens in Spain: Civil Society and the Popular Origins of the Transition 1960–1978*, New York: Palgrave Macmillan, 2011.

Rankin, K. N., "The Praxis of Planning and the Conditions of Critical Development Studies," in N. Brenner, P. Marcuse and M. Mayer (eds.), *Cities for People not for Profit: Critical Urban Theory and the Right to the City*, London: Routledge, 2012, pp. 219–229.

Raymond, H., "Habitat, modèles cultureless et architecture," in H. Raymond, J. M. Stébé and A. Mathieu Fritz (eds.), *Architecture urbanistique et société*, Paris: Éd. L'Harmattan, 1974, pp. 213–229.

Richards, M., *Un Tiempo de Silencio. La Guerra Civil y la Cultura de la Represión en la España de Franco 1936–1945*, Barcelona: Critica, 1999.

Ródenas, C., "Migraciones Interiores 1960–1985: Balance de la investigación y análisis de las fuentes estadísticas," in J. de la Torre and G. Sanz Lafuente (eds.), *Migraciones y coyuntura económica del franquismo a la democracia*, Zaragoza: PUZ, 2008.

Rodríguez Cortezo, J., *Desde la calle. La Transición cómo se vivió*, Madrid: Visión Net, 2007.

Sambricio, C., *Madrid, vivienda y urbanismo: 1900–1960*, Madrid: AKAL, 2004.

Siguán, M., *Del campo al suburbio. Un estudio sobre la inmigración interior en España*, Madrid: C.S.I.C., 1959.

Siguán, M., "Las raíces de la emigración campesina," *Estudios Geográficos*, 27, 1966, 533–539.

Simancas, V. and Elizalde, J. M., "Madrid, Siglo XX," in *Madrid: cuarenta años de desarrollo urbano (1940–1980)*, Madrid: Ayuntamiento de Madrid, 1980, pp. 11–21.

Sheller, M., "Mobility," Sociopedia.isa, 2011, available at http://www.sagepub.net/isa/resources/pdf/mobility.pdf/.

Stanek, L., *Henri Lefebvre on Space: Architecture, Urban Research, and the Production of Theory*, Minneapolis, MN: University of Minnesota Press, 2011.

Santiáñez, N., "Cartografía crítica del fascismo español: Checas de Madrid de Tomás Borrás," *Res publica*, 13–14, 2004, pp. 181–198.

Steinmetz, G., "Regulation Theory, Post-Marxism, and the New Social Movements," *Comparative Studies in Society and History*, 36(1), 1994, pp. 176–212.

Sugranyes, A. and Mathivet, C., *Cities for All: Proposals and Experiences towards the Right to the City*, Santiago de Chile: HIC, 2010.

Tejerina, B., and Ignacia Perugorria, P. (eds.), *From Social to Political: New Forms of Mobilization and Democratization, Conference Proceedings*, Bilbao: Universidad del País Vasco, 2012.

Threlfall, M., "Gendering the Transition to Democracy: Reassessing the Impact of Women's Activism," in M. Threlfall, M. Cousins and C. Valiente (eds.), *Gendering Spanish Democracy*, New York: Routledge, 2005, pp. 11–54.

Thurén, B. M., *Mujeres en la casa, hombres en la calle?*, Madrid: Biblioteca Básica Vecinal, 1977.

Toral, M., del Vigo, J., Eguiraun, J., Paredes, J. M. and Izarzelaia, A. (eds.), "Movimientos ciudadanos en Bilbao: Rekaldeberri, Otxarkoaga, S. Francisco," *Bidebarrieta*, 10, 2011, pp. 229–248.

Townson, N., *Spain Transformed: The Late Franco Dictatorship, 1959–1975*, New York: Palgrave Macmillan, 2007.

Bibliography   157

Urritia Abaigar, V., *El movimiento vecinal en el área metropolitana de Bilbao*, Bilbao: Instituto Vasco de Administración Pública, 1985.

Urrutia Abaigar, V., "La ciudad de los ciudadanos, Actas del VI Symposium: Movimientos Ciudadanos y Sociales en Bilbao," *Bidebarrieta*, 10, 2001, pp. 11–23.

Van der Steen, B., Katzeff, A. and Van Hoogenhuiuze, L. (eds.), *The City is Ours: Squatting and Autonomous Movements in Europe from the 1970s to the Present*, Oakland, CA: PM Press, 2014.

Valenzuela Rubio, M., "Iniciativa oficial y crecimiento urbano en Madrid 1939–1973," *Estudios Geográficos*, 137, 1974, pp. 593–655.

Valenzuela Rubio, M., "Notas sobre el desarrollo histórico del planeamiento en España," *Cuadernos de investigación: Geografía e historia*, 4(2), 1978, pp. 39–68.

Vega García, R., "Radical Unionism and the Workers' Struggle in Spain," *Latin American Perspectives*, 27(5), 2000, pp. 111–133.

Yiftachel, O., "Critical theory and Gray Space," in N. Brenner, P. Marcuse and M. Mayer (eds.), *Cities for People not for Profit: Critical Urban Theory and the Right to the City*, London: Routledge, 2012, pp. 150–170.

Walker, A. and Porraz, B., "The Case of Barcelona," available at http://www.ucl.ac.uk/dpu-projects/Global_Report/pdfs/Barcelona.pdf/.

Index

Absorption Suburbs (*Poblados de Absorción*) 30, 31, 33
Acción Católica 80
ACTUR (Urgent Urban Intervention Plan) 45
Adell, Ramon 114
advocacy planning 101
alienation, concept of 6
appropriated space 6
appropriation 6, 58, 143
Arrese, José Luis 43
Asambleismo: general assembly 89, 93, 98, 103, 115, 129
Asociación Sindical de Trabajadores (AST) 91, 115
Asociaciones de Cabezas de Familia (Family Associations) 84
Asociaciones de Padres de Alumnos 84
Associations Representing the Parents of School-Children (*Asociaciones de Padres de Alumnos*) 84
Athens Charter 25
Audiencia Territorial de Madrid 98, 100, 103
Autogestion 2, 3, 12, 81, 103, 108–110, 120, 140, 142
Autonomous Community of Madrid 145

Barcelona: demographics 19; Federation of Neighborhood Associations 107; General Plan 23; housing units 29; Metropolitan Plan (1953) 87; Metropolitan Plan (1976) 108, 124, 129, 131; migration to 46; Partial Plan 108, 124; Regional Plan (1963) 87; registered barracas 60; street signs in 22
barraquismo 59
Barreiros Diesel S.A. 51
barrios chabolistas 2, 64, 80, 121

Bidagor, Pedro 3, 20, 23, 25, 26
Bidagor Plan 23
Bilbao: association of Recalde 87; *chabolas* 60; civic associations 85; Controlled Suburb of Otxarkoaga in 31, 86; demographics 20; Federation of Neighborhood Associations in 107; General Plan 23, 24; housing units 29; migrants to 46; neighborhood association in 86; partial plan 24; Recalde association 86, 87, 107; regional plan 33; squatting in 27; street and bridge names 21
Boetticher y Navarro S.A. 51
Borja, Jordi 134
Bread War 118–19, 142
Bringas, José Manuel 124, 126
Burgos trials (1969) 13, 91

Calvo Sotelo, José 21
Candel, Francisco: *Han matado un hombre, han roto el paisaje* 61
Carrero Blanco, Admiral Luis 13
Carrillo, Santiago 91
Casa de Pueblo 89
Castoriadis, Cornelius 108
Cataluña: Citizens' Movement in 134; demographics 20; migration from 46
centre-periphery relation 19
chabolismo 1, 28, 59–60, 87, 103
chabolistas 11
Circuéndez, Antonio 88
Citizens' Movement (*movimiento ciudadano*) 3, 13–15, 82, 108, 114–18, 120
citizenship 9
Civil Guard 60
Civil War (1936–1939) 2, 9, 10, 19

CODEMAR (*Colectivo de defense del marginado*) 123
collective consumption 84
Comisiones Obreras (CCOO) 86, 91, 146
Commission for Planning and Coordination of the Madrid Metropolitan Area (COPLACO) 59
Commissions for Urban Development 29
Communist Youth Movement 92
Consortium of Bread Manufacturers 119
Controlled Suburbs (*Poblados Dírigidos*) 30, 31, 32: in Madrid 31; of Orcasitas 97, 98, 99, 103; of Otxarkoaga in Bilbao 31, 86
Coordinación Democrática (CD) 113
Cort, César 32
counter spaces 78
Cubillo, Luis 31

D'Ors, Victor 27
Development Plans (Planes de Desarrollo) 34, 38 n. 42
direct democracy 108
dominated space 6

Economic Stabilization Plan 28–9
education 48, 86, 108, 121–4
Emergency Education Plan for the Basque Provinces (*Nuevo Plan de Urgencia de Construcciones Escolares para las tres provincias vascas y Canarias*) 86, 107, 108, 143
employment 49, 52
enfranchisement 9

Family Associations (*Asociaciones de Cabezas de Familia*) 84
Federació d'Asociaciones de Vecinos Barcelona 135
Federation of Neighborhood Associations 120; in Barcelona 142; in Madrid 107, 135, 142
Female Section of the Spanish Fascist Party (*Sección Femenina de la FET*) 50, 83
Ferrés, Antonio 73; *Piqueta, La* 61
Ferrovial-Agromán 51
first modernity 41
Fordism 103
Fraga, Manuel 135
Franco, General Francisco 21, 104: conception of urban space 9–10, 20; death of 13, 35, 111; dictatorship (1939–1975) 1
functional zoning 25

Galindo, Paco 88
García de Enterría, Eduardo 100, 101, 102
Garrigues Walker, Juaquin 124
gendered spaces and community of women 72–6
General Metropolitan Plan of Barcelona: Metropolitan Plan (1953) 24–5, 87; Metropolitan Plan (1976) 108, 124, 129, 131
General Plan of Reconstruction (1939) 21
General Plans 20–8, 29; of Barcelona 24–5, 124; of Bilbao 23, 24; of Madrid 23, 24, 33
Giralt Laporta S.A. 51
González, Felipe 112, 135
grass-root organizations 94
gray space 77, 78

Harvey, David 140

informal settlements 11
infraviviendas 27, 60, 97
inhabitance, principle of 9, 143, 144
internal migration 39–54
International Congress for Modern Architecture: Second (CIAM II) 30; Fourth (CIAM IV) 25
Iribarne, Manuel Fraga 83

Juan Carlos, King 113
Junta Democrática, La 112, 113
Junta for the Reconstruction of Madrid 22

Laboratorios Llophar (or Llofar), S.A. 52
Laguna, Julián 32
Land Law (*ley de suelo*) 10, 20; (1956) 28–33, 60; (1975) 34, 35, 102, 103
Laorga, Luis 3
Law of Associations (1964) 83
Law of Local Administration (*Ley de Bases de Régimen Local*) (1945) 21–2, 34, 135
Law of Political Responsibilities (1939) 45
Law of Protected Housing (*Ley de renta limitada*) (1954) 30
Lefebvre, Henri 27, 31, 58, 78, 101, 108, 141; on "alienation" 5; on "appropriation" 6; *Critique of Everyday Life, The* 4, 5; on "domination" 6; politics of spatial change 4–9; *Production of Space, The* 4, 6, 7, 59; *Right to the City* 4; on "right to the city" 110, 143; on "state spaces" (*l'espace étatique*) 5; *Urban*

160 *Index*

Revolution, The 4; *L'Urbanisme aujourd'hui* 59
Llopíz González, Vicente 92
lock-downs 115, 116
López, Pura 95, 96, 102
López Rey, Félix 63, 69, 70, 88, 84, 89, 98, 118, 121
López Rubio, Juan Manuel 135

M-15 13
Madrid: *barracas* in 59–60; *barrios* 31, 86, 92; Controlled Suburbs in 31; demographics 19; General Plan 23, 24, 33; housing units 29; *infraviviendas* 27; migration to 46; neighborhood association 86, 87; reconstruction 26; regional plans of 33; Satellite Suburbs 23, 25; street names 21; *see also* Orcasitas
Madrid Federation of Neighborhood Associations 118
María de Porcioles, Josep (Mayor) (1957–1973) 124
Martínez de Lamadrid, Abelardo 25
Martínez López, Miguel 12
mass squatting *seechabolismo*
Meseta de Orcasitas 1, 86; neighborhood association 97
Miguel, Carlos de 20
minimal house 30
mobility, concept of 42, 53
mobility capital 42
Mola, General Emilio 21
Moncloa Pacts 113, 146
Montes Mieza, José 60
Movimiento 83
Muguruza, Pedro 20, 21, 30, 32

National Housing Plan (1961) 33
National Institute of Housing 3, 21, 30
national reconciliation 114
National Register of Associations 84
National Service for Devastated Regions and Reconstruction (*Servicio Nacional de Regiones Devastadas y Reparación*) 20–1
National Service of Architecture 21
National Social Emergency Plan *seePlan de Urgencia Social* (PUS)
Navalón, José Morán 88
Navarro, Carlos Arias 112, 113
neighborhood associations 13–15, 80, 82–94, 114–18, 119; in Bilbao 86; in La Paz, Entrevías 121; in Madrid 86, 87, 97; in Orcasitas 4, 63, 69, 70, 82, 89

neighborhood commissions (*comisiones del barrio*) 82
Neighborhood Movement 12
new mobilities paradigm 41, 42
new social movements paradigm 12, 14
Nou Barris 124
Nuevo Diario 99
Nuevo Plan de Urgencia de Construcciones Escolares para las tres provincias vascas y Canarias 86, 107, 108, 143

Obra Sindical del Hogar y la Arquitectura (OSH) 30
Occupy 13
Opus Dei 28
Orcasitas 2; Anti-Delinquency Program 143; *barrios* 97; *chabolas* of 60, 61–72; Controlled Suburbs 97, 98, 99, 103; counter-spaces 7; employment in 52; inhabitants 3–4, 11; migrants to 46–9, 50–1, 53; naming of streets in 131; Neighborhood Association 4, 63, 69, 70, 82, 89; original form 1; partial plant 124; Reconstruction Plan in 1973 102; social networks in 52; women in 72–6
Orcasitas, María 97, 98
OrcaSur 1
Organic Law of the State 83

Palencia, José Luis Lorca 121
Palma, barrio of Son Rapinya in 85
Paredes, Jesús Mari 134
Partial Plan for the Reconstruction of the Municipal Area of Orcasitas in April 1971 97
Partial Plans 26, 29, 87, 131, 144; Barcelona 108, 124; Bilbao 24; Madrid 124; Orcasitas 124
Pérez Mínguez, Luis 21
Pla, Juan Francisco 123
Plan de Urgencia Social (PUS) 10, 20, 28, 30
Planning Committee of the City of Madrid 98
Plataforma de Convergencia Democrática, La 112, 113
Poblado Agricola de Orcasitas 122
Poblados de Absorción 30, 31, 33
Poblados Dirigidos see Controlled Suburbs
Prieto, Carles 135
Primo de Rivera, José Antonio 21

Primo de Rivera, José Antonio, dictatorship (1923–1930) 59
public activism 14

radical democracy 108
regional planning 33–6
right to the city 4, 8, 110, 143
RTVE 135
Rueda, Martínez 24
rural culture 53

Sábado Grafico 98
Sáenz de Oíza y Alejandro de la Sota, Francisco Javier 3, 32
Sánchez Rivas, María Teresa 87, 108
Sanjurjo, General José 21
Satellite Suburbs 34
Sauquillo, Paca 91–2, 115
Sección Femenina de la FET 50, 83
self-management, concept of 103, 108, 109
Serra i Serra, Narcís 110
Service for the Repression of Squatting (*Servicio de la Represión del Barraquismo del Barcelona*) 27
sit-downs 116
slums 11
Sobrino, Cristina 116
Social Emergency Plan *see Plan de Urgencia Social* (PUS)
social housing schemes 30
social networks 51, 52; in internal migration 49
Socias, Josep María 129
Socio-Political Brigade 98
Solana, Ignacio 124
Spanish Communist Party (PCE) 14, 112
Spanish Socialist Party (PSOE) 14, 112
spatial mobility 43, 44
spatiality 5

squatter movements 11, 58
squatter settlement 11
squatters 11
squatting, concept of 10–13, 27, 28
Students' Movement 108
Suárez, Adolfo 113, 120 120

Terán, Fernando de 3, 35
Territorial Tribunal of Madrid (*Audiencia Territorial de Madrid*) 98, 100, 103
Tierno Galván, Enrique 110
transformative capacity of squatting 13
transitional spaces 77

UGT 146
Unified Socialist Party of Cataluña (PSUC), third congress (1973) 92
Union of Democratic Center (UCD) 113
Urban Reserve Land 29
urban social movements, definition of 140

Vega, Javier 124
Villanueva Agüero, Antonio 84, 91
Viola, Mayor Joaquim 129

water provision 32, 67–70, 73–4, 85, 89
welfare agencies 50
women: neighborhood associations and 94; in Orcasitas 72–6
Workers and Students' Movement 93
Workers' Movement 15, 80, 91, 92, 108
Workers Syndical Association (*Asociación Sindical de Trabajadores*) 91, 115
World Bank 34

youth delinquency 121–4
Youth Movement 49

Zuazagoitia Azcorra, Joaquín 23

# Taylor & Francis eBooks

Helping you to choose the right eBooks for your Library

Add Routledge titles to your library's digital collection today. Taylor and Francis ebooks contains over 50,000 titles in the Humanities, Social Sciences, Behavioural Sciences, Built Environment and Law.

Choose from a range of subject packages or create your own!

Benefits for you
- Free MARC records
- COUNTER-compliant usage statistics
- Flexible purchase and pricing options
- All titles DRM-free.

Benefits for your user
- Off-site, anytime access via Athens or referring URL
- Print or copy pages or chapters
- Full content search
- Bookmark, highlight and annotate text
- Access to thousands of pages of quality research at the click of a button.

 Free Trials Available
We offer free trials to qualifying academic, corporate and government customers.

eCollections – Choose from over 30 subject eCollections, including:

Archaeology	Language Learning
Architecture	Law
Asian Studies	Literature
Business & Management	Media & Communication
Classical Studies	Middle East Studies
Construction	Music
Creative & Media Arts	Philosophy
Criminology & Criminal Justice	Planning
Economics	Politics
Education	Psychology & Mental Health
Energy	Religion
Engineering	Security
English Language & Linguistics	Social Work
Environment & Sustainability	Sociology
Geography	Sport
Health Studies	Theatre & Performance
History	Tourism, Hospitality & Events

For more information, pricing enquiries or to order a free trial, please contact your local sales team:
www.tandfebooks.com/page/sales

 The home of Routledge books

www.tandfebooks.com